The Commemoration

ALSO BY JJ WINSTON

The Anniversary (Fiction)

The Anniversary and The Anniversary: Guide to Behavioral Health Workbook (Non-Fiction)

The Commemoration

JJ WINSTON

Wins Consulting Press

The Commemoration

Edited by: Eryka Parker, Lyrical Innovations LLC
Michael Payne, Ann Weatherhead

Book cover artist: Leonard "LC" Collins

Book cover designer: Jackson Publishing

ISBN: 978-1-7350903-0-6

10 9 8 7 6 5 4 3 2 1
First Edition

This book is dedicated to my late father and daughter, both of whom have known the excruciating pain associated with sickle cell disease. I hope my words inspire the world to assist in donating blood, time, and money in our collective fight to find treatments and a universal cure.

Table of Contents

Prologue

Melinia lay on her lumpy little cot and thought to herself, *what a difference three years makes.* The sway of Lake Erie moved the small boat back and forth as she struggled through the onset of seasickness. She had been aboard the cargo boat for over two years, but she still found herself fighting nausea. Her thoughts were interrupted when Mimi came into the room. Mimi was a beauty with a deep, dark ebony complexion and long, wavy hair that hung down to the middle of her back.

"Hey there, sleeping beauty. Are you awake?" Mimi quietly asked.

"Hey, Mimi. Yes, I'm up," Melinia sleepily replied.

"Girl, you were knocked out."

"I guess I was tired. I've been working pretty hard."

"Well, guess what," Mimi excitedly said.

"What?"

Mimi smiled. "I have something for you."

"Did you get me some China white?" she asked, referring to a special blend of heroin they had been using.

"Damn, girl. Is that all you have on your mind?" Mimi fussed. "I'm telling you, one day, that junk is going to kill us both if we're not careful. Sooner or later, we're going to have to kick this monkey off our backs, or he's going to take us both out."

"I hear you, Mimi. So, if my surprise isn't China white, then what is it?"

"Close your eyes," Mimi commanded.

Melinia did as she was told and tightly squeezed her eyes shut. "Okay, you can open them now."

When she opened her eyes, she saw a large gift-wrapped box.

"Oh my God. It's a gift! What is it?"

"Open it, and you'll find out."

Melinia sat up and swung her feet onto the floor of the cramped cabin she shared with Mimi and looked up at her roommate. Mimi was five foot eight with long, shapely legs and looked more like a model than a drug-addicted sex worker.

Melinia pulled the decorative paper off the large box. She could barely conceal her excitement as she surveyed the contents of the box. Inside was a short, beautiful black cocktail dress and a pair of black, two-inch stiletto heels. She pulled the dress out of the box and held it up to her body. She turned to Mimi and said, "I'm going to look fierce in this dress, and these shoes are just my size. Thanks so much for the gift, but what is it for?"

"I didn't buy the gifts for you, but I did pick them out."

"Oh. Well, if you didn't buy them, then who did?" Melinia asked, with a puzzled expression.

At that moment, Rique walked into the cabin.

"I bought it for you. Happy Anniversary," Rique announced. "It's been three years since you became a part of my family. I want you to put on that dress and shoes because we're going out to celebrate."

"I thought we had to work tonight."

"All work and no play will make you a dull woman," Rique said as he pulled out a bag filled with white powder. "I say it's time to play, and...that's why I am giving you some of this."

"What's in the bag?" Melinia eyed it cautiously.

"I got your favorite—China white. Now, I want you to get dressed so Daddy can do you right." Rique winked playfully.

Melinia felt her heart racing as she anticipated the high she would get from the white powder he dangled before her. She picked up the dress and rushed into the small bathroom to change as directed. She knew better than to make Rique mad, and he had conditioned her and Mimi to do as they were told.

It had been three years since Melinia had left her home and her family. Not a day had gone by that she didn't regret her decision. She hoped her family was still looking for her and would somehow know she was still among the living. In some ways, she felt as though she was already dead. The arrangement she had voluntarily entered into had become a prison she could not escape. She realized that you don't have to die physically to be trapped in hell.

After she put on the beautiful dress and shoes and made up her face, she emerged from the bathroom to find the entire crew waiting for her. Rique stood in front of the group with a bottle of champagne and several flutes in hand. After opening the bubbly, he filled everyone's glasses.

"Before we do what we do, I want to make a toast to my girl, Melinia," Rique said. "I'm glad she's part of our family. Since we are celebrating Melinia's third anniversary with us, she gets to do the honor of christening this bag of China white that we whipped up with her in mind. Now, let's get this party started right."

Later that evening, as Melinia weaved in and out of consciousness, she wondered if she would ever wake up from the nightmare that had become her life.

Chapter 1

Collide

Of all the therapies known to man, nothing warmed Grandville Tubbs' heart more than good soul food. Having his entire family gathered with him for a meal settled his frantic nerves, especially given what awaited them the next day. With the fifth-year anniversary of his daughter, Jessica's death upon them, getting the family out of the house for dinner at Chicago's Chicken and Waffles, their favorite restaurant, was just what the doctor ordered.

Grandville glanced down at the menu spread on the table in front of him. His eyes settled on a dish named the "Pastor Chris Harris Treat." "Hmmm, this looks good," he said, nodding his head as he imagined how good the lemon-pepper, grilled catfish with sautéed onions, bell peppers, and Cajun red beans and rice tasted.

Juliette, his wife of eleven years, leaned in and glanced at his menu as he pointed to his selection. "Oh, that does sound good, babe. I'm sticking with my tried and true fried chicken breast and waffles. I'll just pinch off your plate to see if I like that catfish."

"The last time you pinched off my plate, you wound up eating half of it," Granville said with a chuckle which brought a bright smile of embarrassment to his wife's flawless, mahogany face set with the most adorable pair of oval, brown eyes he had ever seen.

"Yeah, Mommy always tastes our food," Jonah complained from across the table in their large corner booth.

"That's because you guys don't eat all of your food," Grandville said, coming to Juliette's defense. "Especially you, Jenae. You can never finish your food but always seem to have enough room for dessert."

"But I like dessert, Daddy," Jenae whined playfully, which made her twin, Jolene, laugh out loud along with Jonah.

While the kids continued poking fun at Jenae, Grandville and Juliette decided to have the girls split a meal to avoid having any food go to waste.

Meanwhile, Jabari, the oldest of the bunch, sat staring down at his menu with his hands placed on both of his cheeks.

"Have you decided on what you're going to order, Jabari?" Juliette asked.

"I'm not really hungry," he sighed, keeping his downcast eyes fixed on the menu.

"Maybe you can order something and take it home to eat later," Grandville suggested.

Jabari continued staring at the menu as if Grandville hadn't said anything to him.

"Jabari," Juliette said. When he finally looked up, she said, "Didn't you hear what your father just said?"

The thirteen-year-old sighed and rolled his eyes before dropping them back down to the menu. Juliette's chest expanded and pushed air through her flared nostrils. Before she could unleash her fury on her first-born, Grandville placed a hand on her thigh and shook his head in warning. She shot Jabari a lengthy side-eye, then turned away.

Since his release from Oakhill a little more than a year ago, Grandville had spent a great deal of time with Jabari to rekindle their relationship. Jabari was a quiet adolescent when Grandville went away to serve time for Jessica's death. In the three years he was incarcerated, Jabari had grown into a responsible and smart teenager who his mother and younger siblings came to rely on in his absence. Since his release, their relationship seemed to be going smoothly, as the two bonded over playing video games and attending sporting events. However, things seemed to change a month ago, with Jabari's sudden distant behavior. He barely spoke to Grandville anymore and declined his invitations to hang out with him.

Just last week, Grandville decided to approach Juliette about Jabari's sudden attitude change, which, of course, she blamed on teenage hormones and the fact that a girl at school seemed to have captured his heart and his attention. Hearing this made him feel better, as he had initially thought that Jabari was angry with him. Although, given the circumstances of his sister's death, Grandville would have felt Jabari's behavior was justified.

Just as the tension began to mount, the waitress came to take their orders. Jabari, of course, was the last one to order and still seemed disinterested in eating. Given how often they dined there, Granville had an idea of what Jabari liked and took the liberty of ordering him the Jerk chicken dinner with fries.

"I told you I didn't want anything," Jabari yelled.

Grandville's eyes enlarged as he reared his head back.

"Jabari!" Juliette howled through clenched teeth as her palm hammered down on the black wooden table. "Have you lost your mind, boy? Since when do we talk back? You better apologize to the waitress and to your father before you and I have a serious problem."

Jabari sucked his teeth and blew out a deep breath. "I'm sorry, Dad," he said in a low voice that could barely be heard over the loud rumblings from the capacity crowd.

"Apology accepted," Grandville said in a calm, even voice.

When the waitress asked if she should go ahead and place Jabari's order, Juliette cut in and declined, stating that Jabari didn't deserve to eat due to his disrespectful attitude.

"No, go ahead with the order, ma'am. Sorry," Grandville said with a wave. When his eyes returned to his wife, her gaze was hot enough to melt the gold chain dangling from around his neck. He knew right away that opposing her in front of the children was a bad move, but he was more concerned about Jabari than his wife's justifiable anger toward him. He made a note to apologize to her later.

Very little was said amongst the family of six for the remainder of their time at the restaurant. Grandville felt responsible for instigating the rift between himself and Jabari, who sat with his eyes staring down at his phone while the rest of the family ate. Instead of them going out to dinner to bond as a family in anticipation of the grueling day they had ahead of them, they were all undone by senseless drama.

The long ride back home from downtown Cleveland to their home in Willoughby proved to be even more awkward. With the twins snoring and Jabari and Jonah listening to music on their phones, Grandville and Juliette basically had the car to themselves. He reached over and covered her hand, which thankfully, she didn't brush away.

"Are you mad at me?" he asked gently.

"No. Why do you ask?"

Thank you, Lord, he celebrated inwardly. As raindrops started to speckle the windshield, Juliette smiled and squeezed his hand before urging him to grip the steering wheel with both hands as the highway suddenly seemed slick. He nodded in agreement and focused his attention on getting them back home in one piece. The last thing he wanted was to hurt or kill anyone else, especially on the eve of the one anniversary he didn't look forward to.

Carrying both twins in his arms, Grandville scaled the steps to the girls' bedroom, where he gently undressed them and tucked them in for the night. Before exiting the room, he clicked on the nightlight and pulled the door closed, leaving it slightly ajar. His gesture was more for the sake of soothing his own anxiety about them waking up in the middle of the night with nightmares than for the twins.

On most nights, he would read the girls bedtime stories after tucking them in. Since coming home, those bedtime moments were his way of bonding with the daughters he hadn't even known existed a year and a half ago. With Jessica now gone, having the twins felt like a second chance at raising daughters. As such, he vowed to do whatever it took to protect them, not just from threats outside of their home, but inside as well. In other words, he needed to protect them from the psychotic version of himself, which meant that he had to keep his mind right and his soul pure and clean, all of which he accomplished with prayer and counseling.

As he made his way to their bedroom, Juliette was sitting on the edge of his side of the bed. He closed the door behind him and shot her a cautious smile. "I'm sorry for overstepping you tonight," he said in a preemptive strike to break the tension before it escalated. "I shouldn't have done that to you, especially in front of the kids."

"I know you didn't mean any harm, but you know how I feel about kids talking back to adults," Juliette said tenderly. "But I understand that you want to protect Jabari. We just have to keep those kinds of situations to a minimum. In all the years we've been married, we've never stepped on each other's toes in front of the children. Even when we've disagreed, we've always been a united front publicly."

"You're right. Again, I apologize. I guess I was just trying to placate him. I didn't want him to go the night without eating."

"I would have fed him. I had already planned to order him something online to take with us. I just wanted him to think we weren't going to feed him or let him eat."

"Got it," he said, nodding.

Juliette jutted her eyebrows and patted the mattress, gesturing for him to sit on the mattress next to her.

He sat on the bed and looked over at her. "What's gotten into him lately? Jabari's such a calm, quiet kid. Suddenly, he's been acting a little strange. He's getting really flippant too."

"I've noticed the attitude he tends to have with you, which, for whatever reason, he doesn't really show toward me. I think you need to sit down with him and figure out what's really going on between the two of you."

Grandville lifted an eyebrow as he was shocked and embarrassed that Juliette noticed Jabari's cold demeanor towards him. "What do you think it is? I mean, we haven't had any fights or arguments. Everything's been good since I came home. Or at least I thought so."

"Like I said before, Grandville, maybe it's his hormones. He's thirteen. His body is going through changes. Plus, he does get a little moody around this time of the year."

Grandville dropped his eyes to his lap and sighed. He knew instantly she was referring to the anniversary of Jessica's death, which had them all hyperemotional. This would be his second anniversary with his family, as he had spent the other three years locked in a cage at Oakhill. Since coming home, he and Jabari had gotten along so well that dealing with Jabari's pain in person was new territory for him.

"Do you think he's mad at me for what happened to Jessica?" he asked.

"That's a question you need to ask him, Grandville." She rubbed him on the back, which brought a sense of calm over him, as only she could do. "I know you guys have had some dialogue, but I think a deep father-and-son discussion is warranted here."

"What if he won't talk to me?"

"He will."

"And how can you be so sure?"

Juliette flashed a smile that melted his heart. "He'll talk to you because you're his father and that's what he's supposed to do. It's still early and the rain has let up. Why don't you take him for a short drive? That way, you can bring me back a pint of butter pecan ice cream from Heinen's."

He nodded and sat gazing down into his lap, where his fingers wrestled with each other. Although he had agreed to talk with Jabari, he wasn't quite sure if he was ready to have the kind of conversation he suspected was necessary to get to the heart of the matter. He didn't like discussing Jessica with anyone, not just Jabari. But given that his son's emotions were spiraling further into darkness the closer they came to the anniversary, he knew that it was time to have a talk. Not just for Jabari's sake, but also for his own.

Grandville gently knocked on Jabari's door, which he found ajar. When there was no answer, he pushed the door open and stepped into the empty, cluttered room. As he made his way back toward the stairs, he paused upon noticing a band of light coming from under the door of Jessica's room, which he had purposely avoided until then. He knocked on the door and was surprised to hear Jabari's voice answer.

The moment he stepped into the room, he felt Jessica's presence, and a chilled shock descended his spine, which made every hair on his arms and back stand at attention. "Hey," he said, focusing on his son to keep his eyes from scanning the rest of the room, which remained untouched since Jessica had last slept in it. "What are you doing in here?"

Jabari lifted his head to meet Grandville's gaze. "I come in here all the time, especially around this time of the year."

Grandville nodded. "I need to run to the store for your mother. Figured I'd have you tag along with me so that we can talk."

"I'm good. I'd rather stay here."

Grandville raised an eyebrow and lowered his eyes. "Son, I wasn't asking you to go. I'm telling you. Now get your coat on and come with me. I won't ask again."

Jabari shot to his feet and stomped toward the door. Grandville grabbed him by the collar of his shirt and anchored him in place. "Lose the attitude, son. I don't know what's going on, but we need to re-establish some respect."

"Or what? Are you gonna cut my throat with a chainsaw next?"

To keep from losing his temper, Grandville gnashed his teeth and tugged him back into the room, pulling the door closed behind them. The terror in Jabari's eyes made him feel inhuman. The last thing he ever wanted was for any of the children to fear him as if he were a monster. Thankfully, the voices he occasionally entertained in his head were silent, as he couldn't afford them an audience at that given moment. There was a hurt, broken child who needed him, and he wasn't about to fail him.

"Is this what all of this has been about, Jabari? Are you angry with me for what happened?"

"I'm good, Dad," he said as he flopped down on the bed. "I just wanna be left alone, okay?"

"You're not good, son. I know when there's something bothering you. It's okay to be mad at me. I'm mad at me for what happened." He walked up to Jabari and placed both hands on his slumped shoulders. "I know how much you miss her, and I don't expect you to understand why things happened the way that they did. Maybe one day it'll all make sense. But until then, just know that I'm here for you and will always have your back."

Jabari nodded as tears welled in his eyes. "I miss her," he said, his voice cracking under the stress of his raw emotions—emotions Grandville wasn't used to seeing from him. His teenage tears hit much differently than those that he had shed as a little boy or adolescent. He wasn't crying due to not getting his way or because of a scraped knee. These were tears from the heart—a young, innocent, beautiful heart that Grandville had played a role in breaking.

The two sat down on Jessica's soft, Dr. McStuffins-themed canopy bed, from which her fruity scent still lingered like a ghost. "I'm sorry about what happened. I never would've hurt her on purpose."

"I know," Jabari said barely above a whisper.

"I would've cut my own throat for her to still be here. There isn't a day that goes by that I don't think about what I've done and the people I hurt behind it, especially you."

Jabari looked up with teary eyes brimming with questions. "Why me?"

Smiling, Grandville draped his arm over his son's shoulder. "When I went away to Oakhill, you stepped in and filled the void my absence created. You were just a little boy who had to fill the role of a man before you were ready. It wasn't fair for you to have to do that, but you did. Your mother and I will always be grateful and proud of you for holding this family down while I was gone. You're more of a man than half the guys I know. And I just want you to know that it's okay for you to be sad, hurt, bitter, and angry. Maybe you didn't get the chance to mourn Jessica because you were too busy trying to be there for your mother and siblings. I'm home now, and it's okay for you to release the tremendous weight you've had to carry. So, go ahead and grieve. Just know that my shoulder is available to take your tears."

Jabari rested his head on Grandville's shoulder and sobbed. Grandville wrapped his arms around him and rocked him, planting kisses on his forehead like he used to do when he was younger.

"I'm sorry for being disrespectful, Dad," Jabari said through his sobs.

"It's okay, son. I know your heart, and I'm sorry for breaking it."

Jabari pulled away and dried his eyes—eyes that mirrored his mother's. "I'm okay now."

"Are you sure?"

Jabari nodded.

Grandville chased away his lone remaining tear and smiled. "Then shall we hit the road? Since you barely ate what I bought for you at the restaurant, maybe we can sneak and grab you a Penn Station sandwich on the way back. It'll be our little secret."

"That's cool. I am kinda hungry."

"There's one thing I'd like for you to do before we leave."

"Sure."

"Go apologize to your mother and give her a big juicy kiss and a bear hug. She's hurting too and could use a little extra tender loving care from her firstborn. I'll be out in the car."

"Okay."

The two stood and slowly walked towards the door. "I love you, Dad," Jabari said.

Grandville turned around and smiled. "Not as much as I love you."

Chapter 2

She

Grandville marveled at the beauty of his city while navigating his Suburban off the freeway ramp and onto the downtown Cleveland streets. As he passed the entrance sign of the Rock and Roll Hall of Fame, his heart soared. It didn't matter how many times he saw the sign; he always experienced the same reaction. The Rock Hall would always be a reminder that he was home in the city tucked away on the northern shore of Lake Erie.

Another anniversary was upon them, and his heart was still aching for his deceased daughter, Jessica. He was dealing with the emptiness that accompanies the loss of a child. He chose to fill his time with tending to his other children and loving his wife Juliette with his whole heart. He was on his way to meet his best friend and business partner, Franklin, who had sent a text requesting to see him immediately.

Grandville was nervous, as he had no idea what the urgent meeting could possibly be about. He also couldn't understand why Franklin insisted on seeing him in the office on that day. The anniversary of Jessica's death would always be a difficult time for both him and his family, and he was barely holding himself together.

He and his family would be heading to Oakhill later that afternoon, and Franklin was also supposed to be meeting them there. Rayshawn, Grandville's ex-brother-in-law, and BBA superstar had insisted that the opening of the Jessica Stubbs Mental Health Clinic coincide with the anniversary of Jessica's death. The problem for him and his family was that Oakhill was in Dayton, a three-hour drive southwest of Cleveland. Rayshawn's foundation had built the new state-of-the-art facility and had made sure it was completed in time for the grand opening. Grandville was not comfortable with the clinic being named after his deceased daughter, but Juliette and his sister, Greta, were ecstatic about the idea. Outnumbered, he jumped on board with his support to ensure that the grand opening was a success.

Once a prisoner there, he had now been outside the walls of Oakhill for a little more than a year. The thought of returning to the place where his body had been held against his will for more than three years made his heart race. The silver lining of the visit was that he would get to visit Joe, who was his nemesis turned friend. Grandville was looking forward to seeing Joe and hoped his friend was making progress toward his release.

After parking his car, Grandville rushed into the office he shared with Franklin. He still had not been granted permission by the Supreme Court of Ohio to practice law once again, although he had voluntarily surrendered his law license before going to the Oakhill Correctional Center. Nonetheless, he was still making a very comfortable living by assisting Franklin with the operation of their business. He served several key roles for their company, including a tax adviser and law clerk.

Using his key, he let himself into the office, which he found empty, as was usually the case on Saturdays. Despite the office being closed for business, he and Franklin often met clients on Saturdays by appointment. They did not have any appointments scheduled that day, and Grandville wondered if Franklin had summoned him there to meet a new client.

He walked into Franklin's office and found him looking out the eighteenth-floor window. The picture window that framed the large office provided a spectacular view of Lake Erie and the Flats, a restaurant and club district in downtown Cleveland.

"Hey, Franklin."

Franklin turned to face his long-time partner. "Hey, Grandville."

"Frat, what you know good?"

"So much, it's hard to convey," Franklin said, shaking hands with his friend.

"Did we get a new client?"

"Not exactly. I needed to see you alone about a private matter," Franklin said, gesturing toward the chair in front of his desk.

"Is everything okay, man? You know, no matter what it is, I've got you," Grandville responded, taking a seat.

"That I know. I just need to ask you a question."

"Okay, you've got me here, so go ahead and lay it on me."

"Grandville, I think I've finally found my ride or die. I want to pop the question to her today at the opening of the clinic. But I wanted to make sure it would be okay with you and Juliette first. I'm ready to ask my queen for her hand, and I also want to ask if you would be my best man if she says yes."

Grandville smiled, fully understanding why his friend had wanted to see him in person. "Franklin, of course, I'll be your best man, and you're more than welcome to use the opening to propose to your queen. I just want to know one thing."

"Yes?"

"Who is the lucky girl, and why haven't we been introduced before today?"

Chapter 3

Something About Us

Juliette looked out over her spacious backyard. It was the fifth anniversary of Jessica's death. With the help of the Lord and her family, she had grown stronger with each passing year. Earlier that morning, she, Grandville, and their children had gone to Jessica's grave and left roses from the bushes that grew in their backyard. Ironically, it was the same rose bush Granville was cutting when he accidentally slit her throat and killed her. For the second year in a row, their entire family prayed, laughed, and cried together while spending the morning at Jessica's grave. They had talked to Jessica like she was still among them and retold stories about her antics.

Juliette's emotions were high whenever she thought about the loss of her daughter, but she was thankful that she and Grandville had reconciled. She was blessed to still have her remaining four children. Despite their tremendous loss, she was happy, and her life would be just about perfect if Jessica were still alive and if they knew where her younger cousin, Melinia, was.

Melinia had been missing for three years, and Juliette and the rest of her family had just about given up hope of ever finding her alive. The authorities still had no clue what to make of the mysterious postcard that her aunt had received around the time of Melinia's disappearance. There was also no verification that the postcard had even been from her long-lost cousin.

Feeling overwhelmed by her thoughts of Melinia, Juliette diverted her attention to their upcoming evening. In a few hours, she and her family would be on their way to Oakhill for the grand opening of the Jessica Stubbs Behavioral Health Clinic. Though the pain of losing her daughter was still prominent, she was proud of herself for learning to live again. With the love of God, her family, friends, and her therapist, she was finding the courage to press on with her life.

Her thoughts were interrupted by her daughter Jolene walking into the room.

"Mommy, I know you told me to take a nap, but I don't feel good," Jolene whined.

Juliette pulled her daughter up onto her lap and kissed her cheek.

"I know you're just trying to get out of taking your nap. Is your twin asleep?" Juliette asked.

"Yes, but I really don't feel good, Mommy."

"Okay, can you tell me what hurts?"

"My leg from when I bumped it earlier, Mommy. It really hurts!"

"All right, I'm going to give you some medicine to make you feel better and help you relax. Then you can try to take your nap. A little later, we're going to go out. If you and your sister and brothers behave, we can spend the night in a hotel, and we'll even get to swim in the pool."

"Okay, Mommy," Jolene said, perking up a little.

Juliette took her pretty little daughter into the kitchen and retrieved a spoon from her cabinet. She gave Jolene some children's aspirin before quietly tucking her back into bed, as not to wake her fraternal twin, Jenae.

As Juliette returned to the sun porch, she thought about her youngest children. Jolene and Jenae were the blessings God had given her after losing Jessica. Jolene was stunningly attractive with big, brown eyes, and Jenae was the spitting image of Grandville and his twin sister, Greta, with hazel eyes just like theirs.

Since Grandville's return home, she and Franklin had re-established the easy relationship they'd had before Grandville's incarceration. It was like the one moment of weakness they had during Grandville's absence had been forgotten. They knew what was at stake and that it was never to be discussed. Juliette still hadn't uttered one word about it to anyone, other than her therapist. Her thoughts were once again interrupted when she heard the garage door open. She hurried to the back door, eager to greet her man. Grandville had rushed out of the house as soon as they'd returned from the cemetery, stating he had to meet Franklin at the office. She was anxious to learn what had been so important that Franklin had summoned him to the office, knowing it was the anniversary.

As Grandville came through the door, they shared a quick kiss and a warm embrace.

"Is everything okay?" she inquired, frowning. "You left in quite a rush earlier."

"Yes, sweetie. Everything is great," Grandville replied with a disarming and charming smile.

"Well, what did Franklin need to see you about that was so important, especially today of all days?"

"He had fantastic news."

Juliette fluttered her lashes. "Well, please do tell."

Grandville chuckled and took a seat at the kitchen table. Juliette joined him and took her hands in his. "He's hoping to get married. He's finally found the woman he wants to spend his life with, and he wants to ask for her hand at the opening this evening."

Juliette studied her husband's face as she processed the news. "Really? That's great news. But I didn't know Franklin was in a serious relationship."

Grandville shrugged. "That makes two of us. I have to say, I'm shocked too. But I'm happy for him. He deserves to have a woman who makes him happy. We'll all get the chance to meet her tonight. Are we all packed?"

"Yes, I have everything ready to go. I thought we could have lunch on the way there. After you left, I picked up a sandwich tray and some wings."

"Great. The party limo will be here at three. I can't wait to see the looks on the kids' faces when they realize we're riding to Dayton in a limo bus," Grandville smiled, his eyes lighting up.

"They're going to be ecstatic, and you can bet they'll be tweeting and posting pictures of the limo on social media for all of their friends to see. What time will Montell and Marie be here?"

"I told Montell to get here at 2:30 because I want us to leave on time," Grandville said. "What time did you tell Samantha to get here?"

"She'll be here around 2:15 along with Greta and Derek. They want to have a drink before we get on the road. Is that okay with you? I don't really like anyone drinking around you."

"I know, but don't worry about me. I'm going to have a non-alcoholic beer. I don't want you or anyone to have to walk on eggshells when I'm around. Think about how lucky you all are to have a guaranteed designated driver. Besides, it really doesn't bother me when others indulge. I know my limits. My time at Oakhill taught me that."

"Speaking of Oakhill, how do you feel about returning there?"

"Baby, I'm not going to lie; I'm nervous. If it weren't for the opening, I would never return there."

Juliette nodded. "I know you wouldn't. Thanks for understanding how important this is to your sister and me."

Grandville took her hand and stared into her eyes for a moment before saying, "Juliette, I would do anything for you. You have to know that, considering all we've been through together."

She squeezed his hands and nodded. "I feel the exact same way about you. That's why I want to make one hundred percent sure that you can handle it."

"I can handle anything with you by my side and with the help of God. Also, going back to Oakhill will give me an opportunity to see Big Joe, and I also wouldn't mind seeing Emerson again. I came up with an extra reading assignment for Joe," Grandville stated, referring to his former student at the prison.

"Really, what's the assignment?" Juliette asked.

"I'm going to have him read the biography *Man Child in the Promised Land* by Claude Brown. I think it's the perfect book for Joe. Claude Brown transcends his troubling situation and becomes great, despite what others predict for his future. Joe and many of the men at Oakhill were born with many strikes already against them. I want to motivate Joe and give him hope that, with hard work, he can become productive. I also must admit that I feel good about the money Franklin and I raised through the fraternity. Tonight, I'll have the opportunity to present the Jessica Stubbs Behavioral Clinic with a ten-thousand-dollar check that'll be used to ensure that the inmates who utilize the clinic have commissary to purchase snacks and other necessities. Some meds can mess up your stomach, especially if you take them without food, and I want to make sure the inmates who go to the clinic are actually taking their prescribed meds."

"Grandville, that's great. Will Franklin be meeting us at Oakhill?"

"Yes, he's already on his way there. He's responsible for reserving all the hotel rooms. I really appreciate our family and friends going to Oakhill with us. It really means a lot to me, and I want to ensure our entourage doesn't have to worry about anything."

"You are so thoughtful. Are you worried about seeing Rayshawn?"

Grandville paused as if the question threw him off a bit. He flashed a smile, indicating that whatever thoughts swirled through his head had passed. "I'm a little nervous," he admitted, confirming her suspicions. "I can't help but wonder exactly what he wants."

"What do you mean? What could he possibly want from you? Ray's a multi-millionaire."

Grandville nodded. "True. But what Rayshawn wants can't be bought."

"And what's that supposed to mean?"

"Tonight will be the first time in years that Rayshawn will be in the same room with Greta. You can best believe that he's going to try to talk to her. I guess I'm just not ready for the potential drama that will come along with it."

"Grandville, everything is going to great this evening. Don't start overthinking the situation. Greta knows just how to handle Rayshawn. Besides, Derek will be there with her."

"I appreciate the fact that you're trying to be optimistic, babe. But you don't know Rayshawn the way I do. He'll find a way to get Greta alone so that he can tell her how much he loves her, and you know, that's not going to go over well with Derek."

"Maybe you're underestimating Rayshawn. Maybe he's moved on."

Grandville sighed. "I sure hope you're right because going back to Oakhill is going to be nerve-wracking enough. I sure don't need anything extra to worry about."

"Baby, don't worry. No matter what happens, remember that we have each other. I've got you," Juliette said lovingly.

Grandville's eyes nearly closed as he smiled. "I know you do. That's something I'll never forget."

Chapter 4

Beyond

The sound of the doorbell pulled Grandville from his daydream. He hurried to the front door to let Montell and his family inside.

"Hey, Montell," Grandville greeted as the two former Oakhill inmates embraced. "Thanks for arriving early," he said as he hugged and pecked Montell's wife, Maria, on the cheek.

"No problem. I need to holler at you for a minute privately, so I was trying to beat the crowd." Montel, who was about five foot ten with a medium build and caramel-colored skin, was dressed in black dress pants and a black and white, short-sleeved, button-down shirt. His bright smile and easygoing demeanor always made Grandville feel at ease.

"That's cool. You guys are the first people here, so we have a few minutes."

After taking Maria's light jacket, he sent her toward the sun porch, where Juliette was relaxing. Grandville shook little Monty's hand and sent him toward his sons' room, where they were playing video games. Finally, he sat down with Montell on his living room couch.

"Hey man, can I offer you a drink?" Grandville asked.

"What do you have?"

"The usual: soda, ginger ale, juice, bottled water, and non-alcoholic beer. Juliette also has some alcohol—maybe wine or maybe vodka—but I am not sure."

"I'm still on parole, like you, so the spirits are out. But, considering this is a special occasion and because I have something important to share with you, I'm going to have the non-alcoholic beer."

"Okay, you're choosing fake alcohol as your drink of choice, so this *must* be big news," Grandville chuckled, grabbing the bottles from the fridge.

"Yes, it is," Montell said with a big smile.

Grandville returned to the living room with two chilled O'Doul's in hand. "Okay, tell me what we're toasting to."

"Grandville, you're the first person I'm sharing this news with."

Grandville turned to face his friend, holding off from taking a sip from his mug. "Okay, I think I've been in suspense long enough. Give me the news."

"I'm going to be a dad again. My Maria is pregnant," Montell said excitedly.

"What?" Grandville chirped as his head reared back. "Are you for real?"

Montell nodded as a smile spread across his face.

"Man, that is great news! We definitely need to toast to this," Grandville said, lifting his mug high above his head. "I'm honored to be the first person you've told about the baby. How does Monty feel about the news?"

Montell motioned for Grandville to lower his voice. "He doesn't know yet. We're going to talk with his therapist first to figure out the best way to tell him. Monty has been doing well, and we don't want to do anything that will deter his progress. Maria's pregnancy has caught us both by surprise. We honestly thought her childbearing years were behind her."

Grandville nodded and took a sip from his mug. "Understandable."

"We tried having another baby after Monty was born, but she was never able to get pregnant again. We were scheduled to see a fertility doctor right before I killed the bastard who was abusing Monty. As you well know, I ended up in Oakhill before we could go to the appointment. So, we'll be starting over, plus we're not as young as we used to be. So, this will be a high-risk pregnancy for my Maria."

Grandville could tell how concerned his friend was with the pregnancy and how it would impact his family. "Well, don't worry too much about it. We're going to have a five-star night, and I have a party limo picking us up in about forty-five minutes, so I want you to relax."

Montell took a sip of his beer. "Well, enough about me, man. How are you doing? Today is a pretty big day with it being the anniversary and with the opening of the Jessica Stubbs Mental Health Center."

"Thanks for asking, but despite what today represents, we had a good morning visiting Jessica's grave. We also went out to dinner last night as a family to get us in the right frame of mind about today. To be honest, I'm nervous about going back to Oakhill. But I feel better knowing my family and friends will be with me. How about you? I know Oakhill is the last place you want to be."

Montell nodded. "Yeah, man. I feel the same way you do. I haven't been back there since my release, and the only reason I'm going back in the first place is to support you."

"Thanks, Montell. I really appreciate you doing this."

"Grandville, there's no thanks necessary. You're a part of my family, and I feel honored that you're including us."

"You're the one person who actually understands how it feels to live in a place synonymous with hell."

"At least we get to leave there once the opening is over," Montell said. "Think about all the other guys who are stuck there."

"Yeah, you do have a point. I wonder if Big Joe will ever be released from Oakhill."

"Well, he was at Oakhill for at least a year before I got there, so I'd say he's been there for at least seven years now," Montell stated. "He probably would've already been released if he hadn't spent his time there assaulting other inmates."

Grandville shook his head, remembering the time Joe had set his eyes on him and he'd had to fight him off in the shower. He shook his head again to dismiss the memory. "Well, hopefully, he's a changed man and is working his program to be released soon."

"We can only hope so, but we'll know exactly how he's doing in just a little while."

The ringing doorbell interrupted the two friends' conversation. Grandville got up and opened the door to find a smiling Samantha standing in the doorway with a man he had never seen before.

"What's up, player?" Samantha greeted. "This is Jared, my date for the evening."

"Hey, Samantha," Grandville said as they shared a quick embrace. He turned to the man and shook his hand. "Hello, Jared. I'm Grandville."

"Pleased to meet you, Grandville, and thanks for having me."

"No problem." Grandville smiled at Samantha and said, "Juliette is on the sun porch with Montell's wife, Maria. Montell and I are drinking a couple of non-alcoholic beers. If you want a real drink, I think Juliette has some vodka out on the porch with her."

"Thanks, but no thanks," Jared said, smiling apologetically. "I don't drink. But, if you don't mind, I'd love to hang with you guys."

"Not a problem. Come on in and let me introduce you to Montell. We have non-alcoholic beer and other beverages."

"I'll have the fake beer," Jared joked.

Grandville chuckled. "Okay, let me grab you one."

"Hey, Grandville. Let me get a glass of ice and bottled water," Samantha requested.

Grandville complied, and she kissed Jared on the cheek before setting off in search of Juliette and Maria.

"I'm so crazy about that woman, and I'm going to do whatever I need to do to make her mine," Jared said, watching her take a seat next to Maria outside.

"Samantha bringing you to this event says that she might be feeling you too," Grandville said. "You're one of the few guys she's brought over to meet us and believe me when I say, she's family to us. She and my wife have been the best of friends for years."

"Really?" Jared raised a brow and lifted his beer bottle in the air. "Grandville, you just made my day. From the moment I met Samantha, my spirit told me she's the one. I've tried everything to get her to commit to me, but she keeps throwing up roadblocks. I'm glad to know she hasn't brought a lot of suitors to meet you guys. Makes me feel a little special."

"Good. Glad I helped to make your day. Let me introduce you to Montell, and we can drink our fake beers while we wait for the limousine to arrive."

Chapter 5

Grown Folk

Juliette laughed and talked with Maria, who had just shared that after seventeen years, she and Montell were expecting their second bundle of joy. They both looked up to see Samantha walk out onto the sun porch with a huge smile on her face.

"Hey, how are you ladies this fine afternoon?" Samantha asked as she sat down on the small rocking chair across from them.

"Hey, Sam," Juliette said. "We're great, and judging by that big smile on your face, you are too! I take it you took my advice and invited Jared to join us this evening."

"Yes, he's hanging out with Grandville and Montell. I bought this glass of ice because I want to make sure I hydrate before I have my drink."

"Great, I'm sure the guys are having a great time shooting the breeze. We're pretty much ready to go. The twins are napping, and the boys are in their room playing video games. Greta and Derek should arrive at any minute. Do you want me to make your adult beverage?" Juliette asked.

"Not yet. I'm good for now because I had one at home. I'm going to start with this bottled water. Jared doesn't drink, and it feels great to have a designated driver. Besides, his sobriety saves me a mint. Claude, that last fool I dated, drank like a fish and buying his drinks had my tab off the charts," Samantha declared.

Juliette smiled. "Well, I'm glad you're giving Jared a chance. From what you've told me about him, he seems like a really nice guy."

With a wink, Samantha replied, "Okay, I'll admit, you were right. I guess I could stand to live a little outside my comfort zone. Thanks for reminding me of that fact."

Maria raised her glass. "Cheers to the advice of good friends!"

They all toasted.

"Enough about my love life. How are you feeling, considering what today represents?" Samantha gently asked while sipping her water.

Juliette smiled at her friends. "I'm doing okay. We went to Jessica's grave earlier today and, even though I know Grandville is a little anxious about the opening, I must admit, I'm ecstatic. I really miss Jessica, but having a clinic named in her honor means everything to me. Also, having you ladies along with me makes this even more special for me."

"There's nowhere else I would rather be," Samantha replied.

"Me, either." Maria reached over and squeezed Juliette's hand.

At that moment, Greta came out onto the sun porch.

"Hey, ladies! Sorry, we were running a little behind schedule. What did I miss?" Greta asked, breathlessly.

Juliette reached up for an air kiss from her sister-in-law. "You aren't late. Samantha just arrived a few minutes ago. The limo bus isn't even here yet. It should arrive in a few minutes, and we still have some time before we leave. We'll have sub sandwiches, wings, and snacks for the limo ride. I don't want Grandville or the kids to be around alcohol, so I made sure that the limo is stocked with soda, juices, and waters only. Grandville and I want you all to be comfortable, so I am serving adult beverages in to-go cups here on the porch before we leave out.

Also, we're not coming back tonight, and we have reserved several hotel suites, so I hope everyone remembered to bring their overnight bags."

"Okay. We left ours in the car. Derek will put them on the limo when it gets here," Greta replied. "Is your mother coming with us to the opening, Juliette?"

"No, she's going to stay behind and attend a prayer vigil that's being held for my little cousin at my aunt's church. This is also the anniversary of Melinia's disappearance, and I feel a little guilty that I can't attend, but my family understands."

Samantha gave a warm smile. "We know this is a tough day for you. We just want you to stop worrying about everyone else and let us take care of you. Today is a huge deal for you and Grandville, so we want you to sit back and relax. Now, where's the liquor?"

Everyone laughed.

"Nice transition, Sam," Juliette replied. "It's in the cooler behind the couch. I have vodka, Jack, and white zinfandel. There's also bottled water, cranberry juice, cups, and ice behind there."

"Sit tight. I'll be the bartender and waitress. Now, what are you drinking?" Samantha asked.

"I'll have a glass of wine," Juliette replied.

"No problem, playa. Greta, I'm positive you want a cold glass of your other man," Samantha teased.

"Now who would that be?' Greta inquired.

"Girl, everybody knows you love you some Jack," Samantha teased.

"Soror, I thought you knew. Jack and I are having an affair!" Greta laughed.

"How about you, Maria?" Samantha asked. "I know how much you love your wine. Would you like a glass?

"No, I'm going to sit this one out," Maria replied. "I'm going to have God's drink. A big glass of H-two-oh."

Samantha raised a brow. "You've never said no to a glass of wine when I'm the bartender. What the hell is going on?"

"I have gotten to know you ladies pretty well, so I'm going to share some news with you. But I'm asking that you keep it under wraps right now." Maria looked at each of them.

"I give you my word, I won't tell a soul," Samantha said, signaling a key twist at her lips.

"You can count on my discretion," Greta added.

Juliette nodded as she already knew the news.

"Montell and I are expecting. I'm thrilled, but I'm going to admit I'm scared as hell," Maria confided with a timid smile. "I've only been pregnant once, and that was with little Monty, more than seventeen years ago. Montell and I tried for years to get pregnant but to no avail. I honestly thought after I had Monty that I was barren. After that, I just gave up on being a mother again. I had actually gone to the doctor to get some blood work done, and the doctor's office called this morning and confirmed that I'm two months pregnant. It's still early, so I don't want a lot of people to know, just in case... I mean I *am* over forty years old."

"Aww, this is fantastic news," Samantha exclaimed, hugging Maria. "Let me get our drinks so we can toast to you and Montell's new addition. The baby is going to be just fine, and we are going to claim it in the name of Jesus Christ."

"Preach, Soror," Greta declared, wrapping Maria in her arms. "Like Samantha said, we're going to think positively. There's no room for negative thoughts. This also reminds us that God does answer prayers, and He grants us our blessings in His time, not ours. Congratulations!"

"Thank you. I so appreciate all of you!" Maria's smile was wide, and her eyes danced.

It didn't take long for Samantha to mix their drinks. Juliette decided to do the honor of making the toast. "I want to make a toast to my girl, Maria, who is now carrying the product of her love with Montell. I wish their family, peace, good health, love, and happiness."

The ladies clinked their glasses together, and each took a sip of their drinks. Greta drank hers down in one gulp and said, "I think I have time for one more."

She walked over to the couch and pulled the bottle of Jack Daniels out to pour herself another drink.

"Okay, we know you and Jack are in love, but I've never seen you love on him like this before. What the hell is going on with you?" Samantha asked.

"I'm not going to lie. I'm a little nervous about seeing Rayshawn again," Greta confessed. "I haven't seen him since our divorce, and I don't exactly know how I'm going to feel when I lay eyes on him after all this time. I'm in love with Derek, but a small part of me will always love Rayshawn. He was my first, and we were married for a long time. I really appreciate him using the foundation to turn my vision for the Jessica Stubbs Center into reality."

"Well, Soror, it was a great idea, and I, too, am also grateful that Rayshawn made your idea a reality. We will run interference if you want us to keep him away from you tonight. If we see him trying to talk to you, we can intercede and say you're needed elsewhere."

Greta nodded her appreciation.

Samantha continued, "I can relate to what you're going through. I'm also feeling a certain type of way about seeing Franklin. We never had any kind of relationship, but for years, I've had a major crush on him. It hurts that he never saw in me what I had seen in him."

"But now you have Jared. How's your relationship with him going?" Juliette asked.

"I admit, I'm glad I took your advice and gave him a chance. When we're together, I don't even remember he's eight years younger than me. He's swept me off my feet, but I'm a little nervous about what will happen when he finds out my stance on having children. I have no desire to be a mother right now. Though I'm happy for all of you who are having children, it's not at the top of my priority list."

"Samantha, you're going to have to take your own advice and think positively," Juliette advised her friend. "For all you know, Jared feels the same way you do about being a parent. Why don't you just ask him about it? Not everyone is interested in replicating themselves and becoming parents. Finding out his position on the subject may put your mind at ease."

Samantha sat down and sipped her drink. "I guess you're right. I know that I'm jumping ahead of myself. Right now, Jared and I are enjoying each other's company and it is too early to be getting too serious."

"Speaking of getting serious, I want to let you ladies know that, according to Grandville, Franklin is planning to propose to his girlfriend at the opening tonight," Juliette announced.

"What girlfriend? I thought Franklin was single?" Samantha scratched her head.

"So did Grandville and I. Today was the first time that we learned that Franklin has a girlfriend that he's been keeping a secret. Franklin asked Grandville to meet him at their office on our way home from visiting Jessica's grave. When Grandville got there, Franklin asked his permission to make his wedding proposal at the opening, and, of course, Grandville gave him our consent. We have no idea who the young lady is who's captured Franklin's heart. All he would say about her is that we'll meet her at the opening. He's already on his way to Oakhill because he's responsible for finalizing our rooms at the Embassy Suites and ensuring that everything is in order for our stay."

"Wow, everything is starting to make sense," Samantha said. "No wonder Franklin never responded to my advances. He had a secret lover. Well, I definitely feel better about him never giving me the time of day now. I get it, he's in a relationship, but what I don't understand is why he kept it secret."

"We'll see everything for ourselves in a few hours," Juliette said.

At that moment, Juliette heard the faint ring of the doorbell and assumed it was the limo bus, arriving right on time. Luckily, everyone in their entourage was at their home, ready to go.

"Okay, everybody! Drink up. I'm sure that's the limo bus. Time to get going," Juliette said to her guests.

Chapter 6

Let it Ride

Grandville was laughing, talking, and enjoying a few drinks with his guests when the doorbell rang. He hurried to the door and opened it to find the limo bus driver, dressed in all black and carrying a chauffeur's cap in his hands, standing in his doorway.

"Mr. Stubbs, my name is Grayson, and I'll be your driver for the next two days."

Beaming a welcoming smile, Grandville gave the man a firm handshake. "Nice to meet you, Grayson."

"The bus is equipped with state-of-the-art technology, which includes flat-screen televisions, a play station that is stocked with assorted video games, and wi-fi. The bus is also stocked with beverages. I was instructed not to stock beer wine or alcohol, so the bus is dry, but if you change your mind, I can always stop at a liquor store."

"Thank you, Grayson. We won't be changing our minds. Those who indulge are enjoying their spirits as we speak. Let me start gathering everyone so we can get on the road."

When Grandville turned around, Juliette was standing there with the twins, who still appeared to be groggy, along with his sons and Little Monty.

"Jonah, please take your sisters and get them buckled up in the limo," Juliette ordered. "Jabari and Monty, I want you young men to help the limo driver with getting everyone's luggage onto the bus. Then bring this tray of sub sandwiches and this cooler with chicken and salads onto the bus. The adults will be right out, and then we can get on the road."

Juliette then kissed Grandville on the cheek and said, "Sweetheart, it's time to get this party on the road. Are you ready?"

"I'm ready. Let's get the adults."

It wasn't long before everyone was on the bus, enjoying the food, along with all the amenities offered onboard. The twins were seated in front of one of the bus's six flat screens equipped with wireless headphones. They watched the animated movie *Frozen 2,* oblivious to everyone else. The boys continued their video game marathon on another flat screen located in the corner of the bus. The adults watched the Cleveland Indians game on the flat screen in the center of the bus. Colorful lights illuminated the vehicle's interior, and the mood was festive as everyone laughed and conversed. Everyone was having a great time when, out of nowhere, Jared turned the conversation from baseball to basketball.

"I'm having a fantastic time," Jared said. "I work so much; I don't take time to have fun very often. I already feel like I've known you all for a long time, even though we just met. I want to thank you for making me feel welcomed. Before we make it to the opening, I want to ask a question."

"Jared, you better not be about to ask me to marry you," Samantha said playfully.

He looked at Samantha for a moment, amused. "I would right here and now if I thought you would say yes. But I know you aren't there yet. Don't worry, because I'm still on the job and I plan to make you see why you should be all mine. But seriously, I have a question related to etiquette for when we arrive at the event," Jared stated, sounding mildly uncertain.

"There is no such thing as a stupid question, so go ahead and ask away. We promise not to make fun of you, isn't that right, Samantha?" Grandville playfully teased.

Samantha placed her hand on her chin as if pondering Grandville's question. The group laughed.

"Okay," Jared chuckled uneasily. "I just want to be honest and let you all know that I'm a huge Rayshawn Robinson fan. Would it be inappropriate for me to ask for his autograph while we are at the event? I don't want to come across as star-struck or do anything that would reflect poorly on Samantha."

"Rayshawn is used to being asked for his autograph because he's one of the greats when it comes to the game of basketball," Grandville said. "However, knowing him as well as I do, he'll probably decline any autographs requests today because he'll want to ensure that the focus is on the new clinic and not on him. Tell you what, though. I'll make sure you receive a personal introduction, and I'll also use discretion to also make sure you receive an original Rayshawn Robinson autograph by the end of the evening."

Jared's face lit up. "Thanks, I really appreciate that, Grandville. As I said, I'm a huge fan."

"Not a problem. Consider it done since you're a friend of Samantha.

Smiling, Jared turned to his left and said, "Speaking of great basketball players, I almost missed the fact that I'm sitting next to Derek Dolan, one of the University of Cincinnati's best-kept secrets. I hear the school is planning to retire your number. I'm hoping that before we end our trip, you'll also give me your autograph. There is no telling where you would have gone in your basketball career had you not suffered that ACL injury."

Everyone, including the boys, quieted down and directed their attention toward Derek.

"I didn't realize you played basketball in college," Greta stated, clearly stunned by Jared's statement.

Derek's body shifted. "Yes, Jared is right. I did play in both high school and college. When I was young, my whole life was basketball. I've been six foot five inches since I was fifteen and very athletic when I was young. I ate, slept, and lived the game, but after my injury, I was unable to play anymore. I'm still good, but I'm no longer great. I've spent my career working with various professional sports teams because basketball is the one thing I know and understand. I learned a long time ago that basketball is just a game. Life is real, and I don't take any of it for granted because things can change in an instant."

"Testify," Grandville said. "There are no truer words. I know exactly how it feels to have your life change in an instant."

"Me too," Juliette remarked.

"Same over here," Greta said. "Just this instant, I realized though I love you, there are a lot of things we still don't know about each other. I had no idea you played basketball in college or that you attended the University of Cincinnati."

"I guess we never really talked about our college years," Derek replied. "But, God willing, we'll have a lifetime to learn more about each other. I love you, too, and I don't care where you went to high school, college, or graduate school. Right here and now is all that matters to me." He leaned over to stroke her cheek.

"I feel exactly the same way," Greta responded, and the two interlocked their fingers.

"Okay, love birds. Enough of the mushy stuff, or you'll have all of us in here crying," Samantha said, throwing up her hands. "Derek, I also didn't know you attended the University of Cincinnati. One of my good friends went there, and we're all around the same age. Her maiden name is Donna Baldwell."

Derek's eyes enlarged with recognition. "Yes, she's a member of the Gamma's and one of my late wife's best friends and sorority sisters."

"Did you ever play against Rayshawn before your injury?" Samantha asked.

"Yes, our teams played each other once or twice in college. After I finished college, Trish and I were married. We headed out to California so I could work for the LAs. Shortly after we arrived, we learned we were expecting our first child. When she was seven months pregnant, Trish was murdered while walking into a convenience store that was being robbed."

Everyone gasped and shook their heads.

Derek nodded his gratitude, then continued, "I stayed in California, partly because I was hopeful that, one day, the authorities would apprehend my wife's killer. Rayshawn was drafted and ended up on the LAs about a year after her death, and despite my boyish looks, I'm a few years older than you guys," Derek joked.

"Derek, let me say how sorry I am for your loss." Samantha's hands wrung as her empathy showed in her eyes.

He nodded again. "Trish's murder didn't get a whole lot of media attention here in Ohio, but for a while, the story of her death dominated the news in Los Angeles. The authorities still haven't caught her killer. I could've allowed my pain to stop me from loving again, but then I met Greta. Even when she was with Rayshawn, I felt a connection to her that I had never felt with anyone else, including Trish. I feel extremely blessed that the Lord sent her my way when I returned to Cleveland. I'm hoping that you'll join us at our wedding on Valentine's Day."

Grandville nodded. "You know we'll be there."

"I'd love to be there—if Samantha invites me," Jared stated.

"Well, right now, you're in a probationary period. If you make it past then, you'll be my boo as well as my date for the wedding and reception," Samantha joked.

"Okay, I'm in pursuit of becoming a permanent employee. Hope you don't pass on a good thing," Jared joked right back.

"In the words of one of the best music groups of all times, the Debarges, time will reveal," Samantha said.

Chapter 7

You Know I'm No Good

Melinia continued battling the relentless waves of nausea as the small cargo liner cruised over Lake Ontario. As she stood on the deck and looked at the grayish-blue water, she contemplated jumping in and ending the pain that seemed to permeate every pore of her body. She recently recognized she had been having thoughts of ending it all more frequently. This frame of mind had landed her in a very dangerous place. As strong as her urge was to jump, she knew that doing so would be unfair to her family, who she knew was doing everything in their power to find her.

"Hey, Melinia," Mimi greeted as she entered the deck. "Rique sent me up here to get you,"

"Hey, Mimi, I didn't realize you were here."

"That's because you were in deep thought. You look sad. I know the life that we've chosen is hard, but I need you to promise that you won't give up."

"Mimi, I'm not going to lie to you; I'm depressed," Melinia stated sorrowfully. "Every morning when I look in the mirror, I hate myself. I've completely destroyed my life. I had everything, and then I fell in love with China white and look at me now: a junkie who is now a slave of a drug dealer and wannabe pimp. The things I've done for a hit makes me shudder."

"I've also performed acts I'm not proud of, just for a hit of heroin, but what I refuse to do is think about it," Mimi stated, with a hand on her hip. "We've done what we've needed to do to survive. We've been places we never would've had the opportunity to see if we didn't live here with Rique. I mean, he's not so bad. He buys us beautiful gifts and gives us more freedom than some of the other girls. Also, because of what you did for him and his family, he treats you better than he treats the rest of us. You are my best friend, so whatever negative thoughts you have swimming around in that beautiful head of yours, please put an end to them. And don't you dare think about leaving me here alone."

"I can't promise I won't ever leave, but I can promise you I am not leaving today. What does Rique want?" Melinia asked her friend with cautious eyes.

"He wants us to help fillet the fish that were caught today. Now come on, we don't want to make him angry. He's actually in a good mood, and I want to keep him that way."

Melinia followed Mimi out onto the main deck, where Rique had assembled his whole posse.

"We caught some beautiful walleye today," he said. "I'm going to need everyone to pitch in and get them cleaned and filleted so Remy can fry them for dinner. Our spread will include greens, macaroni and cheese, and hush puppies. I have a third party interested in purchasing the surplus. We're on a serious time crunch; there are only three hours left until our rendezvous. We have to meet our third party so he can pick up what we caught and prepared. We will be arriving at the port tomorrow, at which time, we'll be working very hard. So tonight, let's have some fun and relax. There will be a little contest between Melinia and Mimi. Whoever can fillet the most fish will receive this bag of China white." He smiled as the group hooted and hollered. "And the loser has to perform a freak show with Remy, which will be recorded and released for distribution."

In the past, Rique would use the crew's special blend of heroin as an incentive to motivate his sex workers to compete against other members of the crew in various contests. The sole winner would receive the coveted China white. There was only one thing that motivated Melinia more than her desire to get high, and that was the opportunity to spend time with Remy. She was more than willing to sacrifice her next fix to spend some alone time with him. He had never had sex on camera, and Melinia wanted to make sure that if he had to participate in the freak show, it would be with her.

Melinia knew the recent catch could pose problems for the crew because they did not have a commercial license to fish in Lake Ontario. Legally, they were only permitted to catch six walleyes per day. There had to be more than a hundred and fifty fish in the large pile. Melinia knew that Rique needed to get rid of them in case the authorities decided to board their cargo boat. She had been a passenger on the boat for years, and in that time, the authorities had yet to board the vessel. She was sure that this was due to the large payoffs that Rique religiously made. Even though a visit was highly unlikely, they could never be too careful.

She looked up and caught Remy watching her intently, then felt herself quiver. She had fallen in love with him, and with him being Rique's younger brother, she had yet another reason to hate herself and for what she now stood for. Remy was very attractive. He was six feet tall with a muscular build and smooth, dark-brown skin. He had short, black, curly hair, and when he smiled, which was not often, it was like a soft light shining into her dark world.

After a moment, she looked to her right and saw Mimi who had caught the eye contact between them. They gave each other a quick look before Mimi nodded slightly in acknowledgment. Then she returned her attention to their shared task, using her filet knife like she had been raised by a fisherman. She was much quicker than Melinia, who moved painstakingly slow. But she was no dummy. She knew she had to do just enough to make Rique believe that she was competing or there would be a problem. As she cut up the fish at half the pace, she thought back to the previous year. It was the only time she and Remy had been intimate. She longed for a repeat of that beautiful night and the following day. She hoped her plan would result in her release from bondage.

She found herself reminiscing about the only time she and Remy had been intimate. She had been on the boat for more than a year when Rique announced that it was Remy's birthday and that she was to be his "present." She knew this meant that Remy could do whatever he pleased with her. Melinia was irritated that Rique felt he had the right to treat her like an object to be freely passed around. But she knew better than to let Rique know how she felt. The pain on Mimi's face when Rique beat and abused her in front of Melinia always served as a reminder and kept her in check. Whenever Melinia did something wrong, Mimi paid the price and she would be forced to watch. Melinia hated to see her friend cry and suffer due to her disobedience. So, she swallowed her feelings and went along with the program, looking forward to partaking in her favorite pastime afterward. Soon, she would be higher than a kite from the smack that Rique always supplied.

She lay on the bed, waiting for Remy to enter the back unit that Rique had turned into a bedroom. When Rique came in, he was followed by his cousin Raul. Melinia couldn't stand him, but for whatever reason, Mimi was in love with him. She sometimes even enjoyed the acts he and his friends would force her to do.

Rique gazed at her with a smile on his face. "Hey, Melinia. Change of plans. I'm going to let Raul hit it before Remy. And because

I'm such a nice guy, I'm also going to let you get a hit of this uncut China white."

Melinia despised Raul, but she knew that saying no to his proposition would cause Rique to have Raul rape her on camera. Again, she agreed to go with the flow.

"Daddy, you know I am down for whatever," Melinia replied, attempting to make her voice sound as sexy as possible.

"Good girl. Now, come over here and let Daddy give you a hit of this good, good," Rique coaxed.

Melinia rolled out of bed and sashayed toward Rique. She stood still while he sprinkled the white powder onto the small dresser, which was in the corner of the room. She then leaned in to inhale the white substance. Immediately, she was consumed by the high as it slammed into her body like a freight train.

"This shit here is the good, good. It's so good that I can't shoot you up with it," Rique said. "This here has to be snorted or smoked because if you shoot it, Raul would have to revive you before he can enjoy what you are about to give him. Remy doesn't want to be on camera, so I'm going to let Raul hit first. The freak show will be live on the website, so make sure you make it believable. If you're good and make my boys scream, I'll make sure you get three more hits of this good shit. Do we have a deal?"

Melinia smiled up at him. "Daddy, you know we do."

"Good, now go over there and lay on the bed. Then close your eyes," Rique commanded.

After doing as she was told, she heard Rique give instructions to Raul in Spanish. Although she spent quite some time with Spanish-speaking people, she still didn't understand the language, but she knew their words involved something sexual in nature. The Sandego boys were from the Dominican Republic, and Spanish was their primary language. Rique and Remy were brothers, and Raul was their first cousin. The three of them made up a strange motley crew that ran drugs and a small sex ring from the Caribbean all the way to the Great Lakes. The Sandego boys always conversed among themselves in Spanish, but Rique and Raul also spoke excellent English. Remy never spoke in English, and before that evening, Melinia was under the impression that he didn't comprehend the language. Now, she knew better.

She was so high that she was barely conscious. She was not fully aware of what Raul was doing when he began his assault on her body. Rique directed him as he walked around, filming their illicit copulation with a handheld video camera. When she opened her eyes, reality set in as she saw Remy standing in the corner completely naked. He was carefully watching what Raul was doing to her body. She hated herself for what she had become and how she allowed her body to be brutally used in exchange for the white powder that she constantly craved. Rique was her sole supplier of the little bags of white powder that was affectionately known as China white. It was the perfect blend of fentanyl, heroin, and cocaine. Remy was the crew's mixer, and the Sandego boys were well known for their blend that was commonly sought after on the streets of several major cities.

Melinia locked her eyes on Remy as he stood in the corner, witnessing Raul's sexual attack on her body until the tears in eyes blurred her vision. She was tired of being abused by various men so that Rique could make his money. But the high that his powder provided her motivated her not to struggle against them. She had given up her fight. What they did to her body was not sexual for her, but a means for her survival. She planned to make Rique's crew howl like she had been directed in order to receive extra hits. She hoped they would help her forget about all the savage acts she allowed against her body and soul. After Raul mercilessly pounded into her for five minutes, she clenched her muscles and heard him scream out in ecstasy, while simultaneously speaking in Spanish. She closed her eyes in relief at the signal of the end of his sexual assault. As he retrieved himself, she noticed the used condom. He stood and Rique turned off the camera, indicating that the show was over.

"Melinia, that was great. We made a mint on the live show, and we'll make even more once the DVD comes out. Because you've been such a good girl, I'm going to give you an extra hit. You can have two now and two after you hook Remy up," Rique said.

"Thanks, Daddy," Melinia replied, getting off the bed and moving her bruised body over to the dresser.

"Today is Remy's birthday, and I want you to show him an exciting time so you can get your last two hits."

"No problem, Daddy," Melinia slurred.

"Yeah, this is that uncut China white. It's the shit, ain't it? Got you flying high. I want you to take Remy up to the sky with you. Now lay your beautiful ass back on that bed," he slapped her behind, sending her on her way.

Remy, who was still standing in the corner, looked frightened as Rique spoke to him in rapid Spanish. Then he hesitantly walked over to the bed. Rique quietly exited the room, leaving them alone. Melinia patiently waited for Remy to begin touching her with her eyes closed and tears streaming from them. After five minutes passed by, she opened her eyes to find Remy staring down at her.

"I'm sorry about what Rique makes you do. I know that he lets men hurt you," Remy whispered in English with a heavy accent.

"Wait a minute, I know I'm high, but you're speaking in English. I thought you didn't speak or understand it," Melinia whispered back.

Remy nodded. "Yes, I can. My brother and cousin don't know that I've learned. Rique would never allow me to spend time alone with you if he knew. So, please keep my secret."

"Sure, I'll keep your secret, if you promise to keep mine. I hate myself because of who I've become. I really don't want to do this, but I'm sure you don't want to hear my problems. Just tell me what you want me to do to please you. You look like a guy who enjoys a half and half. I'll do whatever you want. All I ask is that you don't make me do anything freaky," Melinia begged.

Remy slowly reached out his hand, using his fingers to wipe the tears from her eyes. "Please don't cry. I don't want you to do anything but relax. You have given my family and me something that we will always treasure, and for that, I am very grateful. I'm sorry that my brother keeps hurting you."

Melinia nodded, then dropped her head. "It's okay. I probably deserve everything that's happening to me. I mean, karma is a real bitch, just like me."

"I don't know what the word karma means."

"It means that I've done some horrible things in order to get high and prevent myself from becoming dope sick. All the bad things that I've done are coming back to haunt me," Melinia said.

"Chica, we have all done things that make us feel ashamed, but you have also done good things. My family feels grateful to you for what you have done for my sister, and because you have helped, we are all doing better. Soon, the karma you speak of will come to you, and you will be happy, yes?" he asked. His eyes lit up as he gave an eager nod.

"Yes, I suppose. Are we going to do this? I'm so tired, all I want to do is sleep," Melinia stretched, but stopped abruptly as her bruised body protested.

"Chica, you are in pain. Please go ahead and rest. We have all night."

Grateful for his response, she closed her eyes and quickly drifted off. She slept like a baby and did not awaken until several hours later.

She opened her eyes and found herself wrapped in Remy's muscular arms. As her eyes adjusted to the darkness, she gazed over to see Remy's large, brown eyes staring at her. She recognized the potent longing he had for her. She had never allowed the johns she tricked with to kiss her. A French kiss was even more intimate than the acts she had allowed on her body. It was much different for her than lust or the act of sex. She tried to tell herself that it was the drug's influence that made her feel a connection to Remy that she had never shared with anyone else. That was why she hadn't stopped him as he leaned down and kissed her with deep passion.

After he pulled away, he whispered, "Chica, I know those other men hurt you. I promise I will never hurt you. You have felt so much pain. All I want to do is make you feel good like you deserve."

He gently turned her over onto her stomach. She complied, but she fully suspected that he would roughly abuse her body like all the others. But he surprised her by massaging her shoulders and back, using his fingers to trace the large dollar sign tramp stamp that Rique had branded on the back of her shoulder. It indicated that she was the property of him and their crew.

"Chica, just relax." She tingled as she felt the warm breath in her ear as he whispered to her.

Melinia closed her eyes and enjoyed the massage along with the euphoria from her latest hit. The combination had her feeling as though she were riding a cloud, despite how badly Raul had abused her earlier that night. After he finished the massage, he kissed delicately, from head to toe, treating her like a woman who was loved. She no longer felt like a whore who had bartered her body for drugs, and for a short time, she forgot all about the complexities of her life and her current situation. During the intimate moments they shared together, she focused on experiencing every sensation as if it were her last time.

Remy's large hands felt warm and soft on her skin, despite the calluses he'd earned from hard labor on the boat. They felt like they had been made specifically to please only her as they eagerly ventured all over her body. She moaned her satisfaction as he suckled upon her small breasts while massaging the increasing warmth that spread between her legs. Shortly after, he eased himself into her slowly, as if timidly savoring the feel of her. As he began his leisure strokes, she bit down on her lower lip to absorb the powerful waves of ecstasy that threatened to overcome her. He ran his fingers through her hair, and she dug her nails into his back as their bodies moved in synchrony. Struggling to read his eyes in the darkened room, she searched them for validation of the pleasure she felt. Did he feel the electricity between them as well, or was it only her?

His penetrating look assured her that it was not only her. She realized that the elation surging within her was indeed reciprocated. He leaned down and kissed her neck softly and intertwined his fingers with hers as quiet gasps escaped his soft lips. Upon the sweet confirmation of his feelings for her, she succumbed to the intensifying pressure welling up within her. He continued his rhythm, assisting her with getting there. As she released a guttural moan, the force of her sprouting fountain felt like it would burst right through her seams. Each muscle grew taut as she lifted her back off the air mattress, fully entranced in the power of the moment. As a gentle sense of calm descended upon her, she felt her muscles release, one by one. For the first time in over three years, she had experienced an orgasm from penetration and it was divine.

She attempted to get up and take care of him, but he stopped her. Instead, he wrapped her in his strong arms and spooned her until she fell into a peaceful sleep. In the early morning hours one year ago, she and Remy had connected in a way that transcended sex, and she knew she would never forget it.

The next day, she was allowed to spend the day with Remy. As a member of the Sandego crew, he had many jobs, but his main job was operating the cargo boat. He took her on a tour of the helm of the boat, and when no one else was around, he quietly spoke English to her.

"See, chica, these instruments help me guide la barca. These numbers are the coordinates where we will be docking," he said, gesturing toward the boat's instrument panel. "This has been the best birthday I have ever had, and it is all because of you. Thank you. Please don't forget that my family does not know that I can speak English, so you must remember to keep my secret and never tell them."

"Don't worry. I won't tell anyone," Melinia assured him.

"Good, because the only reason Rique let you spend last night and today with me is that he thinks we can't communicate with each other. If he finds out, he will punish you and Mimi. Also, after today, he won't let us be together alone. He doesn't want me to fall for you. So, when we see each other, you can't act too familiar with me, or he will hurt you."

Melinia nodded, looking up into his eyes to confirm she could be trusted.

Remy gave her a warm smile and held out his arms. "Now, give me a hug before they come back."

At that moment, Melinia noticed that several envelopes had fallen out of Remy's pocket. He bent over and picked them up, placing them next to the steering wheel of the boat.

"When we get to port, I must mail these for Rique. He wrote them in English. I am hoping one day to learn how to write in English, too."

"Maybe someday I will get the chance to teach you."

"Chica, I would like that. But, right now, I have to focus on preparing to port in less than one hour."

Melinia watched him pick up a clipboard with the coordinates of their destination and got an idea.

"Hey, I'll be right back. I need to run to my quarters and get your birthday gift," she breathed into his ear before kissing him on the cheek.

He looked back over at her and smiled. "Chica, you *are* my gift. I don't need anything else."

"Thank you. But I promise I'll be right back."

"Okay, but hurry up. Time is winding down, and my time with you will soon be over."

Melinia made it back to her room in record time. She pulled open a drawer and found a postcard and a stamp that she had hidden in the box where she kept her tampons. In another drawer, she pulled out a bracelet made of yarn. She had talked one of her johns into giving her those items in exchange for extra services during the crew's last visit to the Bahamas. If Rique ever found out that she possessed them, he would beat Mimi within an inch of her life. Despite the risk to herself and her friend's welfare, Melinia knew that this might be her one and only chance to get a message to her mother.

When she returned to the hull of the boat, Remy said, "Chica, you took a long time. We are about to pull into port."

Remy had been preoccupied with preparing the boat and hadn't seen her sneak his clipboard and pen from the side of the steering wheel. She kept up a casual conversation with him as he stared ahead, guiding the boat toward the port. Meanwhile, she quickly copied the number from the clipboard onto the back of the postcard. Then she wrote the address of her mother's home on the front. Remy had just explained to her that the numbers: 265128N786423W were the coordinates for Port Lucaya. In her rush to get the numbers down, she hadn't included commas or periods. Besides, if the postcard was intercepted, her captors would realize that she had written it and what her motive was. She'd hoped that her mother would recognize her penmanship and assume that the number represented something important. Maybe she would give it to the police, and they would discover that it was the coordinates where she and the crew would be for the next three weeks.

She knew it was a long shot, but she had to take the risk. She slipped the postcard into the stack of envelopes, hoping and praying Remy wouldn't be able to read English and would pay little attention to what he was mailing off.

"Hey, lover. You might want to put these letters back in your pocket before Rique comes up here," Melinia suggested.

"Good idea. You took so long what did you do, *make* my gift?"

"Yes, I did just that. Now, put your wrist out."

Remy did as he was told, and she fastened the yarn bracelet around his wrist and said, "Every time you wear this bracelet, think of me and the fantastic time we had on your birthday."

Remy looked at her, displaying that handsome grin of his. "Oh, I will never forget."

Melinia was so caught up in her walk down memory lane, she hadn't heard Rique speaking to her.

"Hey, Melinia, do you hear me talking to you?"

"Sorry, Papi. I didn't hear you. I zoned out for a sec," Melinia replied, giving him her full attention.

"I said you're the loser," Rique said, staring at her. "Mimi won the China white. She filleted sixty-five fish, and you've only done forty-five. You've also cut up the lowest amount of fish out of everyone here. You know this means you'll be on tape tonight with Remy."

She maintained a poker face, knowing he would gauge any type of reaction. "Yes, Daddy. But I thought Remy didn't participate in the freak shows."

"Everyone in the crew participates, including my little brother. So, I'm going to need you to fall back with the noise and stay in a bitch's place. Don't be questioning me," Rique said, still staring her down.

"Daddy, I'm sorry. I didn't mean any disrespect."

"I know you didn't because I won't tolerate it. But since you asked, you should know that this will be Remy's first time on tape. And because he is familiar with you in a biblical way, I want you to teach him the ropes."

"No problem. What time will we do the show?" Melinia asked.

"We'll tape around nine. We'll eat a great dinner that Remy will prepare for us, relax for a little while, then get down to business." He turned toward the rest of the crew. "Okay, everyone, listen up. Tomorrow we will be pulling into port. Tomorrow night we're going to have dinner with Romanita, and then we will entertain a few people who are here for a bachelor party on the smaller boat. So, I want everybody performing at their best."

"Daddy, do you mind if I go to my quarters and take a nap?" Melinia asked quietly. "I'm very tired."

"Yeah, that's fine. We'll eat at 7:30. So, make sure you're on the main deck at that time, cleaned up, and ready to perform."

Melinia walked to her quarters to prepare to put her detailed plan into motion.

Chapter 8

Where Are We Now

Before Grandville knew it, he and his entourage had arrived at the Embassy Suites located near the Oakhill Correctional Center in Dayton, Ohio. Franklin had already booked their rooms, and he was waiting for them in the lobby.

"Hey, frat. Long time, no see," Grandville greeted his friend with a handshake.

"Hey, everyone. Did you guys enjoy the limo ride here?" Franklin asked.

Everyone nodded and smiled.

"Yes, we had a great time, but it would have been better if you were with us. How was your trip down?" Grandville asked.

"Uneventful. It's almost time for us to make our way to Oakhill. Everybody, here are your room keys," Franklin said as he handed out keys to Samantha, Greta, and Maria. "All of our rooms are on the eighth floor. Grandville, you have two rooms that connect, which should give you and Juliette room to spread out with the children."

"Franklin, thanks again. Planning our hotel stay for us has really lifted a load off me. I appreciate you."

"No, Grandville, I wanted to do it. I also want to thank you for allowing me the opportunity to ask Sabrina's hand here tonight."

"I can't wait to meet her. She must be one hell of a woman to get you to the altar. You have always made it clear that you're unwilling to settle for just anyone," Grandville said.

"Yes, she's one hell of a woman and more. I promise you are going to really like her. She's meeting us at the opening and will be spending the night here at the hotel. She'll have her son with her, and this will be my first time meeting him. So, I'm nervous for several reasons. I hope he likes me."

"Who wouldn't like you? You'll be fine. Just try to relax and remember to be yourself. Maybe Sabrina's son can hang out with Jabari and Jonah. How old is he?"

"He's in his early twenties. He'll probably be hanging out with us fellas. But we don't have to worry about that now. It's time to get over to Oakhill. Rayshawn's people want to start the program on time."

Grandville gave a curt nod. "Okay, I'm ready. Let's gather everyone and get on the road."

It was only a ten-minute ride to Oakhill from the hotel. Grandville took a deep breath as he exited the limo into the summer night air. He turned around and looked at the prison while his group was ushered toward the entrance of the clinic, which was directly across from the institution.

As he walked into the shiny, new building, he saw Warden Jenkins, his counselor, Mr. Bolden, and a few other Oakhill officials lined up at the entrance. They were shaking the hands of the attendees as they walked in. Walking inside, Grandville took in the large crowd of people from all walks of life, circulating amidst a media circus. Bright flashes blinded him as photographers snapped his picture. He felt his breathing quicken as his anxiety kicked in. Just then, he felt Juliette squeeze his hand, and he remembered to exhale.

His group was ushered to a long, reserved table, directly across from the stage. Servers dressed in black and white uniforms circled the room with various appetizers and drinks. Grandville was overwhelmed by the activity in the room, along with the large number of people attending the event. As he took it all in, bewildered, his beloved wife whispered into his ear, "Everything is okay."

Juliette called Jabari over to where they were seated and said, "Jabari, I want you, Monty, and Jonah to keep an eye on your sisters. Your father and I will be moving around the room a lot. I want you and the young people in our entourage to remain at this table unless I tell you to move," she said, her voice stern.

Jabari nodded and returned to where all the children were seated with their eyes glued to various devices.

Juliette then turned her attention to Grandville and said, "Remember to just breathe. I'm right here with you. Together, we are going to ensure that Jessica's name is synonymous with good. Soon, the program will start and it won't be as loud in here," Juliette reassured her man.

Grandville nodded, practicing the mindfulness exercise and breathing techniques that his counselors taught him to use in stressful situations. He paused when he heard a familiar voice call his name.

"Stubbs, you're looking great!" Grandville looked up to see Officer Emerson standing behind him. "It's good to see both of you! When I heard this was happening, I immediately took the evening off to be here with my wife and son. He's still one of Mr. Robinson's biggest fans."

Grandville immediately stood up and shook his hand. Officer Emerson had become a friend and confidant over the years Grandville had spent at Oakhill. "Officer Emerson! It's great to see you. Thanks for making such a great effort to come tonight. I heard the tickets were pricey."

"That's okay. I've been working lots of overtime," Emerson said. "Besides, the proceeds from this shindig is going to a great cause. I'm glad to see you're staying out of trouble and back at Oakhill for a good reason. I'm hoping you and Juliette will allow me to introduce you to my family."

"We would be honored to meet your family. Please lead the way!" Grandville took Juliette's hand to help her up from the table. They then followed Officer Emerson, who led them through the large crowd to a table at the back of the room. A petite, brown-skinned lady sat conversing with a lanky, light-skinned teenage boy.

"This is my wife Amanda and my son Andrew," Officer Emerson declared with pride. "Family, this is Grandville and his lovely wife, Juliette. The clinic is named after their late daughter, Jessica. Andrew, Mr. Stubbs is responsible for getting you your Rayshawn Robinson jersey and signed ball."

"Hello, it's so good to meet you both," Grandville said as he and Juliette shook hands with Officer Emerson's family.

Rayshawn emerged from the parted crowd, sandwiched between two tall, buff men who Grandville assumed were bodyguards. The men looked up and smiled at Rayshawn as he made his way toward them.

"Grandville, it's so good to see you and Juliette. It's been too long," Rayshawn said as he kissed Juliette on the cheek and patted Grandville on the back.

"It's good to see you too, Rayshawn," Juliette said. "We want to thank you and your charity for building the new clinic and for naming it after our Jessica."

"It's what I wanted to do," Rayshawn said. "I also loved my niece, and I am hopeful that the clinic will help us all with our healing process. I'm going to need to talk with Grandville for a few minutes to go over the program before it starts."

"Not a problem, but please get him back to me quickly," Juliette said.

"I will," Rayshawn said as he began to lead Grandville away.

"Hey Rayshawn, before we go, let me introduce you to Andrew and his family," Grandville said. "Andrew is your biggest fan and has your signed jersey and ball."

"Hello, Andrew," Rayshawn greeted, extending his hand to the young man before turning to Officer Emerson and his wife. "It's good to meet you all. I appreciate you, and I'm so glad you were able to make it tonight. Andrew, we're going to take a picture a little later."

"Thank you, Mr. Robinson. I-I would be honored," Andrew stammered.

"Then it's done. Come on, Grandville. We're about to start the program," Rayshawn stated.

As Grandville walked with Rayshawn toward the podium, his nerves had him shaking in his boots. He was unclear on what Rayshawn and his charity expected of him that evening. He and Franklin planned to express their gratitude by presenting the clinic with a check. They also had a small surprise for Juliette. Besides that, he had little else to say.

Rayshawn said, "Grandville, I'll begin the program by welcoming the guests and explain the mission of the foundation. Then, the charity staff will explain their inspiration for the design of the building. Next, you'll speak. You can say as much or as little as you like about Jessica and why we're here. Then you can introduce Franklin. After Franklin is done, I'll make the closing remarks. When the program is complete, we will cut the ribbon together, eat, take pictures, and hopefully spend some time visiting. I've missed you guys."

"Thanks, Rayshawn, we've missed you too. I'm a little overwhelmed by all of this, so the quicker we can get this done, the better," Grandville responded.

"Cool, then let's get this party started."

When they reached the stage, Franklin was waiting along with several people whom Grandville assumed were part of the charity's staff.

"Hey, frat. I'm sure Rayshawn has hipped you to the order of the program. Just relax, and soon we'll be back at the hotel, chilling by the pool. It's normally closed at this hour, but I paid for extended access for our party. We'll have private use of the facility's amenities this evening. I figured we could have a pool party and just hang out."

"Franklin, you always know just what to do. That's a great idea. It's burning up outside, and the kids are going to have a ball. I hope everyone brought their suits!"

"I'm sure those who want to swim will have their suits. You know the sisters are probably not going to want to swim because they don't want to get their hair wet," Franklin laughed.

"Right. I can hear Juliette's voice now. 'Sisters are superheroes and water is like kryptonite to our hair,'" Grandville mimicked his wife. "But all jokes aside—Juliette did bring her swimsuit. She says she's going to take the kids swimming and promised to get in the pool with the twins. Early tomorrow morning, I plan to return to visit Joe. The warden pre-approved it through my treatment team. I know how it feels to be an inmate at Oakhill, and I wouldn't have made it through without you and Montell. Maybe if Joe knew that someone cared about him, he'd get himself together."

"You're a really good man, my friend," Franklin said.

"So are you, Franklin. Speaking of good people, is your girlfriend here and are you ready to propose?"

Before Franklin could respond, Rayshawn came over and said, "We're on."

The lights flickered on and off a few times, signaling for everyone to take their seats.

"Friends, we want to thank you for coming to the grand opening of the Jessica Stubbs Behavioral Health Clinic," Rayshawn began. "Your choice to spend time here with us this evening will aid many of the male residents here at Oakhill with changing the course of their lives. The ticket sales from this event have resulted in a thirty-thousand-dollar donation to the Mental Health and Drug and Alcohol Treatment program. The Robinson Foundation has been a leader in developing socially progressive programs. Some of our other programs provide annual four-year college scholarships to more than thirty high school students. With the help of those scholarship recipients and their loved ones, we have built a dozen playgrounds statewide to provide our youth with safe places to play in their neighborhoods. This evening will begin with a short program followed by dinner and fellowship. Next, I would like to introduce Ms. Locke, who is the Executive Director of the Rayshawn Robinson charitable foundation, to say a few words."

Grandville swallowed back his fear as he tried to focus on Ms. Locke's words. He didn't know how long she had spoken or what she even said because, before he knew it, she was introducing him to the crowd. As he walked to the small podium, he resolved himself to own his truth.

He adjusted the microphone and spoke directly from his heart.

"As many of you may know, Jessica Stubbs was my daughter. It's an honor for my family and me to know that, although Jessica has passed on and is now with the Lord, her name will always represent healing to those who suffer from behavioral health issues like I do. I want to thank God, first and foremost, for allowing me to be well enough to stand before you today. I would also like to thank my wife, Juliette, my sister, Greta, and my children and my friends for standing with me and being my rocks this evening. I also want to thank my friend Rayshawn and the Robinson Foundation for honoring my late daughter by building and funding this great facility and for naming it after her.

"I know how it feels to be an inmate in need of behavioral health treatment. I know firsthand how it feels to be in a place in your life that is so dark and hopeless, you don't even know if it's worth getting up every day. The staff here at Oakhill has helped me understand my mental health condition, and they have taught me techniques to help me confront and control my symptoms. They've also helped me realize that living life is a gift. I am the man that I am today partly because of the time I spent here at Oakhill. I want to personally thank my counselor, Mr. Bolden, for the countless hours he spent helping me to come to terms with my issues. I also want to thank the members of my Oakhill Survivors Group for supporting me and helping me realize that I'm only a victim if I allow myself to be one. The treatment that I received here guided me to make positive changes, return home, and reconnect with my loved ones. The new Jessica Stubbs Behavioral Health Clinic will help many on their journey to find a place in their recovery that works for them. I want to thank my friend, Montell, for everything he has done to help me. I truly believe that God has a plan for us all and that it was part of His plan for us to meet. Montell and I became friends when I moved into the cell next to him while we both were serving our time here. At this time, I want to ask my business partner and best friend, Franklin Lowe, to join me."

Grandville scanned the crowd and found Franklin seated at a table with a beautiful woman who looked vaguely familiar. It didn't take long for Franklin to join him.

"This is Franklin Lowe, my business partner, friend, and frat brother. Without him, I am not sure that I would be here today. His friendship has been invaluable to me, and I want to thank him publicly in front of all of you good people for all that he has done to support my family and me," Grandville announced, shook his hand, then stepped aside.

Franklin gave a grateful nod and stepped up to the microphone. "Thanks so much for the beautiful introduction. I want to reciprocate and thank Grandville for being my best friend and to remind him that, I too, would not be the man that I am without his continued love and support. I also want to thank the Robinson Foundation and the Oakhill officials for their work toward rehabilitation as opposed to strictly enforcement. We recognize that the men here have been convicted of a crime, but we also recognize that they are people with aspirations, hopes, and dreams for the future. Grandville explained that he personally witnessed some Oakhill inmates suffer from the side effects associated with taking medications on an empty stomach. That is why members of our fraternity, Alpha Kappa Omega, would like to donate this check for ten thousand dollars so patients who receive medications here at the clinic can also enjoy complimentary beverages and snacks to help prevent side effects."

Franklin presented the check to Ms. Locke, who accepted it with a wide smile.

The crowd cheered, and when they quieted down, Franklin continued, "When Grandville was released from Oakhill, we realized that housing options in Cuyahoga County that support former inmates with behavioral health issues were few and far between. Seven years ago, Grandville's wife, Juliette Stubbs, launched the Better Tomorrow program, which offers housing for women in Cleveland who are suffering from behavioral health issues. Grandville and I have a nonprofit corporation that recognizes housing is a necessary success component for inmates who will be released from Oakhill. Ms. Stubbs' Better Tomorrow housing program offers not only safe, drug-free housing options, but also additional support, such as vocational and educational training, and twelve-step programming. We have encouraged Ms. Stubbs to consider extending her program's access to men as well. As such, we are hereby presenting her with the deed to a four-suite, newly renovated apartment building located in Euclid, Ohio. Ms. Stubbs, please join us on stage."

Grandville marveled at his wife's beauty as she walked up to the podium to receive the deed to the apartment building with a stunned look and a huge smile on her face as the audience broke out in thunderous applause.

"Juliette, we also want to give you this check for ten thousand dollars," Franklin declared as he handed her the deed and cashier's check. "We would like to help you help men in our community suffering from behavioral health issues and with substance abuse disorders. We want you to know that our fraternity has raised five thousand dollars and our nonprofit matched it."

Juliette smiled at him and gave Grandville a long hug before returning to her seat.

"Now, before I relinquish the microphone to Mr. Rayshawn Robinson, I would like to ask Dr. Sabrina Sullivan to please stand," Franklin stated.

After a few seconds, Sabina slowly stood, looking both puzzled and confused. At that moment, Grandville remembered when and where he had initially met her. She was one of the psychiatrists who had examined him when he was in the state hospital before he was admitted to Oakhill. Franklin detached the microphone and stepped away from the podium. He took a few deliberate steps toward Sabrina while the large, inquisitive crowd looked on.

His voice boomed into the microphone. "Doctor Sullivan, there are no words that can express just how much I love you." He made his way down the side steps while maintaining eye contact with her. Once he reached her, he took her hand and got down on his left knee in front of his surprised girlfriend.

He continued, "I'm a praying man, and my prayers to the Lord were for Him to send you to me. I'd like to ask here, in front of all these good people, that you give me your hand in marriage and consent to spending the rest of your life with me."

Sabrina pulled Franklin into her arms and showered him with kisses.

The crowd, assuming her answer was affirmative, began clapping and cheering. Rayshawn and the charity staff looked on, baffled at how the program itinerary had changed in a blink of an eye.

The crowd reminded Sabrina of her duty by chanting, "Say yes, say yes."

Sabrina yelled, "Yes, of course!"

Franklin slipped the three-carat diamond ring onto her finger, and the couple embraced in a passionate kiss. The crowd erupted once again as Franklin and Sabrina returned to their table. Seated there was a young man who Grandville assumed was Sabrina's son. Grandville was sure that he had never seen the young man, but something about him seemed familiar.

Rayshawn took the microphone from Franklin and returned to the podium. "Well, congratulations, you two. We are all wishing you a lifetime of happiness together. That was touching and beautiful. At this time, I'm going to ask Greta Stubbs Robinson to please join me," he directed.

Greta stood up hesitantly, then approached the podium. Grandville watched Rayshawn's body language, trying to figure out his agenda.

"I was under the impression that I was the only one with a surprise planned this evening. I guess I was wrong," Rayshawn joked as Greta made her way to the stage.

Greta stood timidly next to Rayshawn, who gazed down at her with a look of pure love as he continued to address the crowd. "The Rayshawn Robinson Foundation is presenting this plaque and gift certificate for a day at the spa to Ms. Greta Stubbs Robinson as an expression of our gratitude. Many of you may be unaware that the concept for the Jessica Stubbs Behavioral Health Clinic was actually Ms. Robinson's idea. Watching Mr. Lowe propose to the love of his life reminded me of the day that I proposed to this beautiful woman standing next to me. We've been through a lot together, and though we're no longer married, I want everyone here to know I'll always love her, and she'll always be a part of my family and me."

Rayshawn then turned and looked down at Greta. "Greta, I want to take this opportunity to apologize and to tell you that I'm sorry for everything. I know when we were married, I didn't treat you right. I took you for granted and didn't honor my wedding vows, and for that, I'm deeply sorry. I also want to apologize to Grandville, who is my brother and one of my best friends, for being so self-absorbed that I missed the fact that you were struggling with your own issues. Maybe if I had been there for you, the way you have always been there for me, Jessica would still be here. I want you both to know I love you and you will always be family to me."

There was scattered applause as Ray handed Greta the plaque and hugged her stiff body.

Ray took a few moments to compose himself, then said, "So, this concludes our formal program. The wait staff will be serving dinner momentarily, so relax, mingle, and have a great time."

The room fell nearly silent. Greta's tears streamed down her face as she rushed away from the podium. Juliette, Maria, and Samantha were waiting for her at the base of the stage, and the trio took her hands and headed out of the room.

Before Grandville could leave the stage, Rayshawn cornered him. "Hey, I'm sorry for putting you and Greta on the spot. Part of my sex addiction recovery is to make amends with everyone I've wronged. I guess this wasn't the right platform for such a private matter. But you made it pretty clear the last time at Oakhill that you didn't want me to contact Greta and that you didn't want to be bothered with me. I didn't know when I would get another opportunity–"

Grandville was beyond angry, but before he could respond, Rayshawn said, "Grandville, I know you're angry, but please hear me out."

Grandville breathed in and out and focused his mind on the present, just like he was taught in his mindfulness classes. "Okay, Rayshawn, I'm listening."

"Look, I'm aware Greta's engaged to someone else, but I want you to know that I can't let that happen without a fight. Regardless of our legal marital status, she'll always be my wife, and I'm not going to just walk away from her."

"Well, I guess you don't have a choice. You had your chance; now be the man you weren't when the two of you were married and allow my sister to be happy," Grandville demanded.

"I can't, and I won't just stand by. I've stepped aside and waited, and absolutely nothing has happened. I've learned a lot during my sex addiction counseling, and I want to make it up to Greta and to you for how I treated you."

"Rayshawn, you don't have to do anything. Greta will always have love for you, and so will I. Like you said before, we'll always be family, but the one thing I've learned is if you love someone, sometimes you have to let them go. I'm not perfect, and like you, I've made lots of mistakes. After Jessica's death, I was lost and alone here at Oakhill. I didn't think Juliette would want to still be with me after what I did to our daughter."

"Grandville, what happened was an accident," Rayshawn reassured him.

"Yes, but it was caused by my choice to keep the symptoms of my illness away from my family. It also happened because I was drunk, trying to self-medicate and shield my issues on myself and others. I had to prepare myself to let Juliette go—if it came to that. I can honestly say that I love her enough to respect her wishes if she chose to walk away from me. I'm asking you to do that. Let my sister go because truth be told, she's already gone," Grandville sternly advised his former brother-in-law.

"Grandville, you'll always be my brother, and I'm going to try, but I don't know if I can let go," Rayshawn said. "It's one thing to divorce me, but it's a whole other game when she's trying to marry someone else."

"I'm not sure what you mean by that, but that better not be a threat," Grandville sniped. "Please, Rayshawn, stay away from my sister." He shot him a warning glare as he turned to search for his wife and sister.

Chapter 9

No Halo

Melinia was ready to put her plan into motion. At exactly 7:30, she was seated at the dinner table as directed, dressed to slay, and looking incredible. The whole crew was seated around the rectangular table, with Remy seated directly across from her. The look they shared when no one was paying attention made her tremble. She was anticipating her performance with him after dinner, cherishing the idea of spending time alone with Remy. She planned to use all of her tricks to make Remy roar on camera for the world to see. She was hopeful that when the show was over, she and Remy would be given the opportunity to spend time alone. She knew the odds of Rique allowing it were almost zero, but a girl could dream. Melinia was in deep thought as she scarfed down her food like an Ethiopian refugee.

"Hey, Melinia, you seem awfully hungry," Rique said through a mouthful of food.

"Yes, this is delicious," she replied.

"Well, I'm glad you like it, but don't eat too much because I don't want any problems with your performance due to overeating," Rique advised. "We're going to start filming around 9:30, and my little brother is gonna get downright personal with your punta. You ready to make him scream for the camera?"

"Yes, Daddy, you know what I do."

Rique then began speaking to Remy in rapid Spanish, and Remy gave her a lustful stare while she attempted to act nonchalant.

"Listen up, crew. After dinner, Remy and Melinia are going to freak on tape," Rique announced. "This is Remy's movie debut, and all of you are invited to come to the Bone Room to watch. But this is going to be a live show, and I am going to need spectators of our movie madness to be quiet. Word has it that Mimi is going to share her winnings with the whole crew."

While the crew clapped and whistled, Rique whispered into Melinia's ear. "At two tomorrow afternoon, we're having a private lunch with Romanita. Make sure you look presentable so you can spend time with my sister and Rafael. I'll be unavailable for most of the day because Roberto and I have business to discuss," Rique directed.

Melinia nodded and swallowed hard. She knew this day would come sooner or later, and she was still trying to figure out her response. Romanita was Rique and Remy's little sister and the only woman the Sandego crew seemed to love, respect, and adore. When Melinia first joined the crew, she met Romanita and her fiancé, Renaldo, at their home in the Dominican near the village where the Sandego family grew up. The couple was expecting their first child and were ecstatic. Three weeks before their wedding, several masked men broke into their house and raped Romanita in front of Renaldo, then killed him in front of her. The trauma from the sexual assault caused Romanita to lose the baby. After the violent event, she fell into a deep depression. Melinia came along and helped Romanita's recovery from her personal devastation. Over time, Romanita was able to heal and learn to lead a purposeful life, once again.

After the attack, the Sandego crew relocated Romanita to the Grand Bahamas. Her new home was a 4,000-square-foot private villa surrounded by a large fence and an armed guard hired by Rique and paid for by the crew. Word on the street was that the rape and murder were retaliation for Rique ripping off a low-level cocaine dealer whose territory was near Romanita's childhood neighborhood.

Rique had asked the dealer, Juan Martinez, to stop dealing in his childhood community. Juan refused, so Rique arranged a robbery to reinforce his message. When Juan found out who was responsible for the theft of his money and cocaine, he exacted revenge. Romanita seemed unaware of the business her brothers and cousin were in and Rique always seemed anxious to keep it that way. As far as Romanita was concerned, Melinia was a hired hand who worked on Rique's boat. Melinia maintained that story whenever she was with Romanita, and because she had done such a convincing job, Melinia was also one of the only people outside of the Sandego family that Romanita could speak to.

"Daddy, is it possible for me to act out a storyline with Remy?" Melinia asked timidly. "I have a few ideas that will spice up the show. I'm not trying to step out of line, but I believe if you allow me to take the lead, I can increase our views and increase sales."

"I keep forgetting you went to college. I'm going to allow you to take the lead, but remember to bring the heat."

"I always do," Melinia purred.

Soon, the crew made their way to the Bone Room, which was housed in one of the empty rooms turned into a makeshift movie studio. The Bone Room had two massive bones mounted over a queen-size bed. The crew crowded around Mimi, who had tied a tourniquet around her arm in preparation for Raul to shoot her up with the China white. He was melting it down with a spoon and a lighter right before her eyes.

"Hey, Melinia. Before you start, do you want a hit of this white?" Mimi asked.

"Yeah, let me just snort a couple. If I shoot, I'll be too out of it to perform."

"True. Come on over here and get your hits," Mimi ordered.

Melinia sashayed across the liner to where the crew had congregated. She bent over to take her hits when Raul reached over and started groping her behind. She knew resisting or struggling would be fruitless, so she remained completely still while he ground his erection into her backside.

"Chica, you are looking good tonight. Maybe I should do the show with you," Raul sneered.

"Raul, get off of my girl and come over here so I can give you your surprise," Mimi scolded.

"I don't know if I want it. I might want to dig your girl out," Raul said, his voice deep and raspy.

Rique happened to walk in and picked that moment to put everyone in their place.

"Raul, get your hands off the girl and sit down somewhere," Rique directed. "Melinia, go over to the bed, we're ready to begin the magic. The rest of you shut up because this show will be live, and like I already said, we're going to make this movie available for purchase."

Everyone did as they were told, and Melinia got on top of the mattress and patiently waited for Remy to join her.

She was dressed in black, lacy lingerie and knew she was looking and smelling good. She glanced at the glass of ice on the small nightstand next to the bed. The prop was an integral part of her plan. Then she closed her eyes and waited.

It didn't take long for Remy to appear. Rique counted down to indicate the show was beginning. Remy sat on the edge of the bed and waited for Rique to give the signal. Immediately afterward,

Melinia began her seduction. She crawled toward him and then began kissing his neck. She reached under the pillowcase and retrieved a pair of handcuffs and a blindfold. As she kissed his neck, she gently handcuffed him.

Next, she placed the blindfold over his eyes and whispered in his ear, "Relax, lover."

She felt the tension immediately dissipate from his body as she laid him down on the bed and began licking down his chest to his manhood. She clenched a piece of ice in her teeth and slowly traced his nipples. She then used it to circle his manhood. Remy moaned when the ice touched his skin, finding the way she manipulated his body steamy and sexy. She expertly began an oral assault of his manhood, and when he was fully erect, she placed a condom on him. Rique captured the details of Remy's stunned expressions with his video camera.

Melinia straddled his erection and rode him like the stallion he was. She pulled out every sexual trick she knew in order to please him. Every time she felt Remy coming close to ecstasy, she slowed her pace, teasing him. Before long, Remy screamed out his pleasure in Spanish. She looked down and realized the condom she had placed on Remy before their sexual encounter had begun was gone. She was alarmed as she felt the wetness of Remy's semen run down her legs. Rique saw it also but continued to film while Remy tried to normalize his breathing.

Rique ended the tape and Melinia jumped off the bed and rushed out of the liner toward her quarters. The first part of her plan had worked perfectly. Now she had to wait to see if the second part could be put into motion. Only time would tell, but with the way things were going, time was not on her side.

Chapter 10

Moral of the Story

Juliette picked at the chicken on her plate and anxiously watched Grandville as he tried to smile through his irritation with Rayshawn's impromptu confession. The entourage was eating while a jazz band, made up of Oakhill inmates, entertained them. Juliette found herself tapping along with the upbeat music. Juliette and Grandville were both ready to go but decided the best way to handle the situation was to act like Rayshawn's confession of love to Greta was a part of the program. Juliette was able to calm Greta down by reminding her why they were at Oakhill that evening. Rayshawn's confession also validated what Greta had already known, Rayshawn was filled with regret for his action, which had ultimately caused her to walk out of his life.

"Listen, player. You're going to have to go back out there and behave as if Rayshawn's words don't mean a damn thing," Samantha advised.

"Yeah, girl, you wouldn't want Derek to think you still have feelings for Rayshawn," Maria cautioned.

"I agree with Samantha and Maria," Juliette said. "How you handle this moment will impact the future of your relationship with Derek. Also, this day is about Jessica, and we need to go back out there and remind everyone out there why we are all gathered here."

Greta listened to her girls, washed her face, and let her friends reapply her makeup. She was laughing and talking with Derek, and the rest of the members of the group like Rayshawn's words had meant nothing to her.

Juliette put her gaze on her man, and it wasn't long before they were staring into each other's eyes.

Grandville leaned over and whispered into her ear, "Are you okay?"

She nodded, and before she could respond, she spotted Franklin with a beautiful woman who looked vaguely familiar. Alongside them was a young man who bore such a striking resemblance to her husband; it was uncanny. They all began walking toward them.

"Hey, fam. I want to introduce you to my fiancée, Sabrina, and her son, George," Franklin said.

Juliette immediately jumped up and gave both Sabrina and George a warm hug.

"It's so good to meet you both. Sabrina, congratulations on your engagement."

Grandville shook George's hand and hugged Sabrina. "Sabrina, it's so good to see you again and under much better circumstances."

Before Juliette could greet Sabrina as well, a woman she didn't recognize ran up to her. It seemed Sabrina recognized her, and they embraced.

With a puzzled expression, Juliette turned to Grandville and said, "I didn't realize you'd met Sabrina before."

"I didn't realize it, either, until I got a closer look at her when we arrived. She was one of Dr. Stanley's residents and was studying to be a psychiatrist during my trial," Grandville advised.

"Small world. Did she examine you?" Juliette inquired.

"Yes, she met with me a couple of times, but my legal team decided not to pursue a mental health defense."

Once the woman walked away from her, Juliette said, "Sabrina and George, it's a pleasure to meet you both." She gave them both hugs, then said, "Sabrina, Grandville just told me that you examined him while he was preparing for his trial."

"Yes, that's when we met," Sabrina warmly replied. "I'm sorry I didn't get a chance to meet you while helping his legal team prepare for his case, but I'm so glad I'm getting the opportunity to meet you now."

Juliette nodded and smiled. "Yes, and we'll be getting to know each other better during the festivities at the hotel this evening."

Franklin began introducing Sabrina and George to the rest of their group. Greta stood up to hug Sabrina and George. When she looked at George, she said, "Sabrina, what a handsome son you have. You barely look old enough to have a son this tall!"

George smiled and said, "Thank you. I get that a lot when I meet new people. I guess I have a young-looking mom."

"You know that black don't crack," Greta playfully said.

Before George could respond, Officer Emerson, who was standing amongst them, spoke up.

"Stubbs, me and the family are going to be taking off soon. I was hoping you would speak to Mr. Robinson about taking a picture with my boy. Also, I was hoping to meet your children."

Grandville called his children over. "Here are my sons and my daughters. Stubbs children, please say hello to Officer Emerson."

"Hello," the kids said in unison.

"Hello, Stubbs children. You're a great-looking bunch."

"Thank you," the kids replied in unison, then cracked up laughing at how corny they sounded.

"Officer Emerson, let me grab Rayshawn and I'll meet you back at your table," Grandville directed.

It didn't take long for Grandville to spot Rayshawn towering over a crowd of his fans. He walked right into the middle of the crowd and said, "Hey, Rayshawn, let me holla at you for a moment."

"Of course. Please excuse me," Rayshawn said as he walked away from the crowd.

"Hey, I would really appreciate it if you could take a picture with Officer Emerson's son," Grandville requested.

"Of course. I would do just about anything for you and your sister. I don't know if you realize it, but you and Greta are my oldest friends," Rayshawn said.

"You are also our oldest friend, but you can't possibly love us the way we love you. Despite my instructions, you continue to make Greta uncomfortable. I love you like a brother, but don't ever forget that Greta is my twin, and no matter what, I'll always be down for her." Grandville's stern tone matched his expression.

"I'm down for her, too," Rayshawn passionately replied. "And, though you have advised me to leave her alone, I'm going to respectfully let you know that I'm going to have to defy your instructions. You made a mistake, and Juliette forgave you. What would you do if Juliette, who is the love of your life, was with someone else? You and I both know that you would do whatever was necessary to make it right. I love Greta, and though I fucked up, I am going to make sure she knows that."

"Greta knows you love her, but she's trying to move on. Believe me when I say that she loves you too. Remember, if you love something, let it go. If it comes back, it was yours. If you really love Greta and me, then let her go. If Juliette left me, I would have no choice but to come to terms with it, particularly if she were engaged to another man. You don't have a choice, either," Grandville stated. "My sister has been through enough, so I am going to tell you this for the last time: leave her alone. Your friendship is important to me, but trust and believe that if you continue to hurt my sister, I'll drop you like a bad habit. Then you'll lose one of your best friends *and* the woman of your dreams."

Rayshawn nodded like he understood.

"Hell, you're an eligible bachelor," Grandville stated encouragingly. "I know you've got a thousand chicks just waiting for the chance to do anything with you. Do you and play the field. When the right woman presents herself, you will know. Learn from the mistakes you made with Greta and move on. Now come on. Officer Emerson and his son are waiting." He shook his head, hoping he'd made himself crystal clear.

The pair made it to the table, and Rayshawn was gracious as he took pictures with the Emerson family and gave Officer Emerson's son basketball tips. It wasn't long before the warden interrupted them to advise Rayshawn that he was needed elsewhere.

After Rayshawn walked away, Officer Emerson pulled Grandville to the side and said, "Stubbs, I want to thank you for introducing my son to his idol, Rayshawn Robinson, and for arranging for the pictures. I also want to tell you I'm very proud of you. I knew you would do great on the outside. I'm grateful I was given the opportunity to get to know you. If you ever need anything, all you have to do is ask."

"Thanks for your kind words, Officer Emerson, and thanks for your offer. Actually, I do need something from you."

"Okay, Grandville. Lay it on me."

"I haven't been allowed to keep in touch with Joe due to the terms of my parole. I've been sending him reading assignments, but I haven't been allowed to receive any correspondence from him. I would really like to know how he's doing. Is he working his program, or is he still running around, bullying and assaulting the other inmates?" Grandville asked.

"Actually, Big Joe has become the model inmate at Oakhill," Officer Emerson remarked in a proud voice. "You'd be proud to know that your impact on him has had a long-lasting, positive effect."

"I'm not sure what that means," Grandville said, puzzled.

"It means that Joe has become a scholar. He spends all of his free time in the library, and he even started a chess club where he teaches the other inmates how to play. Speaking of the devil, he's standing right behind you," Officer Emerson declared with a warm smile on his face.

Grandville turned around to see a grinning Joe standing behind him with his arms outstretched. Grandville couldn't conceal his shock as Joe pulled him into a bear hug and almost lifted him off the floor.

"Grandville, it's so good to see you! I really missed you," Joe exclaimed. "Thanks for sending me the reading assignments. I completed them all, Teach!"

"Wow. Joe, that's great. I'm so glad to hear that you are doing so well," Grandville said, crossing his arms while staring at his friend.

"Grandville, I'm doing better than well; I'm doing great. I just found out I'm being released soon. My dream of following the examples you and Montell have set is finally being fulfilled. Speaking of Montell, is he here with you?"

"Of course he is," Grandville replied, scanning the room for his friend.

"I really need to see him, and with your permission, I would love to meet your family," Joe requested. "I really feel as though I know them after hearing you talk about them in our group."

"Sure, we're all sitting on the other side of the room. I must say, I'm a little surprised the prison officials aren't following you around," Grandville said.

"Oh, you can best believe I'm being monitored. I'm wearing an ankle bracelet that has a tracking device inside of it that can shock me with a thousand volts. Plus, everyone here is being monitored by closed-circuit cameras. The prison recognizes that you have been instrumental in helping me reform and has graciously allowed me to attend the event tonight. They also wanted to reward me because I got some of the other prisoners from our support group and your former students at Oakhill to join me in donating to Jessica's building fund through the Robinson Charity. Together, we raised over a thousand dollars, and we're each listed in the program as financial supporters," Joe excitedly relayed.

"Joe, that is awesome," Grandville cheered. "I really appreciate you all for your hard work. Let me introduce you to my wife, Juliette."

After Grandville ushered Joe over and made the introductions, Juliette smiled and greeted him warmly. "Joe, I'm so pleased to finally meet you; my husband speaks very fondly of you."

"Well, I think the world of your husband," Joe complimented. "He's been instrumental in helping me become a better person. I was so mad at the world, and he helped me see that we all have problems. As a result, I'm being released from Oakhill in a couple of months. I'm excited, but also scared."

"I'm sure the way you're feeling is normal," Juliette reassured.

At that moment, Montell approached them. Juliette squeezed Joe's arm and wished him luck before heading back to the table.

"Oh my God! Montell, you look great. Freedom certainly looks good on you," Joe complimented, pulling him into a hug.

"Well, thank you, Joe. I'm hoping it won't be too much longer before you are allowed to wear freedom, too," Montell said, smiling.

"Actually, I'm being released from Oakhill soon. But before I leave, I really needed to see you," Joe said.

"Really, whatever for?" Montell asked, lifting a brow.

"I want to tell you how sorry I am for trying to assault you when you were at Oakhill," Joe stated humbly. "You are one of the only people I've wronged and haven't made amends with. I want my future to be different from my past, and both you and Grandville have helped me see that change is possible."

"Thank you, Joe. That really means a lot to me," Montell replied, shaking his hand.

"No, I want to thank both of you for all you've done to help me. I also have a request," Joe said as his voice quieted.

"Okay. We can't promise we can grant your request, but we are listening. What is it?" Grandville asked.

"I heard during the program that your charity presented your wife, Juliette with a new building where she will be offering men like me housing," Joe stated with hopeful eyes. "I'm excited about being released, but I won't have anywhere to go after the halfway house. As you know, I'm estranged from my family. The halfway house is supposed to help me with housing after I'm released, but I'm prayerful that you and your wife will allow me the opportunity to be one of your first residents if your facility is up and running by then."

"Joe, the program is not in operation as of yet, but let me speak to Juliette about what we may be able to do in the meantime," Grandville said.

"Grandville, thanks so much. I really appreciate you considering me, and I promise that if you give me a chance, I'll be a model resident," Joe lobbied for himself.

"I hear you. I'll let you know before your release," Grandville promised.

Joe smiled and nodded. "Much appreciated, Grandville. I can't ask for more."

Chapter 11
Bad Guy

Melinia peered out the window of the luxury car as it zigzagged down the dirt roads of the large tropical island. The sun was shining brightly in the sky, but Melinia knew that as the morning faded into the afternoon, the rain that came every day on the island in the summer would soon arrive. The rain only lasted for a few minutes, and after it ended, the sun would emerge again, and it would be hotter and more humid on the island than before. As she rode in the vehicle, she thought about how the daily rain represented the problems that continued to plague her and were analogous to her life. She could only hope that the issues that continued to rain down on her would come to an end so sunshine could again shine in her life. Her thoughts were interrupted by Rique's words, as he was the only other occupant in the vehicle.

"Hey, Melinia. Your performance last night was fire. What you did to Remy was so hot, our internet traffic was significantly increased. We have got some new hits on some of your older shows that we have posted. Later, I'm going to reward you with a taste of this new blend of China white that Remy cooked up," Rique said.

"Thanks, Papi. You know what we do," Melinia said, feigning delight.

"Yeah, I know that family takes care of each other, and I want you to know that I consider you to be as close to me as my own blood.

That's why we have to have a heart to heart right here and now," Rique said, his tone turning serious.

"Okay, Papi. Whatever you say," Melinia nervously replied. She was suddenly afraid and had no idea where the conversation was headed, but she decided to play along.

"I've been watching you for the past few years, and I have been trying to figure out what would make a girl who has a college education and appears to be relatively smart want to join my crew. Melinia, I'm sure you're aware that there are a lot of people who are looking for you." Rique said inquisitively.

"I'm not sure what you're talking about, Papi." Melinia's tone was cautious.

"Melinia, cut the 'Papi' shit and stop playing with me. I just saw a flyer stating there's a ten-thousand-dollar reward for any information on your whereabouts. That means that you have a blood family who loves you and is trying to find you. So, I did more digging and learned that besides your loved ones, you also have some pretty bad people who are looking for you just as eagerly. My understanding is that there is a twenty-five thousand dollar hit on you, and you are wanted dead or alive," Rique sternly said.

Melinia swallowed hard before saying, "Well...I wasn't aware that anyone was looking for me."

"We both know you're lying," he spat. "You came to the Sandego crew because you wanted to disappear. You've apparently pissed off some drug dealer named Lovelle, and he's been looking for you since before you joined our crew. Did you rob him? Is that why he wants to kill you?"

"Rique, I'm telling you...I didn't know anyone was after me. I really don't know what you're talking about!" Melinia did her best to convince him.

"Bitch, I am trying to let you know that you're considered family to the Sandego crew. That doesn't come easily around here. I'm also not going to keep letting you disrespect me by lying to my face. Now is the moment of truth. How do you know Lovelle?" Rique asked sternly.

Melinia dropped her head and then responded, "I swear I didn't know Lovelle had put a hit out on me. I joined because I want to be a part of the crew that produces China white. I fell in love with it, and you and the other members of the crew make it. When I was with Lovelle, he wanted me to be his bottom bitch while he built his stable around me. I didn't want to be his bottom bitch because he didn't have any ethics."

"Are you seriously talking to me about ethics when you give your body to whoever I direct you to?" Rique asked in a flippant tone.

"Rique, you have ethics," Melinia passionately replied. "That's the main reason I left with Mimi to join you. You don't let anyone under eighteen join our crew. Lovelle wanted me to abduct teenagers to be in his crew, and I refused to do it. You're correct, I might give my body away as directed, but I'm an adult. I have the ability to say yes or no to your proposals. Teenagers are minors, and I may be just a whore to you, but I am a whore who refuses to recruit minors to become involved in an adult business."

"I respect that, and I'm glad we're clearing the air because I needed to know what's up. It's my job to protect *every* member of the crew. After what happened to my sister, I have to be aware of any threats that can cause my family harm."

"Rique, I swear that I didn't know Lovelle was after me. I also didn't know my family was looking for me."

"I believe you. When you came to us, I thought you didn't have any blood family. That's why I'm surprised you let Romanita take Rafael instead of leaving him with your blood family."

Melinia sighed. "I'm a fuckup. My mother worked hard to provide for me and put me through college and how do I repay her? By saying, 'Guess what, Mom. I'm putting your hard work and sacrifice to use by selling my ass. I'm using that marketing degree you paid for to the fullest by selling my own body.' My family loves me, but the disappointment I see in their eyes every time they see me breaks my heart. There was no way I could tell them I was pregnant by a random john that I fucked for a hit. I can't even take care of myself right now, so what Romanita is doing for me means everything. Rafael is where he belongs right now."

"Letting Romanita take care of Rafael for you means everything to my family, and to me," Rique declared. "Romanita is my only blood sister, and you have given her renewed purpose by allowing her to care for Rafael."

"Rique, you basically gave me no choice."

"Chica, everyone has choices. You joined my crew when you knew you were pregnant, and you knew what was expected of you when you joined. If I had known that you were pregnant, I would not have let you desecrate your baby's growing place by fucking every Tom, Dick, and Harry that pays. I am not a monster. So, when Romanita was brought here to the Bahamas, it only made sense for you to stay with her and have the baby here. You cost me money because I had to take care of you and provide product for you. You were not contributing to your upkeep. Luckily for you, I was already paying Roberto to provide security and nursing care for Romanita, so it only made sense for him to treat you. Rafael seems to be a smart kid, so hopefully, the effects of your drug use haven't harmed him."

"Like I said, I'm a fuckup, drugged-out whore who sells her ass," Melinia said sadly and focused her attention on the passing scenery through the window.

"Chica, you *are* a whore. There is no question about that. But you are also many other things, including a mother, a college graduate, and a member of the Sandego crew. So, I don't have time for your regrets. We have business here with Romanita, and I want you to remember that you are never to tell her about what we do, or I will kill you myself, then collect from Lovelle for making good on the hit. As long as you do what I tell you, you are under the protection of the Sandego crew, and if anyone attempts to hurt you, there will be hell to pay," he warned.

"Rique, I lived with Romanita for months and never told her anything. I've shown you and the crew that I can be trusted."

"That is true, and this is why I am going to need you to do something else for the crew and me."

"Whatever you need, Rique," Melinia replied obediently.

"Chica, I know I can always count on you," Rique said, smiling. "Romanita has a house guest who is going back to la barca with us. His name is Julio, and I want you to take him under your wing and show him the ropes."

"Does he speak English?" Melinia asked.

"You know I don't like a lot of questions. But, yes, he speaks English, but not as well as I do."

"Rique, in the words of Tupac, I'm down for whatever," Melinia sexily replied.

"I know you are. That's why I'm glad we had this little talk. When we get back to the boat, I'm going to do you right. But until then, I'm going to need you to play your position." Rique sharply ordered.

"I got you."

"Good. Now relax. We'll be at Romanita's in a few minutes."

Melinia laid back and tried to hide how happy she was to know that seeing Romanita also meant she would get the opportunity to see her son.

Chapter 12

Lose Yourself to Dance

After a long evening, Grandville, Juliette, and their large entourage were on the party bus headed back to the hotel. It was after nine, and the members of their large party were tired and in somber moods. What the day had represented was not lost on the large group. It was the anniversary of Jessica's death, and due to the clinic's opening, her name would be known statewide from that point on. Greta and Derek were seated next to each other, but the air around them was strained. Juliette suspected Derek was very uncomfortable with how Rayshawn had openly displayed how much he still loved Greta.

Despite Rayshawn's confessions, Juliette felt the opening went well. In fact, she was still over the moon about the new property Grandville and Franklin's charity had donated to her organization because it offered the possibility for her to grow her business. Her new boarding home would allow her to begin serving the male population. The property was also near A Better Tomorrow, her female boarding home. So she was elated at all the business opportunities in her future.

Grandville had his arm around her, and he pulled her close to him, whispering into her ear, "When we arrive at the hotel, we're going swimming. Franklin has arranged a private pool party, and we'll be able to have a good time and to get to know Sabrina without any distractions."

Juliette smiled and said, "That sounds like a great idea. The kids are going to be so happy. With the twins taking swim lessons, they're going to be anxious to show us what they've learned."

"That'll be great. I can't wait to see what they're learning. You know, it's been a long time since we've been swimming, and I can't wait to see you in your swimsuit and later in your birthday suit," Grandville flirted.

"Likewise, lover," Juliette sexily replied.

Everyone in the limo could feel the tension permeating from Greta and Derek. Samantha attempted to use humor to lighten the mood. "Hey, Grandville and Juliette. Stop with the mushy stuff!"

"I say we take their lead," Jared said and kissed Samantha on the cheek.

"Boy, don't be starting something you aren't prepared to finish," Samantha said.

"Baby, I'm ready to give you all of my love. Girl, I'm tired of playing games, not just a little bit, I wanna give you all of it," Jared sang, giving his best Gerald Levert impression.

"Are you for real? I think you missed a lyric, I'm sure the song also includes something like, 'so many girls, I can't even name,'" Samantha sarcastically replied.

"That part of the song does not apply to me. That's why I didn't include it, like the late Cleveland native Gerald Levert did in his serenade." Jared winked.

Samantha rolled her eyes. "Whatever. A strapping young lad like yourself has to have a lot of women trying to get with him."

"I'll admit that I'm an eligible bachelor, but I was taught that a man chooses his woman, and I choose you," Jared said.

"Whatever." Samantha laughed.

Everyone was focused on Samantha and Jared's exchange and chuckled, except for Greta and Derek. Greta seemed to be in deep thought, and Derek was uncharacteristically quiet. After a few moments, the other adults in the limo seemed to notice the unrest between them, as everyone kept taking peeks their way.

Grandville tried to change the atmosphere and yelled, "Hey, everyone, we're almost at the hotel, and I have an announcement, so I'm going to need everyone's attention."

Their limo driver muted all the televisions.

"Thanks, Grayson. When we get back to the hotel, we're going to change into our swimsuits and head to the pool," Grandville announced. "Franklin has arranged for a pool party, and I also heard that we even have a DJ." He smiled to himself as everyone cheered.

When they arrived at the hotel, the kids took off running toward their rooms, anxious to get dressed for the pool. Even Derek and Greta looked excited.

Once they were back in their suite, Juliette helped the twins into their bathing suits and put swimming caps over their braids. It wasn't long before she was in her swimsuit and joining Grandville and their sons to head downstairs to the pool.

"Girl, I can't wait until you take off that cover so I can check you out in your bathing suit," Grandville flirted.

"Dad, please cut it out. I'm going to be sick," Jabari said.

"Well, if that made you sick, you're going to throw up when you see this," Grandville teased as he pulled Juliette into his arms and kissed her on the lips.

As the Stubbs family neared the pool, they heard music and laughter. When they entered the pool area, they noticed a middle-aged man sitting behind a turntable, which was next to a computer. He was wearing headphones and bobbing his head to the beat while standing in the corner farthest from the pool. Montell and Monty were already splashing around in the pool. Franklin, Sabrina, Greta, and Derek danced to the music, and Maria and George were seated at a table across from the pool.

Franklin walked up to greet them with a smile in a pair of kelly-green swim trunks. "Come on, Grandville and Juliette. Let's dance, and when Samantha and Jared get here, I say we start a Soul Train line."

"Hey, I'm down as long as it's to some old school rap," Grandville replied.

"Hey, Mr. DJ., you heard the man," Franklin yelled out.

The music suddenly changed, and the older adults found themselves rapping the lyrics to "Gangsters Delight" by The Sugarhill Gang. Next, the DJ weaved the old-school with current rap songs. The twins began hopping around when the DJ weaved Pharrell's hit song "Happy" into the mix. It wasn't long before Samantha and Jared joined the party, and everyone was laughing, dancing, and having a great time.

Samantha breezed in, wearing a flowy floral overlay on top of a conservative two-piece swimsuit. "Hey, guys. Sorry we're late. We took an Uber to the store to get non-alcoholic beer, a couple of bottles of wine for the ladies, some water, and juice. We even got some plastic wine glasses so the ladies can sip our wine right here next to the pool."

Jared lugged the small cooler behind him.

"You guys could've taken the limo bus," Grandville said. "But good looking out. After all that dancing, I could go for a cold beverage."

"Me too. After we finish, we should get the kids in the water for a game of volleyball," Franklin suggested.

"That's a great idea." Grandville agreed. All the fellas, including George, grabbed beers and headed toward the pool with the kids following close behind them.

The women looked up to find themselves all alone.

"Ladies, I say this is a great time for us to relax in the Jacuzzi," Maria suggested.

"That's a great idea, and we can have some of this wine I brought," Samantha said, pulling out a bottle of riesling.

They all got into the Jacuzzi while Samantha opened the wine and handed out the flutes. She handed Maria a cold water bottled water. To Sabrina, she asked, "Would you like a glass of riesling?"

"Yes, thank you. I was hoping we could make a toast to my fiancé. I still can't believe Franklin proposed to me tonight." Her excitement was written all over her face.

"I can't believe it, either, since up until today, we never knew you existed," Samantha declared. "Feel free to lead the toast. Then you can tell us all about yourself, including why we've never heard about you until today and why Franklin had kept you a secret for so long."

Chapter 13

What I've Done

T he southern breeze tickled Melinia's skin as she gazed into the Bahamian sky. She and Rique had just arrived at Romanita's home, and he had left her alone while in search of Roberto, the security guard who also lived on the property. It didn't take long for Romanita to emerge from the house and step out onto the deck. Her long hair was tied up in a ponytail, and her shapely body was draped in a white sundress. Romanita was beautiful and could have been a model if she weren't the little sister of the notorious Sandego boys. She strolled right up to Melinia and took her hands. Melinia noticed that she looked rested.

"Melinia, it is so good to see you. How have you been?" Romanita asked, her beautiful, dark-brown eyes twinkling as she stared at Melinia.

"Hi, Romanita. I've been doing okay. Working hard on the boat, trying to make money. It's back-breaking and smelly work, but I'm surviving. I hope you've received the money Rique has been taking out of my check to help take care of Rafael while staying here with you."

"Where I am from, we let the men handle such affairs. I tell Rique what Rafael and I need and he gets it for us," Romanita answered.

"Speaking of Rafael, where is he, and when will I get to see him?"

"He's napping right now. He'll wake soon and then we'll have lunch. Rique is with Roberto and someone named Julio. I figured you and I could have a little girl time alone so that I could properly thank you for allowing Rafael to stay here with me. I'm so grateful for the company he gives me. He helps me to feel not as lonely." Romanita paused as she wiped away the tears that suddenly collected in her eyes.

Melinia squeezed her hands. "I know you are having a hard time, but remember time heals all wounds."

"I don't think the wounds that I received from the worst night of my life will ever heal. I lost my man, my son, and my ability to ever bear children."

"It'll get better, Romanita. For all you know, you'll get the chance to adopt or remarry and have step-children you can help raise."

Romanita's eyes lit up as she sniffled. "I'm so glad that you brought up the idea of adoption. I'm attached to Rafael, and I want to ask if you would consider letting me adopt him?"

Melinia jumped to her feet. "What? Absolutely not! I let you keep Rafael because I felt you needed something to help you to occupy your mind and distract you from memories of the assault and tremendous losses you've endured. But don't confuse my kindness for blindness. I did *not* give you my son. I merely loaned him to you. But I can take him right now if you're overly attached. I'll never let you or anyone else take him from me, and I sure as hell won't give him away like an object!"

"Melinia, I did not mean to upset you, but I love Rafael so much that I dread the day that you will come and take him from me," Romanita said, barely above a whisper.

"You are Rafael's godmother, and you'll always be a part of his life. I'll personally see to it because, without you, he wouldn't even be here. You and I delivered him together."

"Yes, I remember." Romanita offered a weak smile. "I'll go and get Rafael up from his nap so you can see him. I'll be right back."

She stood up and walked back into the house.

Melina was still shaking as she stood alone on the deck, gazing out over the generous property while the sun kissed her skin. What she told Rique on their way there was true. She didn't realize she was pregnant when she initially became a member of the Sandego crew.

Approximately one week after the weekend she had spent with Lovelle and his cousin, the great Rayshawn Robinson, a bed at the Collins Treatment Center became available. During her weekend with Lovelle and Rayshawn, she used a small video camera to tape their sexcapades. She owed Lovelle a lot of money for her opiate habit, and she had planned to use the video to blackmail him into erasing her debt. She had no idea that he would become so angry that he would put a hit out on her. She had put her name on the Collins Center waiting list over a year prior, and although she had enrolled in the rehab program, her efforts were not sincere. She had used the center to hide from Lovelle and his goons. After she entered the rehab, she noticed her weight gain but had attributed it to her getting off drugs for the first time in years.

She was given a pregnancy test when she first entered rehab, and it was negative, so she had no idea she was pregnant. She was very advanced in her pregnancy when she learned the news. She had no idea who her child's father was, but she suspected that it could be either Lovelle or Rayshawn. She was so high the night they had engaged in sexual activities that she barely even remembered the details.

Then she watched the tape. She realized that Rayshawn had taken liberties with her body without her consent. She had been so out of it that she hadn't instructed him to wear a condom. She was just happy that she had a chance to have a sexual liaison with Rayshawn because she had always had a small crush on him. She knew that, to him, she was just another piece of ass, but she didn't care. She had the tape of that night to remind her that even though she was a junkie, she had been intimate with the great Rayshawn Robinson.

When Rique found out she was pregnant, she expected him to be upset, but he seemed to almost be relieved.

"Anybody else would beat you and the little bastard you're carrying to death," Rique explained. "But I'm not a monster. I'm going to allow you to have your baby, and I'm going to ensure that you are both well taken care of. But you're going to have to do something for me."

"Whatever you need, Rique," Melinia said dutifully, with tears running down her face.

"I need you to stay with my sister," Rique directed. "She has been through an unspeakable horror, and I believe the two of you can help each other. After the baby is born, I fully expect you to fulfill your duty to the family and me. I have hired an armed security guard for my sister, who will also watch over you. He will also help wean you off the China white to become strong enough to deliver the baby. When you are with my sister, you are never to tell her about what you do for the family and me. If she asks, you are a hired hand on the cargo boat. Your boyfriend left you, and we took pity on you and hired you. After you began working on the boat, you found out you were pregnant. That's the story."

"Rique, I promise I'll never tell her. Also, I really didn't know that I was pregnant."

"I know you won't ever tell her because if you ever do, I will kill you. The compound you will be living on with my sister is bugged with video and audio surveillance, and I am recording everything that happens in the house. You can think of me as your private 'Big Brother' because anything you say or do while you are away from me, I will know. Also, you and my sister are never to leave the compound.

If you need something, let Roberto know and he will ensure that you get it. Do we understand each other?" Rique asked.

"Yes, Rique. You can count on me."

The very next day, Rique moved her onto the compound, and, for the most part, she stayed away from Romanita, rarely speaking to her. Romanita was extremely depressed and spent most of her time grieving and praying. Roberto was a former nurse in the Mexican military before becoming employed by Rique. His main job was to guard Romanita and the compound. Roberto also weaned Melinia off the China white until her body was no longer dependent on it.

Though she and Romanita shared the same space, she seemed clueless that Melinia was detoxing from heroin. She also seemed unaware of the type of business her brothers and cousin were engaged in. On the night Rafael was born, she and Romanita formed a friendship she felt would last a lifetime. It was March, and out of the clear blue, the Grand Bahama Island was hit with a major storm. The electricity was disrupted due to high winds, and during the midst of it all, her water had broken, indicating she was in labor. She stumbled out of her room and found Roberto, who had just come back into the house from reviewing the outside perimeter of the house.

"Roberto, my water broke, and I think I'm in labor! I need to get to a hospital," Melinia begged.

"Rique has forbidden us to leave the compound for any reason," Roberto explained. "You'll have to have the baby here. Also, the electricity is out, and that means the electric fence and all the security precautions that we have in place are failing. I need to be outside so I can guard the perimeter of the property."

At that moment, Melinia felt a piercing pain in her uterus and screamed out in agony. She crumbled and fell to the floor, gripping her belly. Fear wracked her young mind as she envisioned every possible way things could go wrong. She thought her mind was playing tricks on her when the lightning flashed, illuminating Romanita's figure in the doorway.

"What's wrong?"

"Senorita, I think she is in labor, which means you are going to have to help her deliver the baby. I must go outside. With no electricity, we are sitting ducks," Roberto informed Romanita.

Romanita began speaking in rapid Spanish, and Roberto responded, nodding. Melina couldn't understand them, and she was in so much pain that it didn't even matter to her. Another severe pain hit her, and she screamed out in pain once again.

"Chica, you are going to have to stop screaming. Instead, try to breathe air in through your nose and then blow it out of your mouth. It is going to hurt, but to bring life into this world, we must feel pain."

Melinia looked up to find Romanita's dark-brown eyes fixed on her. She was kneeling on the floor beside her. After she got her breathing under control, Romanita helped her back up the stairs and into her bed. She lit candles that cast a gentle light in the room before gathering towels, a large bowl of hot water, and scissors. Initially, the sharp pains came and went sporadically. But soon, the waves of pain began hitting her in rapid succession, and Melinia was almost delirious as she felt an intense urge to push.

Romanita said, "I can see the baby's head. Now I am going to need you to take a deep breath, bear down, and push."

Although she was scared and nervous, Melinia did as she was told and pushed with everything she had. The only sounds in the still of the night were her grunts and labored breaths in between. Romanita coaxed her to continue and to remain calm while retaining her focus on the end goal: delivering her healthy baby boy into this world. Melinia was grateful for Romanita's leadership and was more than happy to oblige her commands. A few minutes later, she was rewarded with the sound of her son's piercing cry, alerting her that she was the mother of a healthy baby. She could barely make out his tiny silhouette as Romanita placed him into her waiting arms. Seconds later, the lights came back on.

Melinia gazed down at his angelic face for the first time, and a deep wave of love that she had never felt before nearly consumed her. She hadn't heard Roberto come in and was startled when she looked up to find him standing over her, silently taking in her bundle of joy.

"Chica, you and Romanita did good," Roberto declared. "Now that the electricity is back on and our security systems are back up and in place, I can help you. I need you to push one more time so we can get the afterbirth out of you."

Melinia handed the baby to Romanita and lay back down, preparing to push again. Once she delivered the afterbirth, Roberto examined her and determined she was doing well. Before long, her son was clean and hungry. Melinia looked over at Romanita, unsure of what to do. Romanita showed her how to nurse and care for her baby, taking care not to interfere and to allow the new mother and son to bond naturally. The following morning, Rique had a brand-new crib and bassinet delivered along with just about anything a baby could need, sparing no expense. He didn't visit them at the compound until a month later.

After he examined the baby, he sat Melinia down for a heart-to-heart conversation about business. It wasn't until that moment that she realized she had willingly sold herself into slavery.

"The baby is very handsome, and according to Roberto, he is also healthy. Soon it will be time for you to return to la barca to begin paying back your debt to the Sandego family and me. You will not be allowed to bring the baby with you, so you should plan for Rafael's care. What is your plan?" Rique asked her.

Melinia's breath caught in her throat. Did Rique expect her to just give her child away without a moment's notice? "I…I don't have a plan."

"I figured you didn't, so I came up with one for you. Would you consider leaving Rafael with my sister? According to Roberto, Romanita's condition has improved since she's started helping you with his care. I also understand that you have even named her as his godmother."

Melinia nodded numbly. "I think that's a great idea, but I want you to understand a few things."

Rique's eyebrow rose, and she noticed his left eye twitch slightly. "Bitch, tread very lightly. You are in my service, and I'll be giving the orders here, not the other way around."

Melinia dropped her head. "Rique, please forgive me. I didn't mean any disrespect."

"I know you didn't because you know better. Now, what is it?" Rique asked.

"I think caring for Rafael will help Romanita with her depression. Since Rafael was born, your sister has slept in my room with us. She has nightmares just about every night and wakes up yelling and screaming. I appreciate what you and the Sandego family have done for my son and me, and I am ready to repay my debt, but I want everyone to know that I am not ever giving my son away to your sister or anyone else. I believe your sister needs something to keep her mind off what happened to her, and I'm willing to let Rafael stay with her if it helps her with her depression."

"Thank you, Melina. Then it's done," Rique said, standing up. "Rafael will stay with Romanita, and we will visit her and Rafael often.

He is two months old, and I will give you one more month with him, then it's back to work."

"Of course, Rique. But may I ask a question?" Melinia said hesitantly.

"What is it?"

She looked up at him and asked, "What will I have to do to repay you and the family, and for how long?"

"You will need to be with us until Rafael is ready to start kindergarten. I will provide you both with everything you need, including food, shelter, clothes, and your China white. In exchange, you will do whatever is instructed of you. You will entertain who I tell you to entertain, and you won't even go to the bathroom unless I tell you that you can. If this is not acceptable, you can give me ten thousand dollars right now. That should cover what we've already spent on you. After I receive my money, you're free to take your son and go."

"I don't have ten thousand dollars," Melina mumbled, wringing her hands.

"I know you don't. So, it seems you have little choice."

This was how Melinia had found herself trapped in a cell of her own making as a human trafficking victim. She had willingly, yet unknowingly, sold herself there.

Her thoughts were interrupted by a squealing Rafael running and crashing right into her arms. "Hey there, little man. Look how much you have grown. You're turning into such a big boy," Melinia said between showering her son's face with kisses.

Rafael's bright eyes looked up at her as he squealed and melted into a fit of laughter.

"Mama, come," he said, pulling her hand.

"Okay, Rafael, I'm coming," Melina laughed, following her son on his determined little path.

"I told him to bring you inside for lunch," Romanita said as they entered the dining room where Romanita had placed sandwich meats, bread, and salad.

"Please help yourself to whatever you want. You can also help Rafael with making his plate," Romanita offered.

Melinia turned to her son and asked, "What kind of sandwich do you want, Rafael?"

"That and that!" Rafael pointed toward the turkey and ham.

As Melina prepared Rafael's plate, Romanita said, "Last week, Roberto had a doctor come to examine Rafael."

"That's great. What did the doctor say?" Melinia asked, spreading mustard onto a slice of wheat bread.

"Rafael is doing great. He was a bit upset when he gave him his immunization shots, but he was fine after I gave him some baby aspirin and he took a nap. Rafael is hitting all his developmental benchmarks and is in the ninety-fifth percentile for height. You have never told me about Rafael's father. Was he also tall?" Romanita asked, setting a pitcher of fresh-squeezed lemonade on the table.

At that very moment, Melinia gazed over at Rafael and saw what she had never noticed before. Rafael was the spitting image of his father.

Chapter 14

Add to Me

Juliette, Samantha, Maria, and Greta surrounded Sabrina in the Jacuzzi, sipping wine, laughing, and talking. As they spent time getting to know Sabrina, the men and the children splashed in the neighboring pool. Hanging lanterns surrounded the pool area, casting a soft light beneath the night sky. Despite the setting sun, the temperature was still in the mid-eighties. The pool's cool temperature offered them relief from the scorching heat.

The ladies were an attentive audience as they listened to Sabrina explain the details of her relationship with Franklin.

"From the moment I met Franklin, I felt a connection to him that I've never felt with any other man."

"Well, didn't you have a strong connection to your son's father?" Samantha asked.

"No, because George is not my biological son," Sabrina explained. "My sister, Serena, and my brother-in-law, Gavin, adopted him when he was three months old. My sister was seventeen years my senior, and she and Gavin were both killed in a house fire when George was nine years old. My mother was so grief-stricken from my sister's death that she suffered a mental breakdown. Since she was unable to assume George's care, I took him and raised him like he was my own."

Maria's hand flew to her chest. "Wow, George is so very blessed to have you."

"No, I'm the one who is blessed," Sabrina said. "George saved me from having my own nervous breakdown. When my sister died, I didn't just lose my only sibling. I also lost my mother because although she is here physically, she is emotionally unavailable. I know she loves me, but even after all this time, she still suffers from depression and spends a lot of time crying. She's been unable to work or even function on her own. I was hurt because I could not understand why my mother didn't love me enough to fight for her mental health.

"Although my sister has passed on, I'm still here. George also lost the only mother he had ever known, and he also lost his grandmother. Having to care for him and my mother forced me to reevaluate everything about my own life. A good friend of mine suggested that I attend grief counseling along with the National Alliance for the Mentally Ill's Family to Family program. There I learned that the best way to help my family was to accept our reality. I decided to become a psychiatrist because I wanted to help people who are struggling with these types of issues."

"You're a very strong woman," Juliette said.

"So are you, Juliette," Sabrina stated. "I know we didn't meet until today, but I really feel like I know you. Franklin has told me so much about you and Grandville while we've been dating over the years. Since the first day that I examined Grandville and learned of what you had to go through, I've admired you."

Juliette frowned, deep in thought. "Thanks, but why? I didn't do anything spectacular."

"You've continued to live, despite having to deal with the death of your child. I know that it hasn't been easy, but you continue to move forward and haven't let Jessica's death deter you from being a good mother to the rest of your children."

Juliette nodded graciously. "Well, I found out I was pregnant with the twins when Grandville was at Oakhill. I really didn't have a choice but to keep moving forward because I had small children who were depending on me. Now enough about me—I want to know more about you."

"Yeah, give us the skinny on you and Franklin. You can start by telling us when you and Franklin met?" Samantha requested.

"We met shortly after Jessica's accident," Sabrina began. "I was in my psychiatric residency at a forensic mental health facility at the time. Grandville's attorneys were considering using a team there to provide expert testimony for Grandville's mental health defense if his case went to trial. Like I said earlier, I met Grandville when I examined him. It was shortly after the accident, but I got to know Franklin while he worked with my team on Grandville's defense. I don't know if I would have ever met Franklin if not for the Stubbs family's tragedy."

That's when it hit Juliette. She and Samantha had seen Franklin at dinner with Sabrina while Grandville was imprisoned at Oakhill. But Franklin and Sabrina were deep in conversation and hadn't noticed them.

"You know, Juliette and I saw you and Franklin out at a restaurant a couple of years ago. I had forgotten it until now," Samantha said, reading Juliette's mind.

"Yes, my work schedule doesn't allow me to do much cooking, Sabrina laughingly replied. "So, Franklin and I have been to so many restaurants. I'm lucky I don't weigh three hundred pounds by now. When I was in my residency and taking care of George, I just didn't have much time for much else. But Franklin reminded me that no matter what, I always had to eat."

"When did you finish your residency, Sabrina?" Greta asked.

"In May. My program required two additional years of medical education, and I can't believe I finished. I took the summer off, but I just got hired at Cleveland General Hospital. I plan to work there for a few years before starting a private practice on my own."

"You go, Dr. Sabrina! Ladies, I would say a toast is in order," Juliette said as she raised her glass toward the starry sky.

Maria also raised her glass of ice water, and Greta, Sabrina, and Samantha each raised their glasses, sloshing the wine that was filled to the brim.

"Sabrina, it seems like you're a great fit for Franklin," Juliette sincerely said. "Welcome to our family. We're very proud to have you."

Everyone took a sip. Then Samantha broke the silence, as usual. "Sabrina, if you're still interested in forensic psychiatry, I can check with my colleagues in the prosecutor's office to see if you can do some part-time work for us. We need psychiatrists to treat our mental health patients in county jail and to give expert testimonies at trial."

"That would be fantastic, Samantha," Sabrina said with a wide smile. "Thank you. I've suddenly found myself with more time, and I want a nice wedding. I'm going to need to make a few extra dollars to help with the expense," she laughed.

"Not a problem. I got you, girl. You're the first African-American female psychiatrist I've ever met, and you're bringing that black girl magic by shattering those glass ceilings," Samantha complimented.

"I'm just trying to be like you, Ms. District Attorney," Sabrina teased.

The women melted into laughter and clinked glasses again. They stopped short when they heard a piercing scream.

Chapter 15

Bobby James

Melinia had thoroughly enjoyed her visit with Romanita and Rafael. After lunch, she and Rafael had spent hours playing with his Lego blocks and trucks. Afterward, she, Rafael, and Romanita had eaten dinner together by candlelight. Then, she gave Rafael a bath and read him a book about dinosaurs. Rafael's bedroom was filled with educational toys and decorated with bright colors. She gave him a sweet kiss, then tucked him into his race car-themed twin bed.

As Melinia left his room, she knew in her spirit that leaving him with Romanita had been the right decision. Before long, it was time for her and Rique to get back to the cargo boat. Rique, Roberto, and Julio had spent the entire day in the small building behind Romanita's home. They hadn't interacted with Melinia or Romanita all day. It was eleven at night when Rique entered the house and immediately summoned Romanita for a private meeting. About fifteen minutes later, he announced to Melinia that it was time to go.

She stepped outside and was met by Roberto, who escorted her to the car before giving her a goodbye hug that took her by surprise.

"Senorita, I'm so sorry that I didn't get a chance to say hello until now. I'll see you the next time you return," Roberto said.

She nodded numbly. Once she was seated in the vehicle, Roberto put two garbage bags into the trunk. It didn't take long for Rique to join her, accompanied by an extremely attractive man who she had never seen before.

"Melinia, this is Julio. He is going to be working with us on la barca," Rique said.

"Hello," she said shyly.

"Hello," Julio said with a heavy Spanish accent.

Julio looked at Rique, speaking in Spanish. Melinia allowed her eyes to take him in. He was so handsome; he was almost what she would consider pretty. His curly hair, long eyelashes, and dark, sun-kissed skin framed a lean, muscular body. She was used to Rique and other members of the crew carrying on conversations in Spanish and hadn't cared about what they were saying. She was just grateful to have a few moments of peace. She leaned her head against the car window and closed her eyes for a moment.

"Hey, Melinia. Julio was just telling me that he thinks that you're beautiful," Rique said. "He's wondering if everybody on the boat looks like you."

"Please tell him I said thank you."

"Tell him yourself. He speaks English."

"Are you from the United States?" Julio asked.

"Yes."

"I can't wait until I get to go to the United States so that I can meet LeBron James," Julio said.

Melinia laughed. "I also want to meet him one day."

"Maybe we will get to meet him together." Julio smiled, showing a set of straight, pearly white teeth.

"Yeah, and when you guys meet him, make sure you have him introduce me to the pope because your chances of meeting LeBron are about the same, almost non-existent," Rique teased.

"Rique told me you are from Cleveland, Ohio. Have you ever seen LeBron play?"

Melinia shook her head. "No, I could never afford Aviler tickets once he joined the team. I've only seen him on television just like most of the world. He doesn't live in Cleveland anymore, so even if I ever go back home, I'll probably never meet him."

Rique waved his hand dismissively and said, "Okay, enough about sports. Melinia, listen closely. When we get back to the boat, you're to show Julio to his quarters. In the morning, you will show him the ropes. While we're docked here in the Bahamas, I'm going to purchase supplies, and I want you two to be ready to help put everything away. Julio is from my village in the Dominican Republic, where the Sandego family use to live. When we get back to the boat, we're going to show Julio how our crew gets down. Remy just cooked up a new batch of China white. Melinia, I owe you a few hits for the extra work you put in with my sister."

Melinia was doing her best not to act depressed about again having to leave Rafael, because if Rique knew how much leaving her son affected her, he wouldn't let her see him again. She knew he would do anything to avoid any kind of interference to get in the way of her selling her body. She was upset, but she had learned a long time ago to fake it until she made it.

The thought of a hit of the Sandego boys' special mix of China white had perked her up and gave her something to look forward to. She loved her son and truly wanted to give him a good life, but she was unable to, given her current situation. In her heart, Melinia had known he was better off with Romanita until she could create a better situation for the two of them. So, China white was the medicine she needed for what was ailing her. It helped her forget that she was once again leaving her son.

"Thanks, Rique. You know you can count on us," Melinia purred.

"I do know that I can always count on family," Rique said while looking her directly in the eyes.

Melinia nodded her head, understanding Rique's non-verbal threat. She closed her eyes again, attempting to calm her nerves and block out the pain of her separation from Rafael.

When they arrived back at the boat, Rique pulled her to the side and said, "Show Julio to his quarters and bring him on the main deck in twenty minutes."

It didn't take her long to find the shipping container Mimi had prepared for Julio. It would serve as his room while on the boat.

They stepped inside, and Melinia said, "Julio, this is your room. You can put your belongings away later. Please make yourself comfortable because this room is your new home. In about fifteen minutes, Rique is having a small party to toast you as the newest member of the crew. The restroom is right outside this door. You can freshen up, and I'll be back in ten minutes to take you to the main deck."

Julio smiled. "Okay, muchas gracias, chica bonita. Hasta la vista."

Melinia smiled and nodded in recognition of the very few Spanish words she understood. As she walked back to her room, she thought about when she and Mimi had first joined the crew. There had been no toast or any type of pomp and circumstance, and she could not help but silently wonder what Rique had planned for Julio.

Chapter 16

The Other Side

It was a humid evening, and Grandville laughed and talked with his friends in the pool, finding the cool water to be both relaxing and refreshing. He was having the time of his life, creating new and fun memories when he heard a piercing scream from the other side of the pool. He immediately began swimming toward the deafening sound. The pool was dimly lit, so he could not ascertain who was screaming and why.

"What's wrong! Who's hurt?" Grandville asked as he frantically waded across the hotel pool.

"Daddy, it really hurts. It hurts so bad!"

Grandville immediately recognized the voice as one of the twins. He made it to his daughter at the same time that Juliette and all the other women rushed over. Juliette looked frantic and on the verge of tears while the other ladies gasped in horror.

"Everyone just calm down," Grandville said with authority.

He realized that it was Jolene screaming once he got closer. He picked her up and carried her out of the pool. Juliette swam over with them and sat on the side of the pool, trembling. Grandville handed Jolene to her, then pulled himself out of the pool and took Jolene from his wife, who seemed frozen with fear. He carried the screaming child over to a chaise lounge chair and gently laid her down.

He bent over her and said, "Jolene, what's wrong? Why are you screaming and crying? Tell me what hurts."

"Daddy, it hurts," Jolene wailed between frantic sobs. Jenae stood beside her, holding her sister's hand.

"Daddy is going to need you to calm down and tell him exactly what hurts."

"It's my leg," Jolene cried, clutching it tightly.

He examined her leg and didn't see any visible injury. "Honey, Daddy doesn't see anything wrong. Tell me what the pain feels like," Grandville urged.

Jolene only continued to scream and cry, leaving everyone around them scrambling to figure out what was going on. Sabrina made her way through the group and knelt in front of Jolene.

"Hey, little one. It's Aunt Sabrina. I'm a doctor, and I want to help you, but I can't help if I don't know what is wrong. I know it hurts, but for us to figure out what's wrong, we must understand your pain. I need you to breathe in and out with me, and I am going to ask you a few questions, okay?"

Jolene's sobs subsided for a moment as she silently nodded.

Sabrina gave her a warm smile and continued, "If you can answer my questions without screaming, I'll give both you and your twin sister a treat. Do you think you can do it?"

Jolene sniffed and nodded.

"Good, let's start with your age. How old are you and your twin?" Sabrina asked.

"Four," Jolene whimpered through tears.

"You and your sister are some big girls. Do you know how to count?"

"Yes."

"Excellent. I figured so. Which number is higher, one or ten?"

"Ten," Jolene answered immediately.

"How bad is your pain?"

"Really bad," Jolene said.

"Okay. I want you to describe the pain. Does it burn?"

"It feels like something is stabbing me right here," Jolene wailed and pointed to her calf.

"When did you first feel the pain?" Sabrina asked.

"Earlier, before we came here. I told my mommy about the pain, and she gave me some medicine," Jolene said with tears still falling.

"One last question. Earlier when your Mom gave you the medicine, was the pain this bad?" Sabrina asked.

"No, it hurt before, but it hurts more now."

"You've behaved like a young lady far older than four! And because you've kept your word and calmed down, you and your twin are going to come with me to my room so I can give you both your treat. We're going to bring your Mom and have some girl time. How's that sound to you, ladies?"

"Good," Jolene and Jenae responded in unison.

Sabrina looked up and began giving everyone directives, "Grandville, stay here with Franklin and the guys and enjoy the party. Juliette and the ladies are coming with me to my room to tend to Jolene."

"Okay, Doc," Grandville said. He gave her a quick, grateful hug. "And thank you."

"Now, you cut that out. My family and friends all call me Sabrina. Come on, ladies. In the words of my idol Beyoncé, 'girls run the world,' so let's go to my room and do just that," Sabrina said with sass.

Sabrina headed toward the lobby, carrying Jolene in her arms. Jenae was walking between Juliette and Greta, holding each of their hands, and Maria and Samantha followed closely behind. Grandville noticed that all the women had varying expressions of worry on their faces. He was worried as well but decided to try taking Sabrina's advice.

Franklin, who seemed to pick up on Grandville's concern, said, "Come get back in the water with us, Grandville. The girls have Jolene, and she'll be just fine. It's a perfect night to just swim. Let's do some laps."

"Okay," Grandville reluctantly agreed.

Montell gave Grandville and Franklin a few minutes alone by starting a new volleyball game with George, and Jared.

"Hey, frat, how are you holding up?" Franklin quietly asked.

"I'm hanging in there, although, on the inside, I'm a nervous wreck. When Jolene screamed, it brought me back to the moment Jessica died," Grandville admitted while quivering.

"I know it did. Jolene's screaming like that scared us all. But I just want you to know that everything is going to be okay. Sabrina is one hell of a doctor, and she is going to make sure Jolene is physically and mentally fine," Franklin reassured.

"Thanks, frat," Grandville reached over to grab his beer bottle from the side of the pool. "I'm not going to lie; I couldn't only think of the day I hurt Jessica. And did you see Juliette's face? She definitely felt it too."

"Grandville, you and I both know that what happened to Jessica was an accident," Franklin said. "You saw Jolene. She wasn't bleeding or anything, and she's going to be just fine. Just try to relax,"

"I am. But I can't help but be concerned," Grandville confided. "Did you see the looks on Jabari and Jonah's faces? They were terrified. And with Jabari witnessing what I did to Jessica, I'm afraid that no matter how great a father I want to be, that I'll never be able to erase what he saw."

"Well, have you and Juliette gotten Jabari some therapy?" Franklin looked his friend in the eye.

"Yes, we have, and his therapist concluded that he seems to be doing okay. But I'm still worried that what he saw will have a permanent negative impact on him," Grandville stated with a frown.

"Grandville, your kids know what happened to Jessica was not intentional. They've all forgiven you. But none of it will matter if you haven't forgiven yourself," Franklin lectured.

"I hear you, Franklin, but what do you think is causing Jolene to be in pain to the point where she is yelling, screaming, and crying? I'm not going to lie, I can't bear to lose another child, and I don't think that Juliette would survive it, either. If something happens to another one of my children, I don't know what I'll do," Grandville quietly confessed.

"Grandville, we're not even going to go there. Last time I checked, Jolene was breathing, talking, and walking upright. So, don't jump the gun and get upset before we even know what's going on. Jolene was swimming right beforehand, so maybe she caught a cramp. We both know how painful that can be, so try to just take a moment and breathe."

"Thanks, Franklin. You've got a good point. It's probably is just a leg cramp. I have to say that watching Sabrina take charge of the situation, let me know why you fell for her; she is quite a woman."

Franklin grinned. "That she is."

"By the way, frat, when were you going to tell me that Sabrina and I had already met?"

Chapter 17

High Right Now

Melinia surveyed the Bone Room and tried to figure out exactly what Rique had up his sleeve. The only time it was used was while the crew made sex tapes. But according to Rique, that was where the party would be held. He hadn't mentioned that she would be on tape that evening, and according to Mimi, he hadn't said anything to her about a show. So, she wondered why Rique had instructed her to bring Julio there. When she arrived back at the room that she shared with Mimi, she noticed she was waiting for her.

"Hey, girl. Rique called Raul while you all were visiting Romanita. He told me that Rique wanted me to decorate the Bone Room and make it festive because we were having a party for someone named Julio that's joining our crew. Did you get a chance to meet him?"

"Yes, he's from the same village as the Sandego boys and grew up in the Dominican Republic."

"Well, is he good looking, and does he speak English?" Mimi pressed.

"Yes, he's an attractive guy, and he's bi-lingual. But when we joined the crew, Rique didn't have a party for us. So, what do you think is going on?" Melinia asked.

"I'm really not sure. But whatever it is, we're just going to have to roll with it," Mimi replied.

All the members of the Sandego crew were men except for her and Mimi. Most of them were from that same village. Since Rique preferred that few of the crew members spoke English, there was a communication barrier that made it easier for him to control the women he'd put into sexual bondage.

When Melinia and Mimi had first arrived on the boat, there was another female crew member named Carmelita who had shown them the ropes. She had a beautiful, dark-brown complexion, long, straight hair, and a body that most women would die for. She could also speak Spanish and French, as well as English. Her raspy, sultry voice made her accent even sexier to those who paid for her company. During their first few weeks on the boat, Rique would strike both Melinia and Mimi and withhold their China white whenever they disobeyed his commands, which was painful and terrifying for them. The women quickly learned to do whatever they were told to avoid punishment.

Melinia and Mimi had been on the boat for three weeks when Carmelita explained a few things to them.

"The Sandego crew is made up of drug dealers who are known everywhere for their infamous China white mix. Rique figured out that when the crew sells their product, it's a final transaction, and they have to get more," Carmelita whispered. "When he sells our bodies, he can do it over and over because we are addicted to the drugs he provides. He also uses drugs to control us. It's a special kind of hell that we can only hope to escape one day."

Carmelita was just as addicted to China white as Melinia and Mimi. After being on the boat for five months, the crew had docked in Puerto Rico for a weekend. Rique used a speedboat to transport the ladies to the mainland, where they entertained some California businessmen. Melinia was so high she barely remembered what happened. She knew that when they returned to the boat, Rique had jumped in Carmelita's face, yelling at her in Spanish. Melinia and Mimi had no idea what the two were arguing about. Within a blink of an eye, he had smacked Carmelita's face, knocking her to the ground. Melinia and Mimi witnessed the assault but knew better than to intervene or come to Carmelita's aid. They could only imagine the consequences of attempting to defend Carmelita.

A few hours after their fight, Carmelita and Rique left the boat together. When Rique returned to the vessel, Carmelita was not with him. To that day, neither Melinia nor Mimi had any idea what had happened to Carmelita. They had only seen Carmelita leave the boat without her belongings, not even the pictures of her children, who were still in Haiti. After Carmelita didn't return to the boat, they could only assume that Rique had done something horrible to her, reinforcing the lesson for them to never disobey him.

Exactly fifteen minutes after showing Julio his room, Melinia escorted him to the Bone Room, as instructed. There was plenty of food and drinks, and Julio seemed to fit right into the crew, laughing and conversing with the male members in Spanish. The room was not frequented by the crew often because most of the members never participated in the freak shows. Instead, they spent most of their time cleaning and maintaining the boat.

It didn't take long before Rique pulled out the China white. "Okay, Sandego Crew. It's time to do what we do. Melinia, as I told you earlier, you are a soldier, and because I can always count on you, you'll be the first of the crew to christen this bag. Julio, you're next because you are our guest of honor."

"No, I'm good, but thank you," Julio said. "I don't fuck around with drugs. I don't even smoke weed."

"Why, are you a narc?" Rique asked.

"No. I just hate drugs because I have witnessed what drugs can do to a family and a community. I don't want any parts of it," Julio answered honestly.

"Well, guess what. The moment you boarded this boat, you became a part of 'it' and a whole hell of a lot more," Rique said with a chuckle. "You don't have to shoot, but you sure as hell will inhale. You and I are about to hit this good shit. That way I'll know for sure you're not a narc or an undercover DEA. Melinia, take this bag and start preparing your hits."

Melinia did as she was told, and afterward, Rique took the bag from her and handed it to Mimi, who eagerly began preparing her hits. Rique walked over to the small table in the corner of the room and pulled a bag of weed out of his pocket. It didn't take him long to roll a joint while Julio and the rest of the crew watched.

"Julio, do me the honor of lighting up this sticky. I want you to know I heard you and, because I am a fair guy, I don't want you to do something you're not one hundred percent comfortable with. So, I'm going to take it easy on you and let you hit this sticky instead of this China white, which was specially mixed in your honor," he said, slapping Julio on the back. "You don't want to refuse because if you do, it will be an insult to our hospitality, and you don't want us to get suspicious of you. That would really be bad for you."

"I'm not a narc, and when I decided to take your offer and join the crew, I did not realize you were involved with drugs," Julio explained. "I wouldn't have come on la barca if I had. I wanted to go to America to get away from drugs, violence, and poverty. I just want a better life."

"Good for you. I'm not sure what you thought, and frankly, I don't give a damn. All kinds of illegal, illicit shit happens on this boat. The moment you boarded la barca, you gave your consent for whatever happens here. Now you know where we sleep, so you have no choice other than to join our crew. The only way out is death," Rique said, his tone ominous.

Julio reluctantly took the joint and lighter from Rique. He took a big toke, as directed, coughing loudly. After hitting the weed five times, he said, "Now I have smoked it and, as you can see, I am down for whatever if it will get me to America."

Melinia's head was high as she surveyed her surroundings. Everybody seemed to be having a great time. Rique turned on an old school rap tune, and Melinia found herself humming along with the music as she nodded in and out of consciousness.

Everybody was drinking and getting high when, suddenly, Julio began rapping loudly to the music. Melinia noted that the weed he had unwillingly smoked was starting to kick in. Julio began dancing and taking off his clothes, like a stripper.

"Yeah, boy, you're flying high, aren't you?" Rique laughed, nudging the person next to him.

Julio didn't acknowledge Rique's comment as he continued his striptease routine. Soon, he was completely naked and dancing around in his birthday suit. That was when all hell seemed to break loose.

"Hey, fellas, are you all checking out Julio? Now he understands the rules of joining our crew. You've either got to get beat in or fucked in. So, Julio, which way are you trying to join?" Rique asked.

Julio seemed oblivious to Rique's question as he continued to dance and sing at the top of his lungs. Rique said something in Spanish to Javier, a member of the crew who had spent most of his time cleaning the boat and one of the few members who also spoke English. Javier crossed the room to stand next to Rique.

"Judging by what I'm looking at, I think we know how Julio wants to join the crew," Rique said in English.

Rique handed the rest of the joint to Javier and ordered, "Light up this sticky, Javier."

Javier looked nervous but did as he was told. He took several deep puffs of the weed until the joint was gone.

"The crew appreciates the hard work you do on this boat, and I want you to relax and enjoy yourself," Rique told him.

"Thanks, boss. I am having a great time," Javier said.

After a few minutes, Javier also found himself feeling loose. Soon, he too had stripped naked and joined Julio in song and dance. That was when Melinia realized that Rique had laced the weed with ecstasy.

"You boys like my blend of e-weed? It was mixed especially for the two of you," Rique said, his tone dripping with sarcasm.

Both Javier and Julio were so high that they didn't even realize that Rique was speaking to them.

"Javier, I want you to sit on the bed, and Julio, you get onto your knees on the floor," Rique directed.

Both men followed his directions, and soon he had his video camera out, taping the men. It wasn't long before Javier grabbed Julio by his head and forced his mouth onto his erect penis. He held his head down with both hands, and as Julio struggled, Javier continued to sexually assault him. Julio gagged and coughed as Javier pumped in and out of his mouth.

"Julio, you'd better not bite him. If you do, we're going to kick your ass. Then we're each going to fuck you," Rique warned from behind the camera.

Julio closed his eyes, high and barely conscious. It wasn't long before Javier screamed out in Spanish and ejaculated all over Julio, whose tears streamed down his face. He pulled away, attempting to gasp for air.

"Now, Javier, it's your turn. Get down and please Julio like he just pleased you. What do you say, Julio? In the words of the movie *Deliverance*, Javier 'sure has a pretty mouth.'" Rique released a wicked laugh.

"No, boss. I don't want to do it," Javier defiantly said, although he was still high.

"You little punta! You will suck whosever dick I tell you to! Suck it, or you will be in the water sucking shark dick," Rique said, punching Javier right in the eye. He pushed him down to the floor in front of Julio's midsection. "Now start sucking, motherfucker, and the same goes for you. You'd better not bite him, or I'll let the whole crew fuck you, and I'll tape every last second of it."

With tears streaming down his face, Javier said, "Why are you doing this to me?"

Rique responded, "You didn't think I knew you tried to force Miguel to suck you off last week? I know everything that happens on this boat. You like boys to perform oral sex on you, huh? Since that's how you get down, I know you won't have a problem sucking Julio's dick."

"I'm sorry. I wasn't trying to hurt Miguel, but we don't see any other women apart from Mimi and Melinia," Javier sobbed. "You won't let anyone from the crew touch them unless we're on tape. I'm a grown man who needs a sexual release."

Rique nodded. "You're right. No one touches Mimi or Melinia unless I say so. They're a big part of the crew's revenue. You're not going to be bouncing up and down on them for sport. I'm sorry I didn't realize you were suffering, and you should have spoken up. From now on, I will make sure we have a couple of girls hit la barca when we're docked. But that still doesn't excuse what you did. In our village, homosexuality is not accepted but, after what you tried to do, it gave me an idea. I'm going to use this experience to make the crew some money and for a very high price. We'll offer a few dude-on-dude videos. I'm going to edit this video so no one will know that you and Julio were even in it, but if either one of you ever crosses the crew or me, everyone in our village will see your faces on this tape. Now stop talking and start sucking."

After Javier reluctantly performed oral sex on Julio, Rique put up his video camera and gave Melinia another hit. That was all she remembered until the next day when she woke up to Julio standing over her.

"I thought you were my friend. How could you set me up?" Julio asked her angrily.

Chapter 18

All Your Friends

J uliette stared down at Jolene. Sabrina attempted to take her temperature as she continued to cry, and Juliette was still shaken up after hearing Jolene's scream. It was reminiscent of the last time she'd heard Jessica's screams. The piercing sound had plunged her right back to the worst day of her life. She could tell by how Samantha looked at her that she was also worried.

"Hey, Juliette. Come over here and sit down. Finish drinking your wine and give Sabrina some room to work," Samantha said, leading Juliette toward an armchair directly across from them.

Juliette sat down and attempted to stop her trembling. Despite taking deep breaths, she couldn't calm herself. Jolene was in pain, and she had absolutely no idea why. It felt similar to when she couldn't help Jessica after the accident that took her life. Now, another one of her daughters was in excruciating pain, and she couldn't help her, either.

"Sabrina, I am so thankful that you brought your doctor's bag with you. Were you able to get a temperature?" Juliette worriedly asked.

"Oh girl, this bag goes wherever I go! Yes, it's ninety-nine point five. That indicates a low-grade fever. It could be an infection or a virus. Kids carry more germs on them than adults and get sick all the time. But it's usually something they can fight off easily. We're going to monitor Jolene for a while to see if her symptoms leave. If they worsen, we'll need to take her to the hospital. In the meantime, I want you ladies to relax. Let's have another glass of wine. Samantha, there're two bottles of white zinfandel in the refrigerator. Would you do the honor of pouring us more drinks?"

"No problem. While I pour the wine, can use your doctor skills to check on Juliette?" Samantha asked. "I'm worried about her. To me, her color seems off."

"Okay, no problem. But first, I need to give these big girls the gifts that I promised them," Sabrina said as she went into the closet.

"All right, twins. Close your eyes. When I count to three, you can open them," Sabrina said.

The girls clasped their eyes tight, and Sabrina pulled out two large dolls from the closet that were life-size replicas of the twins.

"Okay, girls. You can open them."

Once they opened their eyes, the girls squealed and began to jump and clap as they rushed over to receive their dolls.

"Jolene, you get the doll that looks like your twin, and Jenae will get a doll that looks like Jolene," Sabrina instructed. "There's also an app that allows you to interact with your dolls. I'll give it to your mother, and she can download it on your iPads. Now, have fun playing with your dolls while I talk to your mother."

"Thank you, Aunt Sabrina," The twins said in unison.

"You both are so welcome," Sabrina replied as she walked over to the ladies and took a sip of her wine.

"You're really good with kids," Juliette said. "Thanks for the beautiful dolls. What I can't figure out is how you got dolls that look like them when you've never seen them before."

"I ordered them online a few months back after I talked Franklin into sending me a picture of the twins," Sabrina confided. "I feel like I know each of you, even though I've never met you until today. Franklin is always talking about all of you and has shown me pictures of you for years."

"It's great that Franklin told you all about us, but why do you believe he's never told us anything about you?" Samantha asked what everyone was thinking. "I mean, we never even knew you existed until today."

"Honestly, I think Franklin felt tremendous guilt for falling in love with me since he met me due to Grandville and Juliette's tragedy. We were friends before we became lovers, but I think he was recently reassured that Grandville is okay. That's why he wants to fast track our relationship and get married soon. I love him, and I was starting to get anxious, but all I can say is that God does answer prayers."

"Amen," the rest of the ladies said in unison.

Despite enjoying the conversation with Sabrina and her friends, Juliette could not seem to relax and still felt herself trembling. Her friends soon took notice.

"Juliette, Jolene is going to be okay," Maria reassured her.

"I know, but this is the anniversary of Jessica's death. She was only four-years-old when she passed, and that's the exact age of the twins. Jolene's scream brought me right back to the day I lost my Jessica. When I heard it, I thought I'd lost her, too," Juliette said, gazing down at her shaking hands.

"You may be experiencing symptoms of post-traumatic stress disorder," Sabrina explained. "It can involve flashbacks of memories and mental and physical symptoms like anxiety and shaking. Although it's pretty common, it can be terrifying. I want you to close your eyes and just breathe with me."

Juliette followed Sabrina's directive and breathed in and out. Then she heard Samantha say, "Jolene will be okay. So, drink your wine and let the fermented grapes calm your nerves."

Just then, Jolene interrupted their conversation with another blood-curdling scream, and Juliette could not get out of the chair quick enough to get over to her.

"Jolene, honey. Tell me what's wrong. Why are you screaming and crying?" Juliette asked.

"Mommy, my leg still hurts so bad. Please help me," Jolene wailed.

Sabrina pulled out her thermometer and took Jolene's temperature a second time and then said, "Jolene's temperature is one hundred point one. It's time to take her to the hospital. Samantha and Greta, please let Grandville and Franklin know that Juliette, Jolene, and I are taking a cab to Mercy Youth Hospital. Ladies, please relax and watch a movie with Jenae and let the boys continue to enjoy themselves. There's no reason for everyone to come to the hospital. Please keep everyone calm, especially the boys. One of my sorority sisters is a pediatrician at Mercy, and I'll text her on the way to let her know we're coming. She was going to attend the Oakhill event with us but had to work, so I know for sure she's at the hospital."

Juliette was barely holding on as she cradled Jolene to her chest with silent tears streaming down her face. The ladies rushed over to the bed to gather Juliette's purse and other belongings.

Sabrina leaned over Juliette and quietly said, "Jolene may be in pain, but she's here. If you fall apart, she will too. We don't want Jenae to become more anxious. So, please try to remain calm."

Juliette swallowed back her anguished tears and nodded.

"You ladies go ahead and get Jolene to the hospital, we'll hold it down here," Samantha reassured them.

"Jenae is hungry, so we're going to order room service," Greta said. "Jolene, hurry up and get better because when you get back, Auntie Greta is going to let you order whatever you want from the room service menu."

"Yeah. And when you get better, Aunt Maria is going to re-braid your hair. So hurry back, precious," Maria said lightheartedly.

"Okay," Jolene said in a tiny voice as Juliette slowly stood, still cradling her. With Sabrina in tow, they rushed her out of the suite.

Chapter 19

1000 X's & O's

M ontel could sense that Grandville was feeling stressed about Jolene, so he took over the festivities to allow Franklin and Grandville the opportunity to have a private word.

"Okay, young men, gather 'round. When I was a teenager, I would play in chess tournaments at the park. The winner would receive a fifty-cent piece. In my hand is one of the many pieces I won at twelve years old. We're going to have a contest to see who can find this coin at the bottom of the pool. Can anyone of the young people tell me when the fifty-cent piece was minted?" Montell quizzed.

"In the year nineteen-oh-one," Jonah screamed out.

"No, unfortunately, that isn't correct," Montel said. "Anybody else want to guess?"

"In seventeen-oh-three," Monty yelled out.

"You're close but, unfortunately, also incorrect. The fifty-cent piece was first minted in seventeen ninety-four, and it was produced in large quantities until two-thousand and two. One day, fifty-cent pieces will be collector's items because they haven't been produced in years. I have a whole bag of fifty-cent pieces with me that I won from all kinds of chess tournaments. Now, I'm going to have you turn your backs, and I'll throw this fifty-cent piece into the deep end of the pool. Whoever retrieves it will get to keep it. We are going to start the competition with Monty, Jabari, and Jonah. After they finish, we'll allow George, Derek, and Jared to try. Now let the games begin."

While Montell led the competition, Grandville and Franklin sat in the Jacuzzi and had a heart-to-heart, during which Grandville gained a better understanding of why Franklin had never told him about Sabrina.

"Every time I visited you at Oakhill, I wanted to tell you about Sabrina," Franklin confided. "But I couldn't find the words to tell you that the worst thing that ever happened to you resulted in the best thing that ever happened to me. When I met Sabrina, I finally found my ride or die. There's a zero probability that I would have met her if it weren't for you facing charges. We had no one with the exception of you in common. I got to know her when her residency medical team sent her to present their findings after they examined you. Initially, we were going to pursue an insanity defense on your behalf, but after the prosecutor presented us with your deal—which you ultimately took— there was no reason for us to use their team."

"Franklin, I wish you would have told me and allowed me the chance to be the kind of friend to you that you have always been to me," Grandville said.

"Man, you are and have always been a great friend to me. But, the truth of the matter is, it isn't you, it's me. I've felt guilty," Franklin confided.

"Why?"

"Because you were in hell at the same time that I was finding my very own heaven with Sabrina. I just couldn't tell you or anyone about her because it didn't seem right. I didn't want to share her with anyone until I made absolutely sure that you were okay. I needed to verify that this nightmare we've endured for the past few years had a positive outcome. I figured Jessica's name being used for mental health care at

Oakhill and my becoming engaged on the anniversary of one of the worst days of our lives is one of the most positive outcomes we could hope for, given all that has happened."

Their conversation was interrupted by loud cheering as Jonah retrieved the fifty-cent piece from the bottom of the pool at the same time Jared's cell phone began to ring. Jared left the pool area and, after a few minutes, came back.

"Hey, Franklin and Grandville, let me speak to you both for a moment," Jared said.

"Step on over to our private man cave," Grandville joked.

Jared slid into the Jacuzzi and said, "Samantha just called me. She said Jolene is running a fever, so Juliette and Sabrina decided to take her to the hospital. The ladies are camped up in Franklin's suite and have ordered room service. She said not to worry and that they will keep us updated. They want us to continue the party."

Grandville got out of the Jacuzzi and said, "What hospital did they go to?"

"She didn't say," Jared replied.

"Franklin, can you get in touch with Sabrina and find out? I'm about to be on my way," Grandville declared.

"Are you sure? I'm sure they have it covered. Maybe you should stay here with the guys, like Samantha suggested," Franklin said.

"I appreciate your advice, but I will not have Juliette sitting there worrying without me. There were many times in our past when I couldn't be with her when she needed me. Now that I can be here, I'll be damned if she's at the hospital without me, trying to deal with our sick kid. Also, I really appreciate Sabrina and all that she is doing, but the two of you just got engaged this evening. She should be spending the night with you, celebrating your joyous news. I'm going to the hospital, and I'll gladly send your fiancée back here to you."

"Grandville, if you're on your way to the hospital, then I'm coming along, too," Franklin said. We've been through too much together for me to leave you hanging in your time of need."

Grandville walked toward the pool and watched Derek and George, who were trying to find one of the fifty-cent pieces on the deep end. The group laughed and cheered, then began clapping once George emerged from the water with the coin.

"Those five years of swimming lessons my mom made me take have finally paid off," George boasted with a grin.

Grandville picked that moment to interrupt them. "Gentlemen, I have a quick announcement to make. Can I get everyone's attention?"

The group fell quiet and stared attentively at Grandville.

"Jolene is running a fever, and Juliette and Sabrina have taken her to the hospital," Grandville announced. "Franklin and I are on our way to meet them. When you guys get done with the contest, you are more than welcome to hang out in my suite to play video games and order room service. The ladies are in Franklin's suite watching movies. Jabari, come over here."

Jabari quickly jumped out of the pool and jogged over to Grandville.

"Dad, is everything okay with Jolene?"

"I don't know, son. While your mother and I are away, you are to look after your brother and sister. And I want you all in the bed by one am. Okay?"

"Okay. Can we keep the television on until you and Mom get back?" Jabari asked.

"Sure, no problem."

"Okay. See you all later, Dad," Jabari said as he ran to jump back into the pool.

"Hey, Grandville, don't worry about anything here while you're gone," Montell said. "I'll keep the boys entertained and out of trouble so you can go tend to Jolene."

"Thanks."

As he and Franklin headed toward the limo, Grandville said a silent prayer. It was the anniversary of one of the worst days of his life. He could only hope that whatever was causing Jolene's pain was treatable. He didn't think he or Juliette could survive losing another child.

Chapter 20

Something Keeps Calling

Melinia stared up at an angry Julio and tried to discern if he was really standing there or if she was dreaming.

"Well, are you going to say something?" he asked.

Melinia tried to shake the sleep off and sat up in bed.

Before she could utter a word, Mimi interjected herself by turning on the radio. In a near whisper, she said, "Who in the hell do you think you are, coming into our room uninvited and accusing my girl? We don't know you and don't forget that most of the members of the crew are your friends. Last I checked, you're all from the same village. She didn't set you up; you set yourself up the minute you decided to board this boat. Okay, you sucked a dick; do you know how many dicks me and my girl have had to suck just to survive? I'm going to give you some free advice, don't ever come incorrect to me or my girl again," Mimi declared.

"Listen here, chica. I'm sorry you and Melinia have had to perform sex acts, but this is not what I signed up for," Julio exclaimed.

"This isn't what we signed up for, either! But this is where we've found ourselves, so deal with it," Mimi advised.

"Julio, didn't you say you wanted to go to America?" Melinia asked him.

"Yes, it's my dream."

"Well, this is going to be your most direct path to reach your goal, considering the president of our country is not letting many immigrants into the US. So, what you don't want to do is piss Rique off. He's a real motherfucker when he's angry," Melinia warned.

"Don't ever let him hear you complaining about anything he's made you do, or he will force you to do even more demeaning things," Mimi warned. "What you want to do is stay on his good side."

"One of the last girls to get into it with him is now sleeping with the fishes," Melinia said. "We can't prove it, but we're pretty sure she's no longer amongst the living. But, for the most part, Rique's pretty fair. He gives us lots of product, makes sure the rest of the crew doesn't assault us often, and he pretty much ensures our safety. We've met other girls during our travels who are also part of the human bondage trade, and they are being dogged by their captors. Overall, Rique does seem to genuinely care about us and the well-being of his crew."

"Melinia, when we met on our way here, I thought you and I connected," Julio said.

"Yes, you seem nice, but what kind of connection do you think we formed? All we really said was hello to each other. As far as I'm concerned, you're the family of my captors, being that you're all from the same village. Do you think Mimi and I really want to be here? We're junkies, and as long as Rique and the crew are providing us with product, we'll stay that way because we know what you have yet to learn: nothing in this world is free. Every day, our lives are put in danger, but we willingly joined the crew, so we do what we have to do." Melinia shrugged. "Even if you feel you were tricked, you also willingly joined the crew. Since you believe we have a connection, you should listen to Mimi and me. Questioning anything Rique says or does will get you killed, so you'd better never repeat what you said to us to any other member of this crew. Rique has this whole boat wired with video and audio, so you'd better pray that the radio has drowned out this conversation."

"Oh my God, I can't believe what I've done. I willingly sold my soul to El Diablo," Julio whispered.

"Hey, Julio, it's not all bad," Mimi reassured. "We do go to numerous ports, which gives us an opportunity to see the world. And because you are a man, you most likely won't be forced to have sex unless you are picked to perform a freak show for the camera."

"Even if Rique doesn't make you perform sexual acts, he'll work you like an Egyptian slave. Speaking of which, let me get up so we can be ready when he arrives with the supplies. When you're around him, put on your game face and do whatever Rique requests, because if you don't, it can result in him hurting you. After he's done punishing you, he'll hurt Mimi and me and other members of the crew," Melinia warned.

"Why, if you and Mimi didn't do anything wrong?"

"Because Rique wants you to know that your actions don't just affect you, but everyone on the crew. It's one of the oldest tricks in the book to get people to conform."

After chatting for a bit longer, the three decided to head back out onto the main part of the ship before Rique arrived back on the boat. Melinia and Julio waited on the dock for him while Mimi helped the crew with their tasks. When Rique arrived, they helped some members of the crew bring supplies onto the boat and worked together to put everything away. Afterward, they went to the top deck to avoid Rique and the other members. Melinia was positive that the sound of the wake would make their conversation inaudible. That was when Julio told Melinia his life story.

"I'm the youngest of seven. I had one brother and five sisters. My family doted on me because I am the youngest. They made sure I was given the opportunity to attend school and learn to read and write. Most of my siblings are illiterate, but I was able to teach my sisters simple math and how to read and spell some words. We were very poor, but my family pulled together to make sure I had everything I needed. My brother, Juan, was the oldest, and we were the only boys in my family. Juan personally paid for me to leave our village and attend Dominican American University in San Domingo. I was a good student, and I would have earned my bachelor's degree if Juan hadn't been killed. After his death, my family could not afford to take over my tuition, so I had no choice but to come home.

"When I returned home to my village, I realized that my brother had been earning money for my education by selling drugs. In the meantime, he'd made several enemies who felt that I was now responsible for his debts. My sisters have all married, and I was afraid to try to escape to one of their homes for fear of putting them in danger," Julio said.

"What type of danger?" Melinia asked.

"Thugs began coming around, threatening me and my parents. If I had gone to one of my sisters' homes, I would have endangered them, their husbands, and their children. I decided to get away from the DR for a while, so I reached out to my friend Hector who'd attended college with me. Hector is Mexican, and he put me in touch with his uncle, Anthony, who has a shipping company that regularly goes to the Bahamas. Anthony told me about his cousin, Roberto, who is a part of the Sandego crew. Anthony gave me a choice to work for him or to come to the Bahamas and join the Sandego crew as many of the crew from my village had done. I decided I would be better off with people from my village. Anthony promised that the crew goes to ports in the US. I had just arrived in the Bahamas a few hours before I met you. Roberto had it set for me to leave with you and Rique. I was excited about joining the crew because all I want to do is get to the land of opportunity and have a chance at freedom," Julio said.

Melinia put it all together at that moment. Julio was the younger brother of the man who had raped Romanita and killed her fiancé. She was almost certain that Julio had no idea of the crime his brother had committed and the potential danger he faced from Rique and the rest of the members of the boat, due to his brother's actions. Melinia instantly felt sorry for him, and she vowed to herself that she would try to protect him.

"Julio, that's quite a story," Melinia said. "All I can truly advise is for you to comply with whatever you're asked to do. You have to show Rique that you're down for whatever if it will benefit the crew as a whole."

He nodded. "Got it. Okay, so you know my story. Now, when are you going to tell me yours?"

"There's not much to tell. I'm from Cleveland, Ohio," she began.

"I know this because we talked about it in the car. Tell me something I don't already know about you."

"I have a child," Melinia confessed.

"You are a mama. That's wonderful!"

"It's not really all that wonderful because, as I told you earlier, I'm addicted to China white. My son is a king, and he definitely deserves more than some dope whore for a mother," Melinia declared, shaking her head.

"Melinia, you're so much more than a drug addict, and you can't let your present circumstance define you. Tell me something else about you." Julio tried to change the subject.

"I'm a proud graduate of Kent State University," Melinia said.

"That's good. Because, one day soon, you're going to go back to your life in the US, and having an education is going to help you provide a good home for your baby," Julio reassured her.

"Julio, the one thing you can't afford to have on this boat is hope. It will just leave you disappointed. I've been here for three long years, and I've learned to focus on making it, day by day. Don't think too far into the future. That can be dangerous."

"Okay, I'll take your advice."

"Also, don't ever mention my baby to anyone on this boat and never let Rique or the crew know that you're friends with Mimi and me. Rique is a divide-and-conquer type of leader," she warned.

"I don't understand what you mean."

"He doesn't want us talking to each other. He purposely keeps us separated because he's afraid we might plot against him."

"Okay, I think I get it now. Melinia, when are you and Mimi getting off this boat? You are American, and it would be easy for you to leave when the boat is docked at a US port," Julio said.

"If it were that easy, I would've done it years ago. When we go to the US, we're never docked at port. Rique anchors the boat at least a mile from the port. He uses a speedboat to take us between land and the boat. We're never alone, and even if we were to get away, we'd be putting our lives at serious risk. Rique pays off so many people; it's impossible to know who to trust. Also, if I don't get my daily fix, I'm going to be very sick. I don't think I could survive withdrawal again. The pain is so bad; you feel like you're going to die."

"So, if you want to be a mama to your baby, you're going to have to get off the drugs."

"I know that, but right now, I don't think I'm strong enough," Melinia admitted after a brief pause.

"But you could also overdose and die. Then what would happen to your baby? There're some drug dealers who are putting fentanyl in all the drugs, including marijuana and cocaine. I never knew a lot about drugs, but I had no choice but to become educated on the subject once I learned that my brother was a dealer."

"Julio, I can guarantee you that the Sandego brothers take great care in mixing their China white. Rique prides himself on having his product mixed in a way that reduces the chance of overdose. He also keeps naloxone on the boat to revive us if we were to ever overdose."

"I've never heard of naloxone. What is it?"

"It's a drug that reverses the effects of opiates like heroin, Vicodin, and Percocet," she explained. "It comes in a nasal spray, or you can inject it. Unfortunately, opiates can slow your respiratory system, and the effects are even greater if you use an opiate and then drink alcohol or take Super Valium. Rique has a huge stockpile of naloxone on this boat. He buys kits every time we hit a port. You don't need to have a prescription to get it in most drugstores in the US due to the opiate epidemic."

"Super Valium. What is that?" Julio asked.

"It's a prescription medication. Valium is a type of benzodiazepine."

Julio shook his head. "There seems to be an awful lot to keep up with just so you can get high."

"I've already told you; I don't do it to get high," Melinia replied. "Although I'll admit, I like to fly up in the sky. But I mostly do it to avoid getting sick."

"Well, a lot of people kick it, so what will you need to do to get off of the drugs?"

"I'll have to be prepared to meet the devil because kicking is a hellish experience," Melinia answered sarcastically.

"It sounds like you're already there."

Before Melinia could respond, Mimi appeared on the upper deck and said, "Rique wants to see you both. He's waiting for you in his office."

Chapter 21

Believe in Us

Juliette was uncomfortable as she sat in a chair that felt too small for her body. She was positioned across from Jolene, who was lying in a hospital bed that almost swallowed her tiny body. Due to Sabrina's influence, Jolene was admitted to the hospital and examined by the emergency room pediatrician immediately after their arrival.

Juliette stared down at her sleeping daughter's angelic face while an expression of anxiety and worry marred her own. Sabrina was in the corridor, talking to her sorority sister, a doctor at the hospital, leaving her alone with her child and her thoughts.

She was hopeful that when Sabrina returned to the room, she would bring some encouraging news. Something like, whatever was causing her daughter severe pain was temporary and could be easily fixed. She couldn't help but think the worst, like cancer or another fatal disease. She was trembling and barely holding it together when her king, along with Franklin, came walking through the door. The sight of Grandville made her heart soar and brought tears of joy to her eyes. His presence was reinforcement that she did not have to navigate the storms in her world all on her own. He was there to offer his love and support, which offered her shelter from her woes.

Grandville reached out for her. "There you are. I've been all over this hospital looking for you and Jolene. Come here,"

Juliette ran right into his open arms and melted into his strong embrace.

"I know you wanted me to stay at the hotel with the kids, but I will not have you at the hospital without me. You've spent far too much time alone dealing with the kids and every problem by yourself while I was at Oakhill. I'll never fail to be here for you again," Grandville said into Juliette's ear. He gently grabbed her face with his hands and placed a soft kiss on her lips. At that moment, she felt her anxiety dissipate.

"Thank you, Grandville. I'm not going to lie; I'm really scared. I can't imagine what's causing Jolene to be in such pain. I'm petrified that whatever's wrong will prove to be fatal, and the thought of losing another child has me in a mess. The way she screamed brought me back to the day we lost Jessica. Grandville, I don't think I could go through that again. If something happens to Jolene, I'm sure I'll have a nervous breakdown," she admitted.

Grandville held her at arm's length and looked into her eyes. "Hey, I've already had a nervous breakdown, and I'm here to tell you: having one is no fun. What you're going to do is take your own advice. We're going to talk about whatever the problem is, and then we're going to deal with it together. Let's try to stay positive because the odds of something being fatally wrong with Jolene are very low."

At that moment, a nurse entered the room and looked at Franklin, who was sitting in the corner, attempting to give the couple some privacy.

"You must be Jolene's father. She looks just like you," the nurse gushed as she went over to the machine to check Jolene's vitals.

Franklin's eyebrow raised, and he looked stunned speechless.

Juliette broke her embrace with Grandville and rushed over to Jolene's side. "Actually, my husband is right here. He's Jolene's father," she said breathlessly.

The nurse looked embarrassed as she held her hands up. "I'm sorry." She finished up, then rushed out of the room.

Before their silence could become awkward, Sabrina breezed back in. "Hey, Grandville. I appreciate you bringing my fiancé to the hospital to collect me, but you and Franklin should've stayed at the party," she said. "According to my sorority sister, Jolene is going to be released soon."

"Sabrina, thank you for you looking after Juliette and Jolene for me, but I can't party when my wife and daughter are here at the hospital," Grandville said. "It's you and Franklin who should be partying, so I want you to go with Franklin back to the hotel and celebrate your engagement. Franklin and I took the limo bus here, and Grayson is parked in front of the hospital. He will take you back to the hotel."

"Okay, Grandville, now that I know Jolene will be fine, I'm going to take your advice and leave with my fiancé," Sabrina said. "Oooh, I love how that sounds. I still can't believe Franklin proposed and we are engaged."

Sabrina walked over to Juliette and gave her a hug, then leaned down and kissed a still-sleeping Jolene on her cheek. Franklin and Grandville exchanged goodbyes with their fraternity handshake. After the couples finished their goodbyes, Franklin grabbed Sabrina's hand and quickly led her out the door.

"I'm glad to see she's no longer screaming and is finally sleeping. Did the doctor say anything about what could be causing her pain?" Grandville asked.

Juliette shook her head. "No, but she's running a temperature. The doctors and nurses took a blood sample, checked her blood pressure, and listened to her heart. They've only been in to check on her vitals at this point. Sabrina said Jolene was being released, so hopefully, they've determined that she has a bad virus or something else that's treatable."

Juliette and Grandville sat together on the small loveseat near Jolene's bed. Juliette laid her head on Grandville's shoulder, and before long, she found herself getting drowsy. Grandville had always had that effect on her. His mere presence instantly relaxed her, and she must have had the same effect on him as he was soon snoring. Juliette was almost asleep when Jolene's emergency room pediatrician entered the room. She stood and motioned for him to step outside the room with her as to not disturb her sleeping child and husband.

"Doctor, did you determine what's wrong with my daughter?" Juliette asked.

"Well, it looks like she has a urinary tract infection that's causing her to run a temperature."

"Does a urinary tract infection cause leg pain? Because Jolene has been crying all day about her leg hurting."

"Yes, I suppose the infection could cause some body aches, but we're more concerned about the results of Jolene's blood tests."

Juliette tried to stay calm as she waited for the doctor to elaborate on his concerns.

"I reviewed her family history and saw that you're a hemoglobin-S carrier. Your father also passed away from sickle cell anemia. Is this correct?" the doctor asked.

"Yes, my father passed away when I was twelve due to complications from sickle cell anemia. What I'm not understanding is what my father's death has to do with Jolene."

"Mrs. Stubbs, Jolene appears to have a larger than normal amount of abnormal hemoglobin cells in her blood. Sickle cell trait carriers, such as yourself, have hemoglobin S in their blood, like those who have sickle cell disease. But hemoglobin trait carriers also have a significant amount of hemoglobin A in their blood, which is normal hemoglobin. Because there is a large number of hemoglobin A in your blood, you suffer few or no symptoms of sickle cell disease. There's a good possibility that you've passed your hemoglobin S trait on to your daughter. But what's problematic is that there does not appear to be any hemoglobin A in her blood. This may be indicative of a sickle cell disease diagnosis," the doctor explained.

Juliette felt faint as she attempted to absorb the meaning of the doctor's words. "Doctor, I thought all children are screened for sickle cell disease at birth. I was told by the doctors that both my twins are sickle cell trait carriers. Also, I'm only familiar with sickle cell anemia. I wasn't aware of other forms of sickle cell disease."

"Yes, Mrs. Stubbs, that is correct. All newborns are screened, but even with the best screening tests, every once in a while, a child can slip through the cracks. Also, only a hematologist can make a definitive diagnosis of sickle cell disease, and there are a host of reasons why this wasn't picked up in your daughter's initial screening test. There are several ways a mistake could have occurred. Sickle cell anemia is the most common form of sickle cell disease, but there are a number of variations that are a part of the disease's family. I am releasing her with antibiotics, but you will need to make a follow-up appointment with her pediatrician so she can be referred to a hematologist. In the meantime, be sure to give her plenty of fluids and that she gets lots of rest. If she complains about pain in her leg, give her children's naproxen as it contains anti-inflammatory medication that will help relieve her pain if it's related to sickle cell disease. You can also put a heating pad on the affected area," he advised.

Juliette nodded but was still baffled. "For a child to receive a sickle cell disease diagnosis, don't both parents have to be sickle cell carriers?" Juliette asked.

"Yes, but there are different variants of abnormal hemoglobin cells, including hemoglobin C, hemoglobin F, and beta-thalassemia. Your husband could be a carrier of one of these abnormal hemoglobin and passed it to Jolene. If both you and your husband passed an abnormal sickle cell gene, this could result in Jolene having a sickle cell disease because she will have no normal hemoglobin. You and your husband will both need to be screened, and Jolene will also need extensive blood work before a definitive diagnosis can be made. I'm a pediatrician. I know a little about the various sickle cell diseases, but I can't get specific with respect to your daughter's case or make a conclusive determination without further testing and without a hematologist's confirmation," the pediatrician said.

"Thank you, Doctor. I'm sorry, but I don't know your last name," Juliette said.

"That's quite all right. My last name is Johnson. Now take good care of Jolene and be sure to follow up with her pediatrician. The nurse will be back shortly with Jolene's discharge paperwork. Have a safe trip back to Cleveland," he said with a smile.

"Thanks again. We will."

It only took a few minutes for the nurse to bring Jolene's discharge paperwork. After signing it and receiving a prescription for Jolene's antibiotics, Juliette gently woke a groggy Jolene. Next, she woke up Grandville, informing him it was time to leave. Once awake, Grandville sent a text to Grayson, who confirmed he had returned from taking Franklin and Sabrina back to the hotel. When they walked outside, he was standing next to the limo bus, waiting to escort them onboard.

During the short ride back to the hotel, Grandville said, "Sweetie, I'm so sorry I was asleep when the doctor came. What did he say was wrong with Jolene?"

"Sweetie, no need to apologize," Juliette said. "You fell asleep because you were tired. We've have had a very long day. The doctor said Jolene has a urinary tract infection. We'll need to stop at a drugstore here in Dayton to get her prescription filled because it's only valid here in this county."

"No problem," Grandville said as he squeezed Juliette's hand. "They're all closed right now, but we'll pick it up first thing in the morning. I'm thankful it's treatable. We've been through a lot, but what I want you to always remember is, no matter what's going on, it's always better when we're handling the problems of life together."

"You're so right, Grandville," Juliette replied and leaned over to kiss her man on the cheek.

Back at the hotel, the children were all in their rooms, sleeping with the television on. She tucked Jolene in bed next to her twin, then went into the bathroom to prepare to retire for the night. As she undressed, she could barely look at herself in the mirror, loathing the reflection that stared back at her. She couldn't bring herself to speak the truth about the possibility that Jolene may have sickle cell disease. To think about this reality for her child was just too painful.

She, along with her mother and siblings, had witnessed the excruciating pain her father had endured without warning. On some days, he would be fine, and on other days, he would be in such terrible pain that he would cry out. Juliette was only twelve years old when he had passed away suddenly.

After her father's death, her mother became active with the Cleveland Sickle Cell Anemia Association, and as a result, Juliette learned that she and all of her brothers and sisters were hemoglobin S carriers. They were warned not to have children with individuals who had sickle cell anemia or the sickle cell trait to reduce the probability of passing along the genetic disorder to their children.

When she and Grandville began dating, she shared this critical information with him. He assured her that he was not a hemoglobin S carrier. When she was pregnant with her first set of twins, she and

Grandville were both tested, and to her knowledge, he was not a hemoglobin S carrier. But she had no idea if Grandville was screened for any other abnormal hemoglobin.

When she got into bed, Grandville was waiting up for her.

"Come here, my queen," he flirted as he pulled her close to him. Juliette tried to relax, but she was barely holding on.

"Sweetie, I know Jolene's sickness threw you for a loop, but everything is going to be okay," Grandville tried to reassure her. "We'll pick up her meds before we go back home, and Jolene will be on the mend. Try not to worry,"

"Grandville, I sure hope you're right," Juliette said but, in her heart, what she was sure of was that things would never be right again.

Chapter 22

My Life

Melinia was a nervous wreck as she walked with Julio to Rique's office. She had no idea why he would summon her and Julio to his private quarters. She braced herself for the worst.

"Julio, remember what I told you. Put your game face on and follow my lead," Melinia warned. She took a deep breath and knocked on the door of Rique's office.

"Melinia, come in and bring Julio from the block with you," Rique directed.

Melinia stepped into the small office and found Rique sitting in front of a small chessboard. The pieces were set up, and it did not look as though the game had been started yet.

"Have a seat and let me talk to the two of you for a minute," Rique instructed without looking up.

Melinia was trembling on the inside because she couldn't read Rique's mood by his blank facial expression. She focused her gaze on the chessboard in an attempt to calm her nerves. She and Julio sat down together on a small couch directly across from the table Rique sat behind.

"You guys did a great job putting away the supplies. I'm happy you were waiting for us as I directed. I called you in here to let you both know that I've arranged for a doctor to come on la barca and give everyone a physical. You are to be in your rooms at three this afternoon to wait for the doctor to examine you. Tonight, after the doctor examines everyone, we'll have a big dinner to celebrate Julio joining us. Then we will head back out to sea."

"Okay. Is there anything else?" Melinia politely asked.

"Yes, I have a question."

"Anything," Melinia said.

"Do either of you know how to play chess? I just got this set. I've studied the moves on YouTube and played a few games online, but I want to play with a real person."

"I know how to play chess," Julio spoke up. "It would be an honor to play with you. But, before we move the ivory, I need to ask a question."

"What?" Rique asked, eying him curiously.

"Are you a sore loser? Because if you lose, I don't want to have to worry about you being angry with me and forcing me to suck another random dick...or worse," Julio replied.

"No, I am not a sore loser. I give you my word that if I lose to you, no harm will come to you as a result. I heard that chess is a game of strategy, and I think I am decent at the game. But I want to play an opponent face to face."

"Good. Do you want to play right now?" Julio asked.

"Yes. Come over and have a seat."

Julio did as he was told. As Melinia watched the two of them, she was unsure of what to do. She decided to return to her room and take a nap.

"Well, I know how to play chess as well, but I'm exhausted. I was hoping I could be excused so I can lie down for a little while," Melinia explained.

"You're exhausted?" Rique asked with an incredulous wince. "What the hell have you been doing to be so tired? And why have you never told me that you know how to play chess?"

Melinia paused, her heart thumping in her chest. "We just put away the supplies, like you asked, and I didn't know you were interested in the game until now. Also, I said I knew how to play, but I never said I was good at it."

"That's fair. You can watch our first game and then you're excused."

Julio had Rique in checkmate in ten moves and the game was over.

Rique rubbed his head, staring at the chessboard. "Julio, you're either really good at chess, or I'm really bad."

"I like to think I'm pretty good because you're better than a decent chess player," Julio complemented graciously. "That I can tell. And I would be honored to play with you again if you wish."

"Definitely," Rique replied. "I'm going to want a rematch, but I'm going to play Melinia first. I'll practice with her before our rematch."

"Whatever you want, boss," Julio said, standing up. "Just let me know when you're ready."

"Melinia, I want you to meet me here at my office immediately after dinner, and we will play a game. Also, don't tell the other members of the crew about our games. If I hear anything about me playing chess, I'll know that it originated from one of you. If that happens, I'll punish you both," Rique threatened.

Melinia nodded.

"You can count on our discretion, boss," Julio said.

"Good, now you both can go on to your rooms," Rique said.

On the walk back to her room, Melinia tried to figure out her next move. She had lied to Rique about her ability as a chess player.

She was actually great at it. She crossed her fingers and hoped that her chess skills would help put her in a better position.

"Chica, do you know where we're going when we leave the Bahamas?" Julio asked.

"No. Rique never tells us until we are about to dock at the next port. Sometimes, we're at sea for days and see nothing but water," Melinia explained.

"I hope we go to Miami. I really want to go there."

Melinia shook her head and quietly warned him, "Never let anyone on this boat know that you're excited to go to any specific port. Always act like it's not a big deal, or you could make Rique and the rest of the crew suspicious of your motives."

"So many rules," Julio said, rolling his eyes.

"You have no idea. But rules keep us alive," Melinia replied.

Julio nodded and waved goodbye as he headed to his room. While back in her room, Melinia lay down on her bed, closed her eyes, and waited. She had just dozed off when she felt herself being gently shaken. She opened her eyes to find Mimi standing over her.

"Hey, Melinia," Mimi announced. "The doctor is outside. He's ready to examine you."

Melinia sat up and smoothed out her clothing while Mimi brought the doctor into the room.

"Dr. Johnny already examined me while you were asleep. I'm going up on deck while he does your exam," Mimi said as she exited the room.

Dr. Johnny maintained a private clinic on the island, and once a year, Rique made sure he examined everyone in the crew and paid him in cash. After Mimi left the room, Dr. Johnny began his exam.

"Good afternoon, Melinia. It's been a while since I've seen you. How have you been?" Dr. Johnny asked with a heavy Bahamian accent.

"I'm making it, Doc. How about you?" Melinia politely asked.

"I'm well. Thank you. You're my last patient of the day. I'm going to take in some of my island's amenities and lay on the beach to enjoy the sun. Then have some fun a little later on," he explained.

"Well, we'd better get this exam started so you can go ahead and get your party started," she playfully replied.

Doctor Johnny checked her heart, blood pressure, and other vitals.

"You appear to be doing well. Do you have any particular concerns?" Dr. Johnny asked.

"Just one, Doc. My stomach has felt bloated, and my period seems to be running late."

"Well, that could be an indication of pregnancy. Have you had unprotected sex over the past few months?" Dr. Johnny asked.

"No, but there was an instance where the condom broke."

"Okay, I'll give you a pregnancy test."

Melinia released a long exhale and fidgeted on the bed. "If you think that's best, Doc."

But as Dr. Johnny reached into his bag for the pregnancy test, Melinia smiled on the inside.

Chapter 23

Dazed and Confused

J uliette sat on her sun porch and gazed out over the leaves that were scattered over her lawn. The November sun was bright but offered little warmth, and she shivered, thinking about all the changes she had endured over the past several months.

Thanksgiving was coming in a few weeks, and she was anxious about the holiday season. Grandville was very excited, as Thanksgiving was his favorite holiday. He had always looked forward to kicking off the Christmas and New Year season, and the holidays had greatly improved for her since Grandville had returned home. But, this year, she knew things would be different because, in her world, the sky was darkening, and she knew storms were approaching once again. She could only hope that the love she and Grandville shared could withstand the hurricane force, as it had in the past.

Since the night of Jessica's honorary clinic opening, Juliette had experienced reoccurring nightmares about her deceased daughter. The dreams were so intense and real that she hadn't been able to sleep. Whenever she tried to close her eyes, her guilt and shame consumed her, and she'd struggled to find rest. In her vivid dreams, Jessica had spoken to her.

Her bright eyes were large and pleading as they looked down on her. The gentle breeze lifted her curly pigtails. Her echoed voice played like sweet music to her longing ears, "Mommy, you are lying to Daddy. He loves you and deserves the truth."

And what was the truth she spoke of? The truth was Juliette had no idea if Grandville was Jolene's father or not. The truth was, the potential identity fraud that she had perpetuated on her husband and family would soon be exposed.

As she placed her gaze on the sky, she reflected on how she'd learned the difficult truth.

When the entourage had arrived back home to Cleveland from Oakhill, Juliette made the decision to discreetly investigate Jolene's genetic background. Due to the symptoms she'd recently suffered, Juliette's instinct had told her that Jolene might have been suffering from a sickle cell disease. However, she hadn't wanted to alarm Grandville or the rest of their family. As far as everyone was concerned, the pain Jolene experienced in Dayton had been attributed to her urinary tract infection, per the doctor. Juliette had constantly worried about Sabrina blurting out what the ER pediatrician had suspected about Jolene.

"Sickle cell disease is the most widespread genetic condition in the US, but unfortunately, specialized care for those it impacts isn't as accessible as the care for other diseases," he said sympathetically. "I suggest having a hematologist run some blood tests since both you and your husband are trait carriers."

Sabrina hadn't mentioned anything further about it, but Juliette had driven herself crazy with worry that she would. She had slowly isolated herself from her friends and family, and she had no doubt that they would soon notice something was very wrong.

Juliette had contacted her family's medical group and had copies of their medical records delivered to her female housing facility. She'd spent hours in her small office scouring over them when she should have been writing grants for her future male housing facility, A New Beginning. While reviewing the medical records, she'd learned that genetic testing had confirmed that she and Grandville were both sickle cell disease carriers during her pregnancy with the first set of twins, but the records did not specify which sickle cell gene Grandville carried. The records also indicated that she hadn't sought prenatal care until she was more than six months pregnant. She had advised the midwife who treated her during her pregnancy with Jolene and Jenae that Grandville was their father, who was incarcerated at the time. The medical staff had predicted there was a fifty percent chance that one or both children could inherit her or Grandville's sickle cell trait, a twenty-five percent chance that the children would have sickle cell disease and a twenty-five percent chance that their children would have neither sickle cell trait nor disease.

After learning this, Juliette contacted her sorority sister, a hematologist who was employed at the Sickle Cell Anemia Foundation of Northern Ohio. The two had become friends when she was initiated into her sorority in college. Pamela was a couple of years older than her, but the two had bonded over the fact that they belonged to the same organization and had each lost a parent to sickle cell disease. Pamela's mother passed away when she was sixteen years old, which began her quest to dedicate her life to the eradication of the disease.

Juliette reflected on their phone call two months earlier.

"Soror Pamela, how are you?" Juliette anxiously asked.

"I'm great, Soror Juliette, but you don't sound like the happy, upbeat soror that I know and love. So, tell me what's wrong."

"Soror Pamela, I need to talk to you in person, and I was hoping you'd be available for lunch or dinner with me in the near future," Juliette said.

"Of course, I always have time for you. I'm available right now if you can fit me in," Pamela said.

"Great. I can meet you at Under in a half an hour," Juliette said.

"Okay, I'm leaving my office right now," Pamela said.

When Juliette arrived at Under, Pamela was at a table waiting for her. Juliette hugged her friend and thanked her for meeting with her on such short notice. She took a seat directly across the table from her.

"Soror Juliette, tell me how I can help you," Pamela said.

Juliette explained Jolene's visit to the emergency room for treatment for a urinary tract infection and the issues she was having with the pain in her leg. She then went on to describe how the doctor began asking questions about their genetic history and suggested testing by a hematologist to rule out sickle cell disease. "I don't want to alarm my family, but I want to have her and Jenae tested discreetly," Juliette said.

"I know you're a carrier, but what about your husband?" Pamela inquired.

"When I was pregnant with my first set of twins, Grandville was tested, and we found out that he is," Juliette said as she struggled to stop the tears that collected in the corner of her eyes from falling down her face.

Pamela could see that Juliette was upset and said, "Soror, I've got you. Don't worry, we will get to the bottom of what's going on, and as you know, discretion is my middle name. I'll test your daughters, and it will be our little secret. I suggest you bring the twins to my office to meet with me tomorrow morning so I can take a blood sample. I'm going to have you sign a medical release form that will enable me to review the girls' medical records. Together, we'll figure out what's wrong and what we can do to fix it. Until then, please try to relax because you might be worrying for no reason. Now I know it's the middle of the afternoon, but I say we have a glass of wine."

That was two months ago, and ever since, Juliette had been on pins and needles, waiting for the results of the tests. The morning before, Pamela had called and invited her to lunch at Under, where she was given the news that she had already known in her heart.

When she arrived at the black-owned restaurant and club, Pamela had been waiting for her again.

"Soror Juliette, thanks for meeting with me. I've called you here because I may have the answers regarding your daughter's health. The results of the test only took five days, but it took me this long to try and figure out how the fact that Jolene's sickle cell disease was missed. Unfortunately, the ER pediatrician's suspicions were correct. Jolene does not suffer from sickle cell anemia like our parents did, but instead has a sickle cell disorder called hemoglobin SC disease," Pamela explained.

Juliette frowned thoughtfully. "What's that? I've never heard of it."

"Unfortunately, most people know very little about all sickle cell disorders, even those whose families have been touched by it," Pamela explained. "Hemoglobin SC is the second most common form of sickle cell disease, and about one in forty people have it. According to the American Hematology Society of which I am a proud member, only seventy to one hundred thousand Americans suffer from a sickle cell disorder, and in order to inherit the disease, you must have two parents who are carriers. As you may know, most people are born with normal hemoglobin, known as hemoglobin A, but people with hemoglobin SC inherit one hemoglobin S gene from one parent and a hemoglobin C gene from the other parent."

"So, what you're saying is Jolene inherited the hemoglobin S gene from me," Juliette asked for clarification.

"I am not sure. Your twins could have inherited a hemoglobin S gene from you or your husband and a normal gene from you or your husband. I can't be sure if your husband passed a hemoglobin C gene to Jolene because I would need to test him to make that determination. What I couldn't understand is how the hospital missed that Jolene does not have normal hemoglobin."

"Exactly. Did you ever figure out how they could have made such a grave mistake?" Juliette asked.

Pamela nodded. "Yes, after spending a great deal of time reviewing Jolene's record, I'm fairly certain I've figured it out."

Juliette wrung her hands together, and sweat quickly gathered on her forehead. All of a sudden, she felt as though she were about to faint. Pamela looked at her with concern and said, "Soror, calm down. Here, drink some of your water."

Juliette took a large gulp of the ice water and tried to regulate her breathing. But her fear and panic seemed to overwhelm her.

"Soror Juliette, you're hyperventilating. I think you're having a panic attack." Pamela walked over to the hostess stand and asked for a paper bag. She returned and said, "Breathe in and out of this. I think it'll help you."

Juliette took the bag and did as Pamela directed. After a few minutes, her panic subsided and she began to feel better.

"I feel a little better now. Thank you, girl," Juliette said, fanning herself with the bag.

"Good. I suffer from an anxiety disorder, and I sometimes hyperventilate as well. Most doctors don't recommend this as a long-term form of treatment for this condition. If you continue to have panic attacks, you're going to have to figure out their source so you can properly treat them," Pamela advised.

"Thanks, Soror," Juliette said, flashing a smile. "This is the first time it's happened, but I'll definitely look into it. Before I started falling apart, you said you think you figured out how the hospital missed that Jolene's lack of normal hemoglobin."

"Yes, but I can't be one hundred percent certain. I'm not sure if you're aware, but in the United States, all African American, Latino, and Mediterranean children are tested at birth for sickle cell disorders using the high-performance liquid chromatography screening test, or HPLC test. It identifies which type of hemoglobin is present in a person's blood. It's reliable and accurate, but every once in a while, it produces a false negative," Pamela explained. "This can happen if the child has had a blood transfusion before the test is administered. I reviewed Jolene's records and learned that she and Jenae were born prematurely at thirty-five weeks, and each had a birth weight of four pounds. I read that they were slightly anemic, and the hospital gave them both a blood transfusion shortly after birth. I believe the HPCL test was administered after the transfusion, so, as a result, it didn't pick up the hemoglobin C trait in Jolene's blood. That's likely why the hospital mistakenly concluded that Jolene was a sickle cell trait carrier and did not have sickle cell disease."

Juliette shook her head, dumbfounded by her friend's explanation. "Soror Pamela, what in the world do I do now?"

"Taking care of a child with sickle cell disease is very different from having a parent with the disease. There will be lots of appointments, and it will be very difficult to witness your child experiencing a pain crisis. The pain felt by someone having a crisis is excruciating and so intensely painful that it cannot be put into words. I highly suggest you join a sickle cell support group to help you manage all the demands you'll now have to deal with. We're going to need to confirm Jolene's diagnosis with Grandville's genetic testing in order to be sure he's a hemoglobin C carrier. Luckily, you'll have him there to help you, because having a child with chronic illness along with other children can be very hard to balance. Having a strong support system can make all the difference in the world. The very first thing we'll have to do is get Jolene thoroughly examined and linked to a hematologist. They'll likely want to immediately put her on amoxicillin as prophylaxis because she's at increased risk of pneumococcal infection. The recommended treatment is normally to administer an antibiotic daily until five years of age to reduce their risk of developing an infection. I'll give you a referral for a good hematologist."

Juliette nodded. "How sick do you think Jolene will be?"

Pamela sighed. "There's no way of knowing. Some people experience few symptoms while young and get sicker as they get older. Some never experience pain, and others endure frequent, unbearable pain. The key is preventive care, like making sure she gets her annual flu shots and takes her vitamins, especially folic acid. Jolene's hematologist will design a treatment plan that will help meet her needs."

Juliette thanked Pamela and thought about her dilemma the entire drive home. When she walked through the door, she was surprised to find both Franklin and Sabrina at her home, visiting with Grandville.

"Hey, stranger," Sabrina said, jumping up as soon as she saw Juliette come through the door.

"Hey, Sabrina. How are you?" Juliette greeted, trying her best to sound upbeat.

"I'm great, now that I am seeing you," Sabrina said. "I hate to intrude on you, but when Franklin mentioned he was coming over to see Grandville, I insisted on coming too. I was hoping to talk to you privately."

"Sure, let's go to my she shed," Juliette joked as she led Sabrina to the living room couch. "Would you like anything to drink?"

"I'm good. Grandville got us some water earlier," Sabrina said, taking a seat. "I know you just walked in. Do you need a moment to get settled first?"

Juliette shook her head. "No, I'm good. Let me just grab a bottled water, and I'll be right back."

She walked into the kitchen and quietly leaned her head against the stainless steel refrigerator, taking a series of deep breaths. Lord knew she was mentally drained and wasn't up to having any company, but she wanted to keep up a good front so Grandville wouldn't catch on that there was something going on with her. After a few more moments passed, she retrieved a bottle of water from the fridge and took a deep swallow before returning to the living room.

When she returned to the living room, Sabrina began to speak. "Girl, I'm so excited. I started my new job, and I'm trying to plan the wedding. But I wanted to take a few moments to talk to you about something else."

Juliette braced herself, thinking Sabrina was about to ask her something about Jolene and her diagnosis. She clasped her fingers together to keep her hands from shaking.

"Whatever it is, shoot. I hope I can help," Juliette said.

"Okay, my son, George, has been talking about finding his birth family," Sabrina confided. "I believe I shared with you that George was adopted by my late sister and her husband, and I raised him after they died."

"Yes, you did." Juliette nodded, waiting for her to continue.

"Well, Franklin tells me that on top of you being an attorney, you're also a social worker and have worked with foster and adopted children."

"This is true."

"Great, I'm hopeful that you can help me find George's birth parents," Sabrina said. "Franklin and I want to start our own family, and a few weeks ago, we each had our blood tested in order to be aware of any potential problems. If George found his birth parents, it might help him feel less threatened when we get pregnant."

"I totally understand. Yes, I'd be happy to help you if I can. Did you and Franklin find out if you're facing any potential genetic issues?"

"Yes, we have a few low risks. We learned that Franklin has a rare sickle cell trait called hemoglobin C. However, I don't have any sickle cell traits or disorders, so our children will not have that as an issue. But there is a twenty-five percent chance that they could inherit Franklin's hemoglobin C trait."

Juliette nodded thoughtfully. "Well, the adoption laws in Ohio have changed, and there are a number of ways you can find George's biological mother. You can write to Ohio Vital Statistics to determine if George's biological family is looking for him. You could also get me a sample of his DNA, and we can run it through an ancestry website. Hopefully, that could get some hits and lead us to George's birth parents."

"I don't want anyone, including George, to know I'm looking for his birth parents," Sabrina said. "I'd like to find out who they are before he does. He's always been emotionally unstable, and it got worse after my sister died. But lately, he's been asking questions, and I want to provide him with some answers, but only if it doesn't harm him."

Sabrina promised to send all the info she had for George's birth family. When Sabrina left their home, she appeared to be on top of the world while Juliette felt as if she were at the very bottom.

The night before, she couldn't get to sleep, and when she finally did, Jessica stayed in her dreams, taunting her. It had only been one day since Juliette had learned about Franklin's hemoglobin C trait, but every time she looked at her husband, she felt lower than dirt.

At that moment, she was lost in such deep thought that she didn't realize Grandville had come out onto the porch until he spoke.

"Juliette, for the past few weeks, you've seemed really distracted. Tell me, what's wrong?"

Chapter 24

The Journey Home

Grandville sat in the soul food club, Take 4, which was empty, and silently watched the band set up. The Right Music Experience was getting ready to play a private live concert for him and Rayshawn, who had yet to arrive. One of Rayshawn's fraternity brothers was the owner of Take 4, which was considered one of Cleveland's hippest soul food clubs. It was Tuesday, January 2nd, and Rayshawn was well aware that people normally didn't go out directly after the holidays. So, he'd arranged the event to help his fraternity brother make a profit by renting the whole facility for their meeting, complete with live music.

Grandville had no idea what Rayshawn wanted, only that he had contacted Franklin and insisted on Grandville meeting with him the day after New Year's. The last place Grandville wanted to be was in downtown Cleveland on a cold, snowy January evening. He'd much prefer to be at home with his beloved Juliette to keep an eye on her.

Ever since their return from Oakhill, Juliette had not been quite herself. She'd seemed jumpy and anxious, and he was concerned she was suffering from post-traumatic stress disorder because she had not been the same since the anniversary of their daughter's death. They had experienced a fun holiday season, but Juliette—who usually participated in every holiday party and dinner they were invited to—had been uncharacteristically unsocial.

"I only want to spend the season with you and the kids," she had said.

Other people were also starting to notice that Juliette was missing in action, including Samantha. He had run into her and Jared two days before Christmas at the mall, trying to purchase last-minute gifts. He thought back to their brief exchange.

"Hey, playa. How's it going?" Samantha asked him.

"I'm great, just trying to pick up a few last-minute gifts. What are you guys up to?" Grandville asked.

"Same. This beautiful woman here has agreed to help me pick out gifts for my coworkers. I'm in a secret Santa exchange and need the touch of a special woman to help me pick the right gift," Jared said, squeezing Samantha's hand.

"Well, Samantha is certainly special, so it looks like you've picked the right woman to help you with your gift quest," Grandville remarked, chuckling.

Samantha smiled. "Speaking of special, what's going on with my girl Juliette? I've only spoken to her on the phone, but I've barely seen her in months. I hope I haven't done anything to offend her. She's my best friend, and I would never purposely do anything to upset her."

"I know, Samantha. But, since our return from our trip to Oakhill, Juliette hasn't been herself. I'm worried she may be suffering from PTSD, which has nothing to do with you. Jolene screaming at the pool on the anniversary of Jessica's death may have triggered something."

"Yes, she seemed really upset afterward, but why do you think she's suffering from PTSD?" Samantha asked.

"She's been anxious, distracted, and hasn't been sleeping well. I'm going to try to help her get back to herself by throwing her a surprise birthday party at the end of January, and I'm going to need your help."

Samantha's face lit up. "That's a great idea, Grandville. Tell me what you need and then consider it done."

"Thanks, I'll be in touch. Merry Christmas!" Grandville said as he walked away.

That was over a week ago, and he'd made a mental note to contact Samantha to help him plan an intimate birthday party for his wife. Greta was getting married on Valentine's Day, which was the day after their birthday. She had also been trying to reach Juliette, who was always too busy to talk to her. Greta had called him the day after Christmas out of concern. He was so deep in thought that he hadn't noticed Rayshawn approaching the table.

"Hey, Grandville," Rayshawn said, reaching out to shake his hand. "Forgive my tardiness. I was with my cousin Lovelle and misjudged the commute from Akron."

Lovelle was Rayshawn's cousin, who was rumored to have something to do with the disappearance of his wife's first cousin, Melinia. Grandville had paid a private detective who had determined that, despite the rumors on the street, Lovelle had nothing to do with Melinia's disappearance, but that she may have gone into hiding to get away from him.

"I thought you didn't hang out with Lovelle anymore," Grandville said, trying to sound lighthearted.

"You know I don't have much family left. I know Lovelle can be a trip, but who am I supposed to spend the holidays with? I sure as hell didn't get an invite from you," Rayshawn said, chuckling uneasily.

"Don't start that fam. Juliette and I didn't go anywhere or do anything special this year, anyway. We just spent Christmas and New Year's with our children. Besides, we're hanging out right now. So why did you insist that we get together tonight?"

"You're always in such a rush to get into things. That's that lawyer in you, fam. Let's just relax and enjoy the private concert and great food that my fraternity brother arranged for us," Rayshawn coaxed.

A server came with water and took their orders just before the band began to play. The music was exceptional, and Grandville lost himself in it. After a half-hour of playing and singing, the band took a break. Their food arrived soon after, and it was quiet enough for the men to hold a conversation.

Grandville dug into his food. "This band is awesome. I've never heard them play before, but I'll look for their shows from now on."

"Yes, The Right Music Experience is Cleveland's own," Rayshawn said. "Tonight, I wanted to celebrate all things Cleveland. I have to admit, I miss my hometown."

"I know good and damn well you don't miss this snow and bone-chilling cold weather," Grandville remarked.

"Honestly, I do miss the winter elements, particularly during the holidays. In LA, it never snows, and though I really love the weather there, I still miss home sometimes. Grandville, you're a lucky man to have a wife and children to share the holidays with. I have many regrets, one of which was not having children with Greta, but I was so selfish—only thinking about myself—and now what do I have? Nothing but loneliness and holidays with Lovelle because, without you and Greta, he's all I have left."

"Man, I'm sorry," Grandville said, noting the sadness in Rayshawn's voice. "In time, you'll find the right woman for you and start a family. Despite all that's happened, I still consider you to be my brother. But—and I hate to say it—I recognize that my sister is happier without you."

"Yeah, I understand that. But I can't move on until I can talk to her one last time. I give you my word as a gentleman and on our friendship that I won't overstep. Like I mentioned when I came to visit you in Oakhill, I've been in counseling, and in order to work my steps and find some peace, it's really important that I make amends with Greta. And some of what I need to say is private," Rayshawn said, his tone pleading. "I know you understand. My team will be playing against the Cleveland Avilers. I want to rent out this restaurant and hire this band for a private dinner with Greta. You are more than welcome to join us, but it's important that I be allowed to have a brief, private word with Greta.

Grandville chewed his food thoughtfully and said nothing.

"I also needed to run something else by you," Rayshawn added.

"Damn, Rayshawn, you don't think that was enough?" Grandville joked. "I need to think, man. What else could there possibly be for you to run by me?"

"At the opening, I saw that you and Franklin surprised Juliette with a new rooming house. Word up at Oakhill is that her new rooming home will focus on helping men. Is that true?" Rayshawn asked.

"Yes, it's true. It's called A New Beginning, but she's still working on getting it up and running. Why do you ask?"

"Well, Oakhill wants to partner with a rooming home for inmates who are being released and have received treatment at the new clinic, and I immediately thought of Juliette," Rayshawn said.

"Well, what would the partnership consist of?"

"The Robinson Foundation will give A New Beginning fifty thousand dollars to work with two newly released inmates with the goal of getting them reestablished in the Cleveland area. We want to ensure they have a plan that includes employment goals."

"Okay. Juliette may be interested in an opportunity like that. I'll be sure to run it by her."

"I would truly appreciate that because we're anxious to start helping some of the men who were treated at the Jessica Stubbs Clinic, and I was told that someone you know at Oakhill is being released in the next few weeks. I'm hopeful that he could be A New Beginning's first resident," Rayshawn said.

"Who are you referring to?"

"Someone named Big Joe. I'm told that you were instrumental in helping him to make some positive changes in his life."

Granville smiled and nodded. "Actually, that's true. But Joe did all the work. I spoke to Joe at the opening of the clinic, and he made this same request directly to me after he heard Juliette would be working with men. Juliette and I have discussed it, and we would love for Joe to be her first resident, but Juliette has not begun operating the rooming house yet. We don't want Big Joe's release to be adversely affected because he's waiting to move into a home that isn't ready."

"That's understandable. That's why the Robinson Foundation is ready to write a check right now, if necessary, to ensure we get the rooming house operational by the time Big Joe is released."

"I'm sure Juliette would be extremely happy with your offer to assist her, but what's the catch?" Grandville asked.

"There's no catch. I promise you. It's a win for everyone involved. I just want A New Beginning to be one of the faces of the Robinson Foundation. The men who receive treatment at the Jessica Stubbs Mental Health Clinic will be eligible to win an opportunity to reside at A New Beginning. The Robinson Foundation will pay for their first year of rent and provide money for employment services. We want Joe to be the first inmate released to receive this gift."

Grandville looked at Rayshawn for a moment, then asked, "Why?"

"Because, according to the Oakhill officials, your influence was instrumental in helping Joe. In return, he has helped other inmates. We want this new program to be a success. Besides, it will be a great media opportunity for the clinic to have a former Oakhill inmate who has received treatment there to receive aftercare services from the clinic's namesake's mother. The foundation wants to secure corporate sponsors and capitalize on it. Having partners will allow us to gain more exposure and ultimately help more people. This will also benefit Juliette financially. Before you know it, she will have a chain of rooming houses. I wanted to run both requests by you to respect your request that I refrain from contacting Juliette and Greta directly."

Grandville took in Rayshawn's explanation for a moment before responding. "Thanks, Rayshawn. I'll see what I can do about your requests, but I'm going to need a few days before I can update you." He looked up at the stage. "The band's getting ready to play again. After I receive answers from two of the most important women in my life, I'll contact you directly."

Rayshawn nodded. "Thanks, Grandville. I can't ask for anything more than that."

Chapter 25

Senorita

Melinia sat across from Rique and strategized her next move as he watched her with hawk eyes. Their game of chess was intense, and Melinia was surprised at how good Rique was for someone who had only been playing for a year. Since Rique's initial game with Julio, he and Melinia had been playing twice a week for a month. The two of them had spent so much time playing together that everyone on the boat thought she and Rique had become romantically involved. He had summoned her to his private office every Tuesday and Thursday night from eight until nine. Only she and Rique knew that their private meetings were strictly about chess and little else. During their first game, she knew if she were honest with Rique, it would give her the advantage she needed. So, she delivered the news as part of the second phase of her plan.

"Hey, Rique. I want to thank you for allowing me to see the doctor last month," Melinia began the conversation.

"Of course. As you know, everyone on this boat has an exam at least once a year," Rique said in between moves. "I'm not a monster. I want you and the other people on this boat to know that the Sandego crew does value you and the services that each of you provides to make the crew operational."

"Well, the doctor gave me some news that I need to discuss with you," she sighed.

"Did he give you six months to live?" Rique's joked, his voice dripping with sarcasm.

She looked at him for a moment, then said, "No. Something worse."

He paused and stared at her. "Well, what is it?" he finally asked.

"I'm pregnant."

He reared his head back and twisted up his face. "What? How in the world can that be possible? I've made it clear that no one in the crew is to ever have unprotected sex," he roared.

"Yes, and I give you my word that I haven't let anyone touch me intimately unless he wore a condom. But, when I did the freak show with Remy, the condom came off. We were on tape, so I'm sure you remember," she reminded him.

"Are you saying that you're pregnant by Remy?" Rique asked.

"Yes, I believe I am. He's the only person I've slept with where the condom failed. I know that to you and the Sandego crew, I'm nothing but a strung-out heroin whore, but I want to propose a plan to deal with the situation I now find myself in."

Shaking his head, Rique replied, "I'm listening."

"Allow me to have this child," Melinia pitched. "After the baby is born, I'll allow Romanita to adopt it. That way, she'll get the opportunity to raise a child of her own that is of your blood. All that I ask is that I am named as the baby's godmother and allowed visitation twice a year. I'll also want Romanita to remain Rafael's godmother. But I want Rafael to come with me, and I want to leave the boat. Rafael will be starting school soon, and I want him to be educated in the United States."

"As you said, you are a heroin whore who fucks on my command. Why would I want my sister to have a baby who came from a woman like you?" Rique said.

"Because, despite me being the mother of this child, your brother, Remy, is the father. This might be your sister's only chance to have a child of her own. We both know that having her own child will give her a renewed purpose, and this will help her with her depression."

Rique mulled her words over for a few minutes. "I'll take your proposal under consideration and will let you know at a later time what I've decided. Until then, you are to tell no one about your pregnancy. If you do, I'll make sure that you suffer."

Melinia nodded.

"Now, we are playing chess, so focus on the game," he ordered, peering over the game board.

That was three months prior, and over a game of chess, Rique had accepted her proposal. She had concocted a plan that was heading toward fruition. That was until Rique threw a wrench in it. He made sure Melinia received her China white daily, but he slowly weaned her off of it by giving her less of the drug every week. Melinia knew the baby growing inside of her was likely addicted to the opiates she consumed. If she stopped taking the heroin cold turkey, she would start withdrawal, which could cause her body to abort the baby. So, Melinia blatantly defied Rique's instructions and told Julio and Mimi about her condition, then swore them both to secrecy. The trio's friendship was strong, and Julio kept the ladies abreast of what the rest of the crew said about Rique.

Everything was going so well that Melinia was completely taken off guard when, over a game of chess, Rique announced, "Hey, Melinia. You are now in the second trimester of your pregnancy, so I'm going to need you to put in some work,"

"Papi, what do you need me to do?" Melinia asked.

"You and Remy are going to star in a series of sex tapes," Rique declared. "He's the father of your baby, and because you are already pregnant, there will be no need for Remy to wear a condom. I have recently learned that there is a large market for freaks who get off on watching a pregnant lady get banged bareback. The crew will need to have a way to recoup the revenue we'll lose due to your departure. We'll make a series of tapes and release a new one every few months."

Melinia was upset, but she knew better than to let Rique know it. "Papi, when will we begin taping?"

"Soon. I'm not ready for the rest of the crew to know about your pregnancy, so it will be a closed set."

"What about Remy? What will we tell him? He'll see that I'm pregnant."

"Maybe you should tell him the truth: that you carry his love child."

Melinia feigned shock at his comment. "Excuse me?"

"Cut the crap, Melinia. You don't think I see how the two of you look at each other when you think the rest of us aren't paying attention. I know you're in love with him. What I can't figure out is what you see in Remy that you don't see in me?"

"I have no idea what you're talking about. Do you think I wanted to get pregnant? It's not my fault the condom broke. I just did what you ordered me to do. Remy and I don't have relations outside of the Bone Room. Lastly, you've never given me any reason to think you were interested in me," Melinia said.

Rique scoffed. "We both know that you lie about how you feel about Remy, but there's no way to prove it, so we're going to go with your version of the story. Together, you and I could have made the world our kingdom, but you have a thing for my little brother. So, I'm going to make sure the crew benefits from it."

Melinia was on pins and needles, not knowing exactly what Rique had planned. She hoped the fact that she was pregnant with Remy's baby would deter Rique from making her participate in the sex tapes or tricking with strange men. Even though she'd planned to give the baby to Romanita, she didn't want her children to ever know she had given her body to whoever Rique told her to for a hit. Recording her interactions only memorialized the dirt she was involved in.

Later, she sat on the top deck, listening to music on her headphones. It was one of the few things, including drugs, that allowed her a small measure of escape. She wanted to jump off the boat into the deep, dark water in an effort to find peace. But she was convinced she would go to hell if she took her own life and the life of her unborn child. She also had to find the strength to save Rafael and get him home to the states, where he belonged. She knew that involved her getting off drugs so she could implement the hardest part of her plan, which she hoped and prayed she would be able to pull off.

Chapter 26

Secrets

A sleep-deprived Juliette was exhausted due to Jessica continuing to haunt her in her dreams. Once there was a time when Juliette rarely dreamed about her deceased daughter. But now, every time she closed her eyes, Jessica's angelic face was all she saw. It didn't help that in every dream, Jessica would tell her she was worthless and a liar. Juliette could barely face herself each day, but she had no choice but to push through for the sake of her children and husband. She was trying to hold it together, but despite her efforts, the cracks in her armor were beginning to show. A few months prior, Grandville had point-blank asked her what was going on. She'd told him the truth, but only partially. She clearly remembered the conversation and her response to his question.

"Sweetie, I'm okay. I just haven't been sleeping well," she said.

"I know, don't forget that I share a bed with you. What I want to know is, what is troubling you to the point that your sleep is being affected?" Grandville asked.

Juliette shrugged casually. "I really think I'm dealing with pre-menopause issues that have been affecting my hormones. It's also causing my moods to be all over the place. I'm trying to give my body an opportunity to adjust to the changes."

"Well, whatever you need from me, I'm here for you. Maybe you should see a doctor to confirm what's going on," he advised as he pulled her into an embrace.

"I promise, if it doesn't get better, I'll make an appointment," Juliette said as she returned his hug.

Unfortunately, instead of getting better, it got progressively worse. It was just after the New Year and Juliette had decided to take a break from working on opening the male rooming house. Instead, she focused her efforts on trying to find George's biological parents for Sabrina. She went to her female rooming house, A Better Tomorrow, to check-in with the staff and residents. When she walked in, the smell of food greeted her. She had not been eating right and had been experiencing a loss of appetite due to the anxiety and stress she had been feeling, but as soon as she smelled the aroma of green beans wafting in the air, she was suddenly ravenous. She walked into the kitchen and found Violet, who was the resident manager and the very first resident of A Better Tomorrow, standing over the stove, stirring a large pot.

"Hey there, Miss Juliette," Violet cheerfully greeted. "How are you on this cold, snowy day?"

"I'm great. How are things going over here?" Juliette inquired.

"Everything is great. It's cold outside, so I decided to make comfort food: smothered pork chops, green beans, and mashed potatoes. Are you hungry because I can make you a plate?"

"Yes, I'm starving, but I'll only take a plate if you have enough for all the residents," Juliette said.

"Miss Juliette, we have plenty," Violet said while making Juliette a plate. "Everyone has paid their rent and given their food money for the month, so I stocked up and bought a lot of food. Our deep freezer is almost full. A Better Tomorrow is at full occupancy except for Melinia's room, and I always make a little extra. Before I forget, a social worker lady has stopped by here twice asking for you."

"Do you have any idea what she wants?" Juliette said.

"No, but she said she works for a law firm, and she also left her card. Maybe they have a rich client they want to place here," Violet said as she went into a drawer and pulled out a business card.

Juliette looked at the card, then put it in her purse. She sat down and began eating Violet's delicious food. After taking several bites, she asked, "Hey, Violet, I'm expecting a package. Did anything come for me?"

"Yes, Miss Juliette. I slid it in the mail door, so be careful not to step on it when you open your office door," Violet warned; Juliette was shoveling food into her mouth when Violet asked, "Miss Juliette, are you okay?"

In between bites, Juliette said, "I'm fine, Violet. Why do you ask?"

Violet took a seat at the table across from her. "Because you've lost a lot of weight, and you really haven't been yourself for a while. Miss Juliette, you've been really good to me and the other women here. I made a New Year's Resolution to tell you the truth regarding my concerns because I consider you to be more than just my boss. I consider you to be my friend. I really hope I haven't overstepped, but I am worried about you."

The sincerity in Violet's voice brought tears to Juliette's eyes and made her feel worse for lying. "Violet, thanks so much for your concern. I also consider you to be a friend. I guess I'm having a hard time with Jessica's death. Overall, I'm better than I was when she first died, but some days the sadness, pain, and grief overwhelm me. Ever since the last anniversary, I haven't been able to stop having nightmares about Jessica. I don't want you worrying about me because you have enough on your plate with running things here. I really appreciate you, though."

Violet smiled and nodded. "Thank you, Ms. Juliette. I appreciate you too."

"No, thank you for your friendship and for this delicious food. Now let me go get some work done," Juliette said, setting her dish in the sink and exiting the kitchen.

Juliette headed to her office to begin her research on George's birth parents. Once inside, she pulled out a file that contained information about George that Sabrina had given her. While her computer booted up, she thought about her conversation with Violet and felt guilty. She hadn't totally lied, as she was actually having recurring nightmares about Jessica, but not for the reasons Violet or others would expect.

She knew it was time to resume her counseling with Emily, who had been her therapist for years. She did not know if she could survive the shame of having to disclose the truth to her. She had informed Emily of her illicit encounter with Franklin, but she had not been truthful about when it had occurred. The pressure she felt was immense because she didn't know what her husband, children, family, or friends would think about her once they learned the truth. She was also worried about Jolene because, sooner or later, she would inevitably have another sickle cell crisis. She would be forced to endure excruciating pain that Juliette would bear witness to. She was also afraid the truth could disrupt the progress that Grandville had made mentally and emotionally. She loved her husband and didn't want to hurt him or set him back. However, she knew it was only a matter of time before what she had done in the dark would come to light. She could only pray that their love could withstand the tsunami force the truth would bring into their lives.

She returned her attention to George's file and hoped that the ancestry information contained within the package would shed some light on his lineage. She had limited information about George's birth mother. She knew her last name was Benson, and her first initial was G. She also knew that her birthday was November 1, 1972.

The Ancestors Operation was a warehouse of blood samples. Many were unaware that by using the service, they were voluntarily consenting the use of their blood for whatever the company desired. In essence, they were giving away some of their privacy rights. Juliette was hopeful that one of George's relatives was either unaware of this fact, didn't care, or just hoped that depositing their DNA would ultimately provide a link to their biological relatives. When she opened the envelope and read its contents, she dropped her head. She didn't have to do any more research because she knew exactly who George's birth parents were. As a matter of fact, she was married to one of them.

Chapter 27

When I Was Your Man

Grandville sat at Take 4 and wondered if he were in the movie, *Groundhog Day*, where the main character relived the same day over and over again. As always, he was the first one there and, again, had an opportunity to watch The Right Music Experience warm up for their show. The only difference between that day and the last time he was there was that Greta would be joining him for a meeting with Rayshawn.

On the very next day after his initial meeting with Rayshawn, he'd called his twin and requested to see her immediately. Greta recognized the urgency in his voice.

"Hey twin, is everything okay?" she asked

"Yes, everything is great, but I have a matter I need to speak to you about privately and in person," Grandville explained.

"When and where do you want to meet me?"

"Can you meet me at my office? Franklin is taking a little time off to hang out with Sabrina."

"Okay, I'll pick us up some food from Sam Sylk's Chicken and Fish. What do you want from there?" Greta asked.

"Some catfish with a side of spaghetti."

"Cool, I'll be there at twelve-thirty."

That afternoon, the twins enjoyed a fantastic seafood lunch and had an opportunity to catch up with one another. They also enjoyed some small talk and cracked a few jokes. After they were done eating, Greta couldn't take the building anticipation for another moment.

"Okay, twin. What's up? You know I love spending time with you, but when you called earlier, I could tell by your voice there was something really important that you need to speak to me about."

Grandville wiped his mouth with his napkin and cleared his throat. "I wanted to let you know that I had dinner with Rayshawn last night. He asked me to talk to you about meeting with him." He sensed Greta's apprehension and laid a hand on hers. "Just listen, twin. His team has a game with the Cleveland Avilers, and while he's in town, he just wants to have dinner with us. However, he did mention that he wants to speak to you privately in person. He said he's in therapy, and his counselor says that talking to you is something he needs to do for his treatment."

"Grandville, I don't know how I feel about that. I've been apart from Rayshawn for several years, and I'm not sure what else there is to say."

"Sis, I totally understand. But, if you want my opinion, I think you should do it. I saw your reaction to Rayshawn at the clinic opening when he publicly confessed his love for you. You're about to marry Derek, so I really think it's important to have one hundred percent closure in your relationship with Rayshawn before moving on. But whatever you decide to do, I'll support."

Greta thought in silence for a few moments. "You know what, Grandville, you're right. I guess I have to put on my big girl panties and be a woman about this situation. I'm going to hear Rayshawn out.

I probably also need to say some things to him so we both can move on."

"That's great, Greta."

"So tell me, what's going on with Juliette? I know my girl, and she hasn't been herself for months now."

"I think when Jolene got sick on the anniversary of Jessica's death, it freaked her out, he said. "It honestly upset her to the point that she's having problems with her coping mechanisms. She does everything she's supposed to, like managing the rooming home and taking care of the kids and the house, but she's been very antisocial and anxious. I'm going to be throwing her a surprise birthday dinner to try to get things back to normal, and I may need your help."

"Anything. All you have to do is tell me what you need."

Grandville leaned back in his chair and rubbed his full belly. "I'm also going to surprise her with the news that the Robinson Foundation is giving her a check for fifty thousand dollars to A New Beginning so she can work with two newly released inmates who have received treatment at the Jessica Stubbs clinic."

"That's wonderful, twin," Greta gushed. "Juliette is going to be ecstatic. She deserves to let her hair down."

That was two weeks prior, and since their lunch, he had only spoken to Greta once to confirm the time and date of their private dinner meeting with Rayshawn. Grandville had offered to pick her up, but she had wanted to drive herself. Grandville arrived first, then Rayshawn and Greta arrived at the same time. Once settled, the staff took their cocktail orders and Grandville noted that Greta had ordered a double Jack Daniels and Coke. He could tell that she was anxious.

"Greta, you are looking stunning, as usual," Rayshawn said as his eyes drank her in. "Thanks for agreeing to meet with me. I'm sure

Grandville has already shared with you that I'm in counseling. But what I did not share is that I am a member of Sex Addicts Anonymous."

The twins shared a look, stunned by his announcement.

"It's like Alcoholics Anonymous," Rayshawn explained. "I've been diagnosed with satyriasis, which means I have an addiction to sexual behavior. In my case, it's an addiction to oral sex in particular. Part of my twelve-step program is to make amends with those who I've harmed." Rayshawn turned to Greta and looked into her eyes. "My behavior was unacceptable, and I want to apologize to both of you for violating your trust and for not being honest with you."

Greta remained quiet and nodded her head to indicate that she was listening. Grandville also remained quiet, attempting to digest what he had just heard. The waiter came over and took their orders just before the band began to play. Soon after, the trio got caught up in the music. Before they knew it, the music stopped and the band took their first break.

"That band is awesome," Rayshawn said as their waiter returned to the table, accompanied by a team of staff members to serve their meal. "I don't think I could ever get tired of listening to them. Sitting here with the two of you together is something that I've truly missed."

They silently ate their food when Rayshawn broke their silence and said, "Greta, how have you been doing for the past few months?"

Greta took a sip of water to clear her palette before responding. "I've been great, Rayshawn. As you know, I'm getting married in a few weeks, so I've been busy. How about you?"

"Not so good because I've been missing you and what we had," Rayshawn said matter-of-factly.

"Well, you know what they say, Rayshawn. You don't miss your water until your well runs dry. I accept your apology, but I don't miss the pain I experienced during our marriage. I don't miss the sleepless nights, the betrayal, or broken promises."

"I understand, and I promise, I didn't bring you here to upset you," Rayshawn said.

"Well, why *did* you bring me here?" Greta asked, her voice raising an octave. "What is it that you wanted to tell me?"

Grandville kept his eyes on his plate, opting to stay out of their conversation.

Rayshawn nodded toward the band, who had reclaimed their spot on stage and had begun playing as the leader announced into the microphone, "The great Mr. Robinson has dedicated this next song to the love of his life: Miss Greta."

The band started to play their own rendition of Bruno Mars' "When I was your Man". The words of the song were moving, and when they got to the chorus, they sang, "Now my baby is dancing, but she is dancing with another man." Greta could not contain the tears that streamed down her face. When the song was over, Rayshawn nodded to the band, and they stopped playing.

"Grandville, this is the part of the dinner where I need you to give me fifteen minutes of privacy with Greta. Would you mind sitting at the bar and enjoying some dessert? Or, if you prefer, you can have a drink," Rayshawn suggested.

Grandville looked Greta in her eyes, and she nodded that she was okay with speaking with Rayshawn privately. "Okay, no problem. Twin, if you need me, I'll only be across the room."

At the bar, Grandville watched Rayshawn and Greta closely. He was too far away to hear what they were saying. After a few minutes, he noticed Rayshawn had said something to really upset Greta. She put her face in her hands and cried. Grandville almost leaped off his bar seat to head back, but something in his spirit told him to remain seated. Greta continued to listen as they began conversing again. After a half an hour of what Grandville observed as a spirited discussion, Greta and Rayshawn stood up and hugged. He saw Greta kiss Rayshawn on the cheek while he wiped tears from his eyes. The two of them then walked to the bar where he remained seated.

"Grandville, I want to thank you for allowing me the opportunity to have dinner with you and Greta. Call me soon so we can arrange for the Robinson Foundation to get the money to Juliette. I'm looking forward to moving your friend, Big Joe, into the rooming house. Right now, he's at the pre-release center," Rayshawn said.

"We won't be able to take Joe for at least another month. I'm hopeful that this won't be a problem." Grandville said.

"No, I think that'll be fine," Rayshawn said.

"Thanks for dinner, and you have a safe trip back to Los Angeles," Grandville said.

"No, fam, thank you. No matter what's happened, the two of you will always be my family. I'll be in touch," Rayshawn said.

With that, Grandville reached for Greta, and the twins walked hand in hand out the door.

"Where's your car?" Grandville asked once they stepped outside.

"I took an Uber down. Do you mind taking me home?"

"No problem. My car is in a pay lot down the street."

The twins headed toward Grandville's car while simultaneously trying to stop the strong Antarctic wind that came off the lake from knocking them down. Once they were finally in his car, Grandville turned the heat on high, allowing the car to warm up.

"So, are you going to tell me what was so important that Rayshawn just had to see you tonight?"

"Yes. Rayshawn wanted me to know when he developed his sex addiction to receiving blow jobs."

Grandville fought to keep from rolling his eyes. "Okay, why is this important information?"

"Because, according to Rayshawn, our cousin, I mean...our sister, Gina, had been performing oral sex on him since he was fifteen. She was also his first sexual experience. He said that Gina knew how he felt about me. When he'd spent the night at our house one night, Rayshawn was asleep on our couch. He awoke to Gina performing oral sex on him. After she finished, she told him that I was a nice girl and one day he would be a big star. She'd told him that she wanted him to stay with me, so she was going to provide him with something she knew I wouldn't. Whenever he would come to our house after that, she would secretly do him in the garage. She basically forced him to participate because she was blackmailing him. Gina said that if he didn't let her do that, she'd tell me what she had been doing to him. She convinced him I wouldn't give him the time of day if I found out. After he told me, I explained what happened to me and Gina as children and why I never wanted to perform oral on him."

"Damn, I had no idea. Rayshawn never told me any of that," Grandville said as he navigated the snowy streets on his way to Greta's condo.

"I know. Because, according to Rayshawn, he'd never told anybody. I told him I'm sorry about everything, and I will always love him. I hope he finds a woman who makes him feel the way Derek makes me feel. Derek knows that all I want to do is dance, and he lets me. Rayshawn said he respects my choice and that he finally feels like he can give his blessing," Greta said.

A few moments of silence passed before Grandville asked, "Sis, are you okay?"

"Yes. I'm glad I met with Rayshawn. I feel so much lighter now."

"I'm glad also because you now have some closure. Next Friday is Juliette's birthday, and I need you and Samantha to take her out somewhere so I can get everything together."

"Okay, no problem. I'll call Maria, Sabrina, and Samantha and tell them I need help with some last-minute wedding projects," Greta said as she kissed her twin on the cheek and exited the car.

Chapter 28

Slow Down

Melinia patiently waited for Rique to make his next move on the chessboard. After two agonizing minutes, he finally moved his bishop across the board to land vertically in front of her king. After surveying the board, she realized she had left her king vulnerable. She didn't have any more moves because she was in checkmate, which meant the game was over.

"Checkmate," Rique said.

"Rique, you got me. You've become quite the master of this game," Melinia complimented him.

"Thanks, Melinia. I'm glad we got our game out the way. Now, we have time for you to put in some work. Go on back to your room and make yourself beautiful and meet me in the Bone Room in half an hour. You and Remy are going on tape," Rique directed.

Melinia felt sick because she was going to have to explain to Remy that she was pregnant. She hadn't put on any visible weight and had made sure to wear loose-fitting clothes. But, when she was naked, it would be hard to miss her baby bump. She didn't know how Remy would react when he saw it and had no idea what to expect. She was almost off the heroin, as Rique had reduced the amount he gave her every week. As a result, she was taking less and less of the drug. She felt the withdrawal symptoms, but they weren't as severe as if she would have kicked cold turkey. She had never filmed when her head wasn't high, and she did not know how to make a pornographic movie without the use of an illicit drug. She went back to her and Mimi's room and attempted to find a piece of lingerie that still fit. She was so distraught that she didn't notice Mimi entering. She immediately turned on the radio and adjusted the volume so that Rique couldn't overhear their conversation.

"Hey Melinia, what's going on? Rique just told the crew that you and Remy are going to film in a few minutes. Are you okay?" Mimi asked.

"No, I'm actually not okay. But, right now, I don't have a choice. At least Rique isn't making me do some random stranger. Remy's the baby's father," Melinia rationalized.

"Does Remy know?" Mimi asked.

"I haven't told him, but who knows what Rique has said to him. You know how he loves to play mind games."

"I know this is hard, but keep your head up," Mimi encouraged.

"It's hard to hold your head high when you're a victim of modern-day human slavery, but I'll certainly give it a try," Melinia despondently said.

There was a knock at the door, and Melinia thought Remy might have sent someone from the crew to get her.

Mimi opened the door, and Julio slipped into their cramped quarters.

"What are you doing here?" Melinia whispered. "We told you never to come to our room. Suppose someone saw you?"

"No one followed me, and I know where Rique has hidden cameras. I heard you were going on camera, so I came to get you pumped up. Let's turn up the radio and dance," Julio suggested.

"That's a great idea," Mimi said and turned up the radio.

"Melinia, good news. You won't have to go on film tonight," Julio leaned in and whispered to her.

"Why not?" Melinia asked,

"Because a hurricane is about to hit the Bahamas. Go on to the Bone Room. Rique is waiting for us there. He wants to talk to us, and he sent me to get you. I overheard Remy talking to him about it and that's how I know. This might be our chance to escape," Julio answered.

Melinia didn't respond. She quickly put on a robe and hurried out the door with Mimi and Julio close on her heels. Her son was in the Bahamas, and the hurricane threatened his safety. She could only hope that Rique had a plan to get Rafael, Romanita, and Roberto out of harm's way.

When she and Julio entered the Bone Room, the whole crew was waiting for them. She walked over to the bed and sat on the edge, mentally preparing to remove her robe.

Rique said, "Keep your robe on, Melinia. I brought you all here because I just learned that a hurricane is on course to hit the Bahamas. My little brother, Remy, failed to see this coming, and as a result, we're in a situation where we have very little time to react. Because Romanita and Roberto are there and are members of our crew, we have to go get them."

Rique then repeated what he said in Spanish for the crew. Remy grew upset and began speaking in Spanish a raised voice with Rique, who argued back in their native tongue.

"My brother wants me to explain that a hurricane in January is very rare, and Hurricane Alice is on course to be a category five," Rique lectured. "It'll be the third hurricane to occur in January in recorded history. He also says that this storm is a fluke because hurricane season is usually from July through October."

Melinia was sick with worry and could not help herself when she asked, "So what's the plan? I'm down with my crew, so tell me what you need me to do."

"See, Melinia, that's why I like you," Rique said with a light laugh. "You spoke out of turn, but that's because you want to help our stranded members. The question is, what are the rest of you willing to do? In order to extract Romanita and Roberto, we're going to have to get to them before the storm hits. I want you all to know there is a chance that we might run into Alice," he said in English, then in Spanish.

Everyone began speaking at the same time in both languages.

"Everybody shut up. We can sing together, but we can't all talk together," Rique directed.

Raul began to speak in English, "I love my cousin, but I can't be a part of this mission. Do you remember Hurricane Sandy? We barely made it out alive. We can't risk going anywhere near that storm. Wouldn't it make better sense for Romanita and Roberto to try to ride out the storm? Why put the whole crew at risk for two members?"

"Because Romanita and Roberto are a part of this kingdom and we protect our own, so this meeting is to let you all know that we are bypassing Miami and heading straight for the Bahamas," Rique said sternly. "We're to get there before the storm hits, pick them up, and get out. We don't have much time, and we need all hands on deck." Rique turned to Melinia. "I need you and Mimi to go into the storeroom and locate every life jacket we have on la barca. The rest of you, fall back until I tell you what to do."

Melinia and Mimi hurried down to the storeroom to do what Rique directed.

"Melinia, are you scared?" Mimi asked.

"I'm petrified. We've never been through a hurricane before. I grew up in Cleveland, and the worst I've experienced has been a blizzard," Melinia said.

"I grew up in Detroit, so I'm just like you," Mimi said. "I remember watching the people of New Orleans after Hurricane Katrina on television. It was horrible, and I'm afraid that if this small boat gets caught in a hurricane, we're all going to drown."

"That's why we have to do everything Rique tells us to do so we can survive this," Melinia said.

They rummaged through the storeroom and managed to bring every life jacket they could find to the top deck where the crew was huddled around Rique.

"Okay, listen up, everyone. According to the weather reports, Alice is due to hit the Bahamas in three days, unless the storm changes course. We think we can make it to the Bahamas in a little more than two days, so hopefully, we'll be cool. Everyone go to your quarters and get some rest because I promise you, we're going to need it," Rique instructed.

Later, as Melinia lay on her lumpy little bed, she prayed they would make it through the storm. Her son and unborn child's lives depended on it.

Chapter 29

Pity Party

Juliette opened her eyes to find Grandville staring down at her, "Good morning, birthday girl," he said.

"Good morning, "Juliette whispered.

"I brought you some coffee," Grandville said, motioning to a mug on the table beside their bed.

Juliette gave a gentle grin. "Thanks, husband. You're the best."

Grandville leaned down and kissed her cheek. "I'm my best because I married the best."

There was a knock at the door, and Grandville said, "Come on in."

The door opened, and their children ran into the room and jumped onto the bed. Jabari was carrying a tray filled with breakfast foods. "Happy birthday, Mom," they yelled in unison.

Juliette was touched by the love her family was showing her and hugged each of her kids individually and thanked them for her breakfast. Grandville said, "Okay, Stubbs clan, it's time for you to get ready for school. We're going to let Mom enjoy her breakfast."

The kids all headed toward their respective rooms, leaving Grandville and Juliette alone again.

"Sweetheart, are you going into work today?" he asked.

"Yes, I'm going to stop by A Better Tomorrow for a little while, then over to A New Beginning to meet a social worker from a law firm about two potential residents they want to place there," Juliette said. "I'm not sure how she found out about the male rooming house because it isn't open yet, and I haven't even done any advertising."

Grandville smiled at her. "I was going to save this news until this evening as part of one of your birthday gifts, but the social worker is from a law firm representing the Robinson Foundation. They're going to pay your program to provide housing and work for two former residents of Oakhill."

"Are you kidding me? How long have you known about this?"

"Rayshawn told me a few weeks ago over dinner. This will be great for the clinic and A New Beginning. Joe will be one of your first residents. Rayshawn and the foundation's board members feel that your support of former inmates who received treatment at the clinic will be a great publicity opportunity. He's hoping it will help bring more awareness and funding opportunities for the foundation. Since you already have an appointment with the social worker, I figure I'd better let you know."

"You're so good to me, Grandville. Thank you!!" Juliette exclaimed as she hugged and kissed him.

"My pleasure. I'm also going to go into the office for a little while, but I need you to meet me here at four so the birthday festivities can begin."

"Grandville, I hope you didn't go all out, she whined. "I just want a quiet evening alone with you and the kids."

"Don't worry about what I have planned for you. Just have your sexy self here at four," he directed.

After Grandville left for work, she relaxed while counting her blessings. Before long, feelings of crushing guilt overwhelmed her. Every year on her birthday, she reflected on her past and planned for her future. As she lay there, she realized she couldn't cope with her problems on her own and had finally reached the point where she knew she needed outside help. She picked up her phone and scrolled through her contacts until she located her therapist, Emily McHall's phone number.

The phone rang three times before she picked up and said, "Juliette, you must have ESP because I was just picking up the phone to call you."

"Really?" Juliette asked.

"Of course. It's your birthday, and I wanted to check on you to see how you're doing," Emily replied.

"Honestly, I'm not doing so well," Juliette admitted. "I really need to see you."

"Well, my ten o'clock just canceled. I can give you that spot if you're available."

"Yes, I'm available. I'll see you then."

After letting Grandville and the kids know she was headed out, Juliette was on her way to Emily's office. She turned on some soft music to calm her nerves during the ride. She was filled with anxiety about telling Emily the truth about Jolene, but she knew their session was exactly what she needed.

Once she was seated in front of Emily, everything she'd been feeling for months came pouring out of her in the storm of emotions, which culminated in a deluge of tears and loud sobs. She couldn't catch her breath, and soon she was hyperventilating.

"Juliette, it's okay. Just breathe with me," Emily coached, moving across the room to stand beside her.

Juliette took a few pieces of tissue from the table beside the chair and blew her nose. She began breathing deeply, following Emily's rhythm. Soon, she was feeling better.

"Juliette, you just had a panic attack. Have you had one before?" Emily asked her.

"Yes," she said, still catching her breath. "I've actually had a few of them, but they have only recently begun."

"Well, why haven't you called me? We could have worked on alleviating your anxiety together," Emily said.

"I couldn't bring myself to call you because that would have forced me to face my issues, and I just wasn't ready," Juliette confided.

"Understandable. We social workers and therapists like to refer to it as self-determination. You have the right to deal with your problems whenever you're ready and however you want. I'm just glad that you're here now. Remember, Juliette, anything you tell me will be confidential, with the exception of abuse or your intent to commit a crime or hurt yourself. That would require me to report it under Ohio's Duty to Warn rules. Other than that, what's said here will stay here. I will not judge you, and together we can begin working on a plan to handle the problem."

"Thank you. I just don't know where to begin," Juliette said.

"Begin wherever you feel most comfortable."

Juliette nodded. "Okay. Well, since Grandville's return from Oakhill, everything has been going extremely well in our relationship. He's the man that I married and more, and I'm glad I did not give up on him. We have a good marriage, and he still treats me and the children like gold. I also haven't spotted any signs of a psychotic state or symptoms related to his bipolar diagnosis. He takes his medication faithfully, and his mood is consistent and even. He doesn't seem to drink anymore, and he hasn't smoked. Since he's come home from Oakhill, he's been more relaxed."

Juliette paused for a few moments, and Emily waited patiently for her to continue.

"I guess I'm upset because I'm going to destroy my marriage and all the progress that Grandville has achieved at the same time. Emily, I'm backed into a corner, and I don't know what to do!"

"Okay, Juliette. Can you catch me up to where you are now? If everything is going well with Grandville and your marriage, then what happened? When we decided to alter your treatment plan to an as-needed basis, you were doing great," Emily noted.

"You're right. I *was* doing great, but in the past year, everything has fallen apart."

"So, when exactly did things begin to fall apart?" Emily gently asked.

Juliette composed herself with a deep breath. "This past August, when the Jessica Stubbs Mental Health Clinic at Oakhill Prison was opened. Rayshawn insisted that the party take place at the new clinic on the anniversary of Jessica's death. After the reception, we had a private pool party and were having a great time. Then, all of a sudden, Jolene started screaming at the top of her lungs. Her scream sounded so much like Jessica's on the day that she died that it instantly transported me right back to the worst day of my life," she explained, clenching the tissue in her trembling hands.

A few moments of thoughtful silence passed before Emily urged her to continue. "Why did Jolene scream?"

Juliette explained what happened in the pool and the emergency room doctor's findings.

"Did the doctor suspect that Jolene was suffering from leukemia or some other kind of cancer?"

"No, he suspected sickle cell disease, and I've since confirmed his suspicions," Juliette said as she began to softly cry again. "Now, I'm terrified Jolene is going to die from complications related to the disease, and I'll have to bury another child."

"Sickle cell disease is a difficult diagnosis, and I'm not sure if I ever disclosed to you that my sixteen-year-old daughter also has it. But she's doing well. Although there are only about one hundred thousand people in the United States who suffer from sickle cell disease, I want you to know that there has been a lot of advances made in the area of treatment. What I don't understand is how it's possible that Jolene wasn't diagnosed at birth."

"There was a lab mix up, due to the twins receiving blood transfusions at birth. The hospital staff thought Jolene was a hemoglobin-S trait carrier like me and her sister Jenae. But she actually has a disorder called hemoglobin-SC, which is under the umbrella of sickle cell disease. Those with this disorder have two parents who are carriers and…" Juliette paused, pressing the balled-up tissue to her eyes. "I'm not sure if Grandville is a hemoglobin C carrier, but I know for a fact that he's not a hemoglobin S carrier."

"And?" Emily urged.

"And, there's a possibility that Grandville is not Jolene's father."

Emily nodded slowly, then waited for a beat before asking, "Does Grandville know about Jolene's sickle cell disease diagnosis and the fact that he may not be her biological father?"

"Not yet. But, sooner or later, Jolene will have another pain crisis, and I'm going to have to explain to a doctor in front of Grandville that our daughter has sickle cell disease. On top of that, I've been having dreams where Jessica is calling me a liar and other names. Before this, I hadn't dreamed about her. But now, whenever I close my eyes, all I see is her. I'm barely sleeping. The fact that I betrayed my husband with his best friend makes me hate who I see in the mirror every morning. I think my family and friends can see it, too. Since August, I've been isolating myself, and have only been spending time with Grandville and the kids. I also had a hard time coming to terms with the fact that I even lied to you. I slept with Franklin two days after Grandville went to prison, not three weeks after, like I originally told you. Then Sabrina, who recently became Franklin's fiancée, asked me to help her find her son's birth parents, but not before sharing with me that Franklin is a hemoglobin C carrier. So, now I'm positive that he's Jolene's biological father."

"Okay, Juliette. Please slow down. There's a lot we need to unpack here. I didn't realize Franklin was engaged," Emily said.

"Yes, turns out he and Sabrina have been secretly dating for years, Juliette explained. "He proposed to her on the night of the clinic opening. Sabrina is also the psychiatrist who evaluated Grandville right after the accident. I really like her. She's both beautiful and smart, and they make a fantastic couple. Holding on to all this sensitive information and thinking of all the lives it could potentially impact is making me feel like I'm going to snap at any moment. It's gotten to the point where I hate leaving my house and loud noises now upset me to the point where I feel like I'm going to pass out,"

"Juliette, you've been dealing with a lot on your own, but, from this day forward, we will deal with your problems together. You may be experiencing symptoms related to PTSD and anxiety. You'll need to be examined to ensure that your issues aren't stemming from an underlying physical health issue. I'm going to bring a nurse practitioner in to examine you. Afterward, we'll discuss a short-term prescription for your panic attacks. We'll also design a treatment plan to include therapy aimed at reducing your PTSD, panic, and anxiety symptoms."

"That sounds good. Thank you, Emily."

It was 4:05 before Juliette pulled back into her freshly plowed driveway and marveled at the large snow mounds that lined her house. She'd met with the social worker from the law firm and had stopped by the female rooming house to work on a grant application. She was exhausted and looking forward to taking a nap. Before she could turn her key in the lock, the front door swung open and she was standing face-to-face with her handsome husband.

"Here she is, my birthday Queen!" Grandville cheered. "Come on, girl. I've been waiting for you! I know you've been stressed lately. So, this year, we're going to focus on getting you relaxed. Follow me." Grandville took her hand and led her down the steps into the recreation room in their basement.

The kids usually played there in the winter, but now, she couldn't believe her eyes. Her beautician, nail tech, and a private massage therapist were all set up with mobile stations all around the room.

"I present to you: Juliette's personal day spa. Go on ahead and get yourself situated. I need to get something from upstairs," Grandville ordered as he padded up the steps.

Then Samantha, Sabrina, Greta, and Maria suddenly emerged from the laundry room, yelling in unison yelled, "Surprise!"

The sudden loud noise caused Juliette to flashback to the day of Jessica's death, and she immediately became anxious, which triggered a panic attack. She fell to her knees as she began hyperventilating, barely able to catch her breath.

Sabrina led the group as they immediately rushed over to her. "Juliette, just relax. Everyone breathe with us. Take a big deep breath in through your nose and exhale through your mouth," Sabrina directed. The ladies breathed in sync several times, each with their eyes on Juliette until she calmed down.

"Juliette, we're so sorry. The last thing we wanted to do was scare you. We just wanted to celebrate your day with you," Maria said, bent over and rubbing her back.

"There was no way you could've known," Juliette said with a weak smile. "I'm sorry about my reaction; I've just been having these panic attacks when I'm caught off guard. I guess the surprise was on you. I appreciate you all so much."

"Of course! We're here because we love you. How long have you been having panic attacks?" Greta asked.

"I've had several of them since August. That's why I haven't been hanging with you guys and neglecting my friendships. I just had an appointment with a nurse practitioner who prescribed me Valium to help me deal with my symptoms of PTSD and anxiety. I actually just started seeing my therapist again today."

The ladies nodded, and Samantha said, "Ain't nothing wrong with a little therapy, playa. I'm glad you're getting the help you need."

"Right! And while I have you all here, I want to apologize for not being emotionally or physically available to you," Juliette said, beginning to choke up. "You know I wouldn't withdraw from you guys if it weren't for a good reason."

"Juliette, don't cry," Sabrina soothed, gently massaging her shoulders. "You have nothing to feel ashamed or embarrassed about. We're here, and you never have to go through this alone if you don't want to. I'm glad that you've reached out for help."

Her friends engulfed her in a group hug and, before she knew it, Grandville was back with a tray holding a huge bottle of champagne, flutes, and assortment of fresh sliced fruit, cheese, and crackers.

"Babe, it's your birthday. Why in the world are you crying?" Grandville asked, walking around and offering flutes to everyone.

"It's my party, and I'll cry if I want to," Juliette joked. "No, but for real, these are tears of joy. I'm so glad to see my friends. Thanks for getting us all together."

"No problem. And there are more festivities to come. This is just the appetizer. Now, let's have a toast to my beloved," Grandville said.

The group held up their glasses and collectively toasted the guest of honor.

Later, while the ladies were getting their hair and nails done, Samantha pulled Juliette off to the side. "Playa, I just want to tell you that I am so glad we had a chance to get together. I'm glad I could tell you in person just how much I've missed you."

"Samantha, I've missed you, too. I'm sorry I've been distant; I've just been going through it. For real."

"I'm your best friend, so when you're going through something, I'm going through it too. I want to share some very sensitive information with you, but I'm going to need to swear you to secrecy," Samantha said.

"You already know you can count on my discretion."

"I may have figured out what the numbers and letters represented on that postcard that was mailed to your aunt two years ago."

Melinia's mother, Mabel, who was Juliette's aunt, received an unsigned postcard addressed to her with no return address. There was a series of numbers and letters that appeared to be in Melinia's handwriting, but there was nothing else about the card that indicated it was from her.

"Girl, are you kidding me?" Juliette asked, her eyes widening.

"No, I'm for real. It's a real possibility that the numbers and letters are coordinates to Port Lucaya in the Grand Bahama Island. If the postcard is from your cousin, that may be her current location. I was thrown off at first because she put all the letters and numbers together, instead of separating them. As you know, Jared took me on a cruise on New Year's Eve. While we were on the boat, I took a tour, which included visiting the vessel's control room. I learned how the boat uses coordinates to represent positions while at sea. I don't know how or why, but it just dawned on me that that the numbers and letters on the card might be coordinates. Once I got home, I looked at the picture I'd taken of the postcard on my phone and tried separating the numbers and letters. We still can't say with certainty that the postcard came from Melinia or that the numbers and letters actually represent coordinates, but it's a start."

"Great work, Sam," Juliette cheered. "I really appreciate your efforts in helping us find Melinia. Keep me posted on what you find out."

"I will."

"I'm so glad you and Derek had a chance to spend some quality alone time together. I'm sure things were pretty romantic on that boat. Have you guys taken it to the next level yet?"

"Yes, we have, and that young boy turned ya girl out! We also talked beforehand, and I let him know I have no interest in having kids. He feels the same and even got a vasectomy years ago," Samantha said.

"I'm so glad that you and Jared are a thing. I really like him, and he seems so into you. Do you think Melinia is still in the Bahamas? That postcard was sent a couple of years ago."

"I'm not sure. Unfortunately, a hurricane is headed straight for the Bahamas, so we can't even send officers from the local Human Trafficking Task Force to investigate at this time. But I have a good feeling that your cousin is going to be found."

"A hurricane in January? That's odd, but I sure hope you're right. Melinia going missing has been so hard on me and my family."

"I can't imagine how you and your family feel about Melinia disappearance, and that's why I am telling you this information, even though I'm not supposed to. I just want you to know there's still a chance she's alive and we may be able to get her back. The hurricane is supposed to be some freak storm that almost never occurs during this time of the year. But enough about that. We're going to keep hope alive and celebrate you."

Later that evening, Franklin, Derek, Jared, and Montell came over, and Grandville had a large soul food dinner catered for his friends and family. After dinner, the kids sang karaoke and played on the Xbox while some of the adults joined in on the festivities. Greta surprised Juliette with news of a girls' trip the following weekend for her upcoming wedding. Grandville gave her Lush bath and body products, the kids got her a spa package, and Sabrina, Samantha, and Maria gave her a $300 Nordstrom gift card. She had a great time, and by the time everyone left that evening, Grandville had achieved his goal of giving her a much-needed relaxing evening. At that moment, she felt more relaxed then she had in months. After a hot, long shower together, Grandville made sweet birthday love to her, and she slept like a baby with not a single nightmare.

The next morning, as she lay in her bed, she realized that she loved her husband so much, she was willing to do whatever it took to ensure she'd never lose him.

Just then, Grandville woke up and pulled her into his arms. "Happy belated birthday, beautiful. You ready for some more birthday sex?"

She smiled and said, "In the words of Janet Jackson, I'm down 'anytime or anyplace.' But you know the twins will be up soon, asking for breakfast any minute. So, don't start something you can't finish, Mr. Stubbs," she teased, grinning.

At that moment, they heard a knock at their bedroom door.

"Come on in," Grandville called out.

Juliette sat up and spotted Jolene standing in their doorway, tears silently streamed down her face.

"Sweetheart, what's wrong? Did you and Jenae have a fight? Why are you crying?"

"My arm hurts, Mommy. It really hurts," Jolene whined.

Juliette knew right then; there was a good chance that Jolene's pain was related to her recent sickle cell diagnosis. Her mind raced, and she knew she needed to come up with a story quickly. She just hoped her new story came with a happy ending.

Chapter 30
Know Your Worth

They had arrived at the St Lucaya port, but the waves were so large, Remy was hesitant to dock their boat. They had barely beat the hurricane and arrived right before Alice was due to make landfall, but the waves and wind had knocked their boat around the ocean like a pinball. Melinia was terrified. Despite their best plan, Alice picked up speed and, though they traveled as quickly as the boat would allow, they had only just beaten the storm. But it was difficult to tell by the size of the waves and the howling wind.

Melinia and Mimi had followed all of Rique's orders and made sure everyone had on life jackets. The crew, who were working on the top level of the boat, were attached to safety lines. Rique had directed the women to relocate the boat's supplies, in an attempt to help evenly distribute the weight and assist in stabilizing the boat. Melinia and Mimi were posted on the steps that led to the bottom of the boat, watching the crew fight the waves. Remy expertly steered the vessel in an attempt to keep it above water.

Rique yelled, "Julio, take Mimi and Melinia down to the speedboats. We're about a mile away from shore. Get them onto dry land. We're going to take la barca back out to sea and try to get her away from the storm. You know where Romanita lives. After you take the girls there, I'll be back for you."

Julio, Mimi, and Melinia carefully stepped into the speedboat, and as it was being lowered into the water, Melinia caught sight of

Remy, who was staring directly into her eyes. She didn't know why, but at that moment, she felt it would be the last time she would lay eyes on the love of her life and the father of her unborn child.

Once they were in the speedboat, Julio yelled out, "Chicas, lay down on the bottom of the boat. It won't take us long to get to shore."

Melinia and Mimi followed orders and tried to breathe, despite the water and wind's assault on them. After what seemed like ages, Julio yelled out, "Okay, we're coming into the dock. Get prepared to jump out and run. We have to find shelter before the hurricane hits the shore."

Julio jumped out of the boat and stepped up onto the dock. He grabbed Mimi's hand and pulled her out before reaching for Melinia. The trio trotted away from the water, attempting not to fall on the wet and slippery wooden dock. They spotted a beige building against the gray sky that was boarded up and looked deserted, but they ran toward it anyway. Once they reached the building, they discovered the doors were unlocked. When they stepped inside, they noticed several people in tattered clothing and sparse belongings loitering in the hallway. Julio spoke with a couple of them in Spanish for a little while. The interior of the building had been neglected, and broken glass was scattered throughout the large space. An overwhelming stench of mildew hung in the damp air, and Melinia attempted to breathe through her mouth. She scanned the dark interior and quickly spotted Romanita, who stuck out like a sore thumb from the drab surroundings. She was sitting in the corner, holding Rafael's hand. Roberto was there with them and had his arm around her.

Melinia was ecstatic to see her son and rushed over to him. She called his name and waited for him to recognize her before reaching out to pick him up. Holding him in her arms, she smiled as she inhaled his scent, squeezing him tightly.

"What are you guys doing here? Why aren't you at the house?" Melinia asked.

"Remy called me a few hours ago and told me to bring Romanita and Rafael to the port because the crew was picking us up," Roberto explained.

"I'm so confused. Rique put us in a boat and sent us to shore, telling us to get to Romanita's house. He said they were going to go back out to sea to avoid the storm," Julio said.

"Well, we can't get back to the house right now. The storm is pretty much here. Let's find somewhere here in this building to ride this out," Roberto directed. "When the eye passes over us, we'll make our way back to the house."

The group followed Roberto upstairs to find a suitable shelter. After exploring each room, they found a vacant utility closet, crowded into the small room, and closed the door.

"Why are we squeezing into this small space?" Melinia asked. "Why aren't we in one of the bigger rooms that we passed up?"

"Those rooms have windows, and although they are boarded up, when the storm hits, they'll probably shatter. Then the wind will propel the glass, and we could be hurt or even killed. We came upstairs because if the water comes onto the shore, this building could flood. We'll have to ride the storm out, and we'll have a better chance up here," Roberto said.

"Our American friends have never been through a hurricane, so we have to help them understand the danger we're in and how to survive it," Julio said.

"Thank you, friends. We'll be sure to help you survive your first blizzard if you ever make it to the Midwest during a storm," Melinia joked.

Romanita said, "I've never seen snow before. What's it like?"

"Cold and beautiful, but only if you're inside with heat, food, and a television," Mimi said.

Soon, they could hear howling wind, windows breaking and, the muted screams of people in other areas of the building. Romanita was crying and moaning at the same time. Roberto wrapped her into his arms. Holding on to Rafael, Melinia noticed what she hadn't before. Roberto and Romanita were in love. She silently wondered how Rique would feel about this development. The patter of the rain and the darkness of the utility closet soothed Melinia, and she eventually dozed off. She felt herself being gently shaken awake. She had no idea how long she had been asleep.

"Melinia, wake up. The storm has passed, and we're heading out," Mimi whispered into her ear.

The group cautiously emerged from the utility closet, and Melinia surveyed the damage as they made their way to the stairs. The building looked like a disaster zone with leaves and tree branches littering their path. Once they stepped outside, Melinia noticed large puddles from the flooding Roberto had warned them of. They cautiously waded through the water on their way to higher ground. The rain had stopped, but the sky was still dark, and the clouds hung menacingly. As they hurried toward their destination, Melinia saw small groups of people crying and standing around.

"I parked the car on high ground, near the top of a parking deck. We can only hope the deck is still standing and the car remains intact," Roberto said.

After a few minutes of walking, they made it to the parking deck and were grateful to find the car still in one piece. They jumped inside, and Roberto carefully navigated the debris and standing water as they raced towards Romanita's home. As they pulled up to the estate,

Melinia could see why Rique had insisted on braving Alice to come and rescue Romanita. Trees had fallen down all over the estate, and a huge one was blocking the front door. The windows were blown out, and it was apparent without stepping inside that Romanita's belongings throughout the house had been destroyed.

"The rain and wind will start again soon, so we have got to get inside and try to find somewhere to hunker down," Roberto advised. The group followed him to the back of the house, where they gained entrance through the back door.

"Come on, let's get into the downstairs bathroom. It's the safest place to be during the hurricane," Roberto directed.

The group piled into the bathroom and soon heard the pounding rain and violent wind, indicating that the storm's eye had passed, and the hurricane's fury had resumed. They had been crammed into the bathroom for a few hours when Roberto announced that the storm had passed. The group filed out of the bathroom to find the house's interior in total disarray.

Romanita took one look at her wet and destroyed furniture, carpet, and appliances and began to cry. Roberto and Rafael both tried to embrace her, but she was hysterical.

"They're only material things," Roberto cooed. "They can be replaced, love. But we cannot."

Julio gave them a moment before leaning down to whisper into Melinia's ear, "I'm leaving before Rique and the crew gets here. This is our opportunity to escape captivity. You and Mimi should come with me."

Julio and Mimi were unaware Melinia had an elaborate plan of her own. It had included getting pregnant by Remy, gaining Rique's trust in order to be weaned off the drugs, returning to the Bahamas to deliver her new baby, then running away with both of her children.

But the hurricane had now placed her in a unique position where she could possibly get away without having to wait.

"Hey Romanita, please stop crying," Melinia said. "We're going to help you put this place back together. Julio and I are going to go outside and start picking up some of the debris off the lawn. We'll be back shortly."

They headed toward the back door and out into the muddy backyard before Julio asked her, "So, are you coming with us or not?"

She glanced back toward the house before responding. "Julio, I would love to leave with you, but there are a couple of things you should know before I do."

"Okay, but we don't have much time. To have any chance of escape, we have to get out of here before Rique and the crew arrives," he said.

"I know, but I can't leave without my son."

"Well, where is he?" Julio asked.

"Here. Rafael is my son."

Julio frowned. "I thought he was Romanita's son."

"No, he's mine, and I'm not leaving without him."

"Okay, we'll wait until everyone falls asleep tonight to head out."

"There's something else you need to know before you commit to taking us with you."

"What, Melinia?"

Melinia shifted her weight from one leg to the other nervously. "I'm five months pregnant."

"What?" he blurted out, frowning. "Who's the baby's father? Is it one of the men you were forced to have sex with?"

"It's Remy. And I wouldn't say I was forced. It was a quid pro quo transaction. I provided sex acts, and the crew supplied me with heroin." She paused and noted the shock in his eyes. "Look, I've done what I needed to do to get high. But Rique has almost weaned me off it to prepare me to give birth without the baby being addicted."

Julio crossed his arms and shrugged. "Whatever you need to say to sleep at night. But the truth is: Rique and the crew have made you into a sex slave. Now, this is our chance to escape for good, and I'm not going to blow it. The question you should be asking yourself is if you're coming with me or remain in captivity."

Melinia knew she had a choice to make and hoped she would make the right one.

Chapter 31

Anyone

Grandville was scared. His beautiful daughter was crying hysterically, and Juliette was hyperventilating, shaking, and crying. They were in a private room at Cleveland University Hospital, and he felt as though he had been transformed into an episode of *Tales from the Crypt*. After having a great night celebrating her birthday, he and Juliette had been enjoying a phenomenal morning. He had achieved his goal; his wife seemed to enjoy her birthday celebration and was more relaxed than she had been in months. After their guests left and the kids went to sleep, he had made slow, passionate love to her. Her moans of ecstasy turned him on, and he had anticipated repeating his performance. Then his dream had morphed into a nightmare. He and Juliette had rushed their young daughter to the emergency room.

He was in shock as he tried to absorb the words that the pediatrician had just uttered, "Mr. and Mrs. Stubbs, Jolene is experiencing a sickle cell crisis related to symptoms of her hemoglobin SC disease."

"Doctor, there must be some sort of mistake. Our daughter doesn't have sickle cell disease, so how is it possible for her to have a pain crisis?" Grandville asked.

"I'm sorry, Mr. Stubbs, but according to our tests, your daughter definitely has a sickle cell disorder known as hemoglobin SC. And, frankly, we're trying to figure out why this diagnosis was not declared sooner," the pediatrician stated.

Juliette was so upset, she couldn't speak.

The doctor took notice of her trembles and asked, "Mrs. Stubbs, are you okay?"

"No. I just can't go through it again," Juliette said through soft sobs.

"Mrs. Stubbs, I'm not sure what you mean. Does another one of your other children have sickle cell disease?" the doctor asked.

"No, not to my knowledge," Grandville answered for her. "I'm not a hemoglobin S carrier, so I'm still trying to figure out how it's physically possible for Jolene to be suffering from this disease."

Juliette stood up and took a slow step before crumpling to the floor. As Grandville rushed to her side, the doctor stepped out of the room and notified the nursing station, "We have a code white."

Grandville struggled to hold everything together as he leaned over Juliette's unconscious body.

Jolene screamed and cried out from the examining table, "Mommy, what's wrong?"

The nurses ran into the room and moved Grandville out of the way. They administered smelling salts to Juliette, and she immediately came to.

"Mrs. Stubbs, it appears you fainted. You need to be examined to rule out any underlying issues. Since we're in the pediatric ward, you'll need to be taken to the adult emergency room to be examined," the doctor urged.

"No, I think I'm okay now, doctor. Besides, I can't leave Jolene," Juliette said.

"Well, I can't afford for you and Jolene to both be sick, so go with the nurses, and I'll keep you posted on Jolene's condition," Grandville urged. He kissed Juliette on her cheek, gently guiding her toward the two waiting nurses.

After Juliette left the room, Grandville stared down at his beautiful daughter, and his heart leaped with love. Jolene was a beautiful child with a sweet, gentle spirit. It hurt him to see her in pain. He held her hand as she looked up at him with sadness in her eyes.

Her voice was a whisper as she asked, "Daddy?"

"I'm here, sweetie," he said and squeezed her small hand.

"Is Mommy going to be okay?"

"She's going to be just fine," he reassured. "I don't want you worrying about your mom. I want you to work on getting better."

After a few minutes, the pain medication she had been administered began to kick in, and she closed her eyes, trailing off to sleep. He was left alone with his whirlwind of thoughts and emotions. He was confused, trying to figure out how it was possible for his daughter to suffer from a genetic condition for which he was unaware he possessed the trait.

After a few minutes, the doctor returned to the room. "Mr. Stubbs, we've completed our examination of your daughter. Despite the acute pain she's experiencing, her blood work results have ruled out an infection."

"That's good. But doctor, I thought all children are tested at birth for sickle cell disease."

"Yes, that's true, sir."

"Then how is it possible that we didn't know about Jolene's condition earlier?"

"The only thing I can offer is that, sometimes, mistakes happen. I'm not sure how this one occurred, but I can tell you that you'll need to be screened for sickle cell disease and take your daughter to see a hematologist. We're going to keep her overnight to treat her. Hopefully, she'll feel better in the morning and can be released."

Once the doctor exited, Grandville sat in thoughtful silence, holding his sleeping daughter. After an hour and a half had passed and the nurse assured him that she would remain sleeping soundly, he stepped outside her room and contacted his twin to fill her in on what was going on.

"Grandville, stay there with Jolene and Juliette. Don't worry about Jenae and the boys. Derek is here at your house with me, and we'll order pizza and hold the fort down so you can focus on your girls," Greta reassured him.

"Thanks so much, Greta. I'm going to go check on Juliette. Once I know what's going on, I'll be in touch," he said, disconnecting the call and heading toward the nurse station. He approached the desk where a woman was seated in front of a computer monitor.

"Hi, my name is Grandville Stubbs, my daughter, Jolene Stubbs, is in room one-oh-five. My wife, Juliette Stubbs, was taken down to the emergency room a couple of hours ago, so I'm going to run and check on her while my daughter is sleeping. If Jolene wakes up while I'm gone, can you please tell her I went to the gift shop to buy her some candy?"

The nurse nodded and smiled. Grandville thanked her and headed toward the elevator.

He had seen a gift shop when they were bringing Jolene into the hospital. He stopped there and purchased two bouquets of flowers. One for his beloved Juliette and one for his daughter, along with some candy. As he paid for his items, he got directions to the emergency room waiting room and was on his way.

He searched for Juliette as soon as he arrived in the emergency room. When he did not see her, he went up to the information desk and said, "I'm looking for my wife, Juliette Stubbs. She was brought down here by two peds nurses around two hours ago."

"I'm sorry, but your wife is no longer here," the nurse replied.

"Well, where is she?"

"She's been admitted to the psych ward, which is located on the fifth floor. You can follow the red line to the B elevator," the nurse directed.

Grandville blinked, stunned by the nurse's update. "Excuse me. Did you just say she was admitted to the psych ward?"

The nurse nodded, then said, "Yes, sir. About twenty minutes ago. She was inconsolable and delusional, and after she was examined by a doctor, she was immediately pink-slipped to the psychiatric ward. We had to transfer her immediately."

Without another word, Grandville walked toward the B elevator, trying to figure out what in the hell was happening. In a matter of hours, his life had gone from damn near perfect to spiraling out of control. He felt as though he was living in an episode of *The Twilight Zone*. He couldn't fathom why his wife would be admitted to the psychiatric ward so suddenly. Despite what the nurse had just told him, he was sure that the hospital had made a mistake.

Once he made it to the fifth floor and followed the signs to the psych ward nursing station, he said to the woman seated at a desk surrounded by glass. "Hi, I'm trying to locate my wife, Juliette Stubbs. I was told she was brought here by the ER staff."

"Hello, Mr. Stubbs. The doctor is waiting for you," she said, then pushed a button. The door buzzed opened, and Grandville walked into the ward.

He was greeted by an older white man wearing a white lab coat. "Hello, Mr. Stubbs. I'm Dr. Menefee," he said, shaking Grandville's hand. "Please come with me."

Grandville followed him down a corridor, and they filed into a small office where he was directed to sit down.

"Doctor, I'm confused," Grandville began, shaking his head. "My wife began hyperventilating during my daughter's appointment and was sent out to the emergency room. Next thing I know, she's here in the psych ward. What could've possibly happened to land her here in two hours?"

"Mr. Stubbs, your wife was pink-slipped by the ER staff," Dr. Menefee said.

"Okay...what exactly does that mean?"

"It means they believe your wife needs emergency mental health treatment," Dr. Menefee stated matter-of-factly. "She's against this idea and, as a result, the hospital has initiated paperwork to hold her against her will. We do believe Juliette is a danger to herself."

"Okay. I'm still not understanding why I wasn't notified about this," Grandville snarled. "I stepped away to check in on my daughter and come back to learn that my wife has been pink-slipped."

"I'm sorry you feel that way, Mr. Stubbs. But your wife was just pink-slipped twenty minutes ago. We were in the process of contacting you. I guess we didn't get to you quick enough. Again, I do apologize."

"I want to see my wife."

"Of course."

Dr. Menefee stood and led Grandville out of the office. As they passed numerous patient rooms, Grandville shuddered upon reflecting on his incarceration at Oakhill. Those thoughts faded the moment Dr. Menefee led him to the last room in the hallway corridor. When he opened the door, he saw Juliette perched on the bed, looking afraid and lost. When she looked up and saw him, she stood and barreled directly into his arms, which wrapped around her in a gentle embrace. Smiling, he handed her one of the bouquets.

"Grandville, they said I can't leave," Juliette whined, eying the doctor warily. "I told them I'm fine, and I need to get back to Jolene, but they took my phone and forced me back here."

Grandville followed her gaze. "Dr. Menefee, I'm not sure why you believe my wife is a danger to herself, but I assure you that she's okay. If she's allowed to leave, I'll be with her around the clock. We also have lots of family support at home. Who do I need to speak with to secure my wife's release?"

"I'm not the medical director, and unfortunately, I cannot approve her release at this time," Dr. Menefee explained. "The staff believes that Mrs. Stubbs is in severe distress, and they are adamant she needs to remain under observation. The paperwork has already been initiated." He cleared his throat then aimed his gentle gaze at Juliette. "Mrs. Stubbs, if you want to be released immediately, you can write a letter to the hospital administration. The hospital may release you, or they may decide that you need treatment and deny your request. If that is the case, this matter will need to go before a judge in a legal hearing. Holding you here against your will is a violation of your constitutional rights, and the hospital can only do so with a compelling reason as determined by a court. It's my understanding that both you and your husband are attorneys, so I'll assume you understand the process. But if you don't, I can send the client rights officer in to explain all of your rights to you."

"No, that won't be necessary. May I have a private moment to speak with my wife?" Grandville requested.

"Yes, but only because I have sympathy for your circumstance. In order to visit with your wife, you'll need to arrange it with the social worker, who I'll introduce you to once you're done."

Grandville nodded his appreciation as the doctor exited.

Once they were alone, Grandville noted the look of pain and hurt in his beloved's eyes, and it broke his heart. He silently vowed to do everything in his power to get his wife home where she belonged.

"Juliette, it looks like they're going to hold you. I know you're upset, but I want you to work on getting better and not to worry about anything else. I'll be right in this hospital with Jolene, and Greta is at our house with Jenae and the boys."

Juliette looked at her husband with tears streaming from her eyes. "Grandville, please do everything in your power to get me out of here. And take care of Jolene. I don't think I'll make it if she dies and I'm not with her."

Grandville pulled his sobbing wife into his arms and kissed her softly. "Juliette, my love. Jolene is *not* going to die. There are many people who live full, productive lives with sickle cell disease."

"Grandville, I don't think I can go on if I lose another child."

"Did you tell the nurses or doctor about this?"

"Well, yes. Because that's how I *feel*," Juliette sobbed.

"Okay, okay, baby. I definitely understand, but I want you to put yourself in the position of the hospital staff. To them, you sound suicidal. I also want to remind you that when Jessica passed on, we all lost her—not just you. There's not a day that goes by that I don't feel her loss, especially given my role in it. But I owe you and our other children more than just sitting and wallowing in grief. Jolene is not dead, and she needs you to help speak life into her, not death. None of us know the day or the hour that the Lord will call us home, but we don't want to squander our gift of time by worrying about dying when we should be working on living."

"You're right, Grandville. I'm going to try to take your advice."

"But, I'm confused about one thing that I'm hoping you can help me to understand once you get out of here."

"What is it?"

"How is it possible for my daughter to have sickle cell disease when I am not a hemoglobin C carrier?" Grandville asked point-blank.

Chapter 32

Tomorrow

Melinia looked at her sleeping son and decided to do what Julio had suggested: take her child and run. She and Julio had come up with a crude plan as they worked side by side, attempting to clean up the mess Hurricane Alice left behind.

"The first thing we have to do is get to a phone and call Polaris," Julio stated.

"Who's Polaris?" Melinia asked.

"It's not a who. It's the name for the National Human Trafficking hotline. They connect people like you and me, who are victims of human trafficking, with a safe place to go. They also provide support resources and assistance along the way. You are American, so once Polaris gets involved, they will get you back home."

"How do you know about this Polaris program, and how do we know that Rique didn't pay off the people who run it?"

"I learned about it when I was at the university, but I never thought in a million years I would ever need it. It's government regulated, so if we can get in touch with them, they can help us. It's highly unlikely that Rique and the crew could have paid any member of this organization off."

Melinia couldn't help but feel suspicious. "What kind of name is Polaris for a human trafficking program? It doesn't seem to match what you say the program is meant for."

"It's named after the North Star. Didn't your people use the North Star during the Underground Railroad to escape to freedom during slavery?" Julio asked.

"Yes, slaves did use the North Star to lead them to freedom. Now that you've explained it, I guess the name does make sense. Roberto said the phone lines and cell towers are down all over the island. What if we run away and we're not able to find a phone to call Polaris?"

"It is a chance I am willing to take. The island is in total disarray, so that means that Rique and the crew can't use their cell phones to track us, and we'll have a better chance of escaping."

"Okay. What's our plan?"

"We'll wait until this evening when everyone has fallen asleep; then we'll leave out. We have to find a way to tell Mimi about our plan without Romanita and Roberto overhearing."

"Julio, don't take this the wrong way, but I think we should keep our plan between the two of us," she suggested.

"What do you mean? Mimi is being victimized the same as you and me. We can't just leave her behind."

"She's my best friend and one of the hardest things I'll have to do is leave her, but it's necessary. Mimi is still addicted to drugs and soon, she's going to go into withdrawal. At that point, she'll do anything for a hit. Rique is her pipeline to the junk, and she'll lead him right to us if we take her with us."

"Okay, you make a good point. But what about you? You told me that you're also addicted to what you call junk, but it's known by my people as Héroe."

"It doesn't matter what you call it. Its impact on my life has been devastating. Remember, I mentioned before that Rique has pretty much weaned me off the junk, due to my pregnancy?"

"Well, I'm glad, because the last thing you need is your baby being born with an addiction."

"You are so right. I haven't received a hit in two days, and I'm not going to say that I'm not feeling uncomfortable, but I'm down to such a low amount that the withdrawal is manageable."

"Well, that's good, because we don't need you having major withdrawal symptoms while we're trying to escape. I'll wake you up when it's time to go. We'll take Rafael and head toward the middle of town. We can only hope that we can leave out before Rique arrives. I'm also going to try to sneak Romanita's phone, and we can only hope that service is soon restored so that we can actually use it."

When Melinia and Julio entered the house, they ran into Mimi, who was fidgety and looked pale.

"While you guys were outside, did you see any signs of Rique and the crew?"

"No, all we saw were broken tree limbs and debris," Melinia replied. "We tried to clean up as much of it as we could."

Mimi blinked hard then smiled uneasily. "Hey, I was watching you and Julio, and you guys seemed to be in deep conversation. What's up? Is everything okay?"

"Nothing's up. Instead of watching us, why didn't you come out and help?"

"I didn't come out because I'm dope sick. I don't know what I'm going to do if Rique and the crew don't come through soon."

Melinia shrugged. "Maybe you can try to kick it."

"I can't do it cold turkey. It would kill me."

"Mimi, I've been there. When you're in it, you'll feel like you're going to die, but we both know that opiate withdrawal won't kill you."

"That may be true, but if I don't get my hit soon, I'm going to be really sick. Melinia, what am I going to do?"

"I know what you're not going to do. You're not going to tell Romanita about what you do for Rique and the crew unless you have a death wish. If she ever asks you, tell her you're the cook on the boat. I'm going to run interference for you and try to pull Roberto aside to see if he has something that can hold you over until Rique gets here."

Satisfied with Melinia's plan, Mimi nodded and followed her back inside. Later that evening, Romanita prepared dinner using the few ingredients she could scrounge together, and the group ate by candlelight. Mimi ate very little and asked Romanita for a private area to lay down.

"I think I'm coming down with a virus, so you guys might want to stay away from me, Mimi said. "I don't want to affect you with my bad germs."

"You don't look well. I'll make you a pallet on the floor of the spare bedroom," Romanita offered.

When Romanita went upstairs, Melinia used the opportunity to pull Roberto to the side.

"Hey Roberto, have you heard from Rique?"

"No, the phone service is out, and I have no idea when it'll be back up," Roberto said. "We have a lot of enemies, and I'm going to have to patrol the perimeter of the property by foot to ensure that they don't use this opportunity to attack us. Julio is going to have to help us out."

Melinia looked over her shoulder before leaning towards Roberto. "Hey, listen," she whispered conspiratorially. "I want you to know that Mimi doesn't really have a virus, she's dope-sick. Do you have anything that can hold her over until Rique and the crew arrive?"

"Yeah, I have a little something that should do her right. What about you? How are you holding up?"

She explained how she was almost weaned off drugs due to her pregnancy.

"Really? I can barely tell that you are expecting. I'll slip Mimi something in just a few minutes."

Later, when Melinia went to check on Mimi, she was flying high and said in a slur, "Melinia, when did you plan to tell me that you're going to run?"

Chapter 33

Come to the Light

I t was the day that would determine the direction of Juliette's relationship with the love of her life. She had been in the hospital for exactly one week, and with the help of Emily and the hospital staff, she was feeling strong enough to tell Grandville the truth about her suspicions regarding Jolene's paternity. No more half-truths. She didn't know how he would react, but she was tired of carrying the heavy burden of keeping secrets in their relationship. She was finally ready to come clean.

It had been a very difficult week, but Juliette had decided to take control of her situation. It seemed as if everything in her life was falling apart. She was given the option to voluntarily admit herself into the hospital or to be forced to defend her freedom at an emergency detention hearing. The latter could prove to be detrimental to her future if she lost. According to the Ohio Revised Code, if she was declared mentally ill and involuntarily committed to the hospital for treatment, she would be unable to own a firearm or receive a security clearance in the future. Being involuntarily committed could also pose problems with her professional licenses and potentially place her career in jeopardy. So, when given the opportunity, she voluntarily admitted herself into the hospital and created a treatment plan with her social worker, Tasha Slattering, who was initially taken aback by her unique request.

"Mrs. Stubbs, you cannot work with your therapist while you're in an inpatient facility," Tasha advised. "Ms. McHall is an outpatient therapist and would have to be a member of the staff here at the hospital to consult with you. If not, our malpractice insurance would not extend to her. I'm positive that the administration will deny your request."

"Tasha, I'm very much aware of my rights," Juliette hissed, raising her voice slightly. "According to Ohio law, I must be provided with an independent professional to assist me at my own cost. I'll personally pay Emily out of my own pocket for her services, and I'd like to use the phone right now to contact her. If you decline my request, I'll file a grievance against you and the hospital for attempting to deny my rights. So, can you please go speak to your administrator and get my request green lighted so that we can begin the process?"

Without a word, Tasha hurried out of the room, wearing a pained expression on her face. Shortly afterward, Juliette received authorization to work with Emily, who became an integral part of her inpatient treatment team.

After meeting with Emily one final time, Juliette was able to gain clarity on several issues that had been bothering her. It wasn't until after her admittance into the psych ward that she was afforded the opportunity to be alone with her thoughts. The constant hustle and bustle of everyday life had slowed to a near standstill, thus allowing her to ruminate on all the major events that had happened in a short period of time. She was finally able to figure out how she felt about what was happening to her and her family and the proper way to handle going forward.

Keeping Jolene's paternity and her brief involvement with Franklin from Grandville hadn't been easy, and the pressure of doing so had worn her down mentally. Her reasoning for perpetuating the lies for all those years stemmed from wanting to protect Grandville from the painful truth. She knew that explaining the truth would tear him apart, and the last thing she wanted was to lose him again. Although she did not know if Grandville was a hemoglobin-C carrier, she felt the need to make up the story about how Jolene had the disease, in case he was not a carrier.

After Grandville's release from Oakhill, she vowed to help keep him mentally and emotionally stable. Disclosing that she had slept with Franklin would undo all of the hard work they both put into keeping him emotionally stable and happy. The last thing their family needed was for him to suffer another breakdown.

What if he left me upon finding out about the affair, she thought. *Is confessing to him about one simple slip up really worth tearing down the foundation we've built together over the years? What would my family and friends think of me if they ever found out about my lack of judgment in a moment of weakness with Franklin?*

As she continued to mull over her options, she couldn't decide if confessing was for his benefit or for her own selfish desire to clear her own guilty conscience. Either way, Grandville was bound to get hurt and might never look at her in the same way again.

There was more at stake than just her reputation and Granville's fragile heart and psyche. Disclosing the truth could also potentially cause irreparable damage to Grandville and Franklin's personal and professional relationships. In addition to being long-time business partners, Grandville and Franklin were closer than brothers. As a result of Grandville's psychotic break and imprisonment, he'd lost his law license and relied on his business partnership with Franklin to make a living for himself. That could all go away if the truth ever came out.

In Juliette's eyes, she believed Franklin had done everything in his power to support Grandville throughout his incarceration. He had proven his loyalty and devotion to Grandville time and time again. Friends like that only come around once in a lifetime, and she would never forgive herself if she was responsible for coming between them. Moreover, both she and Franklin had moved on from their transgression as he was now engaged to a beautiful woman, whom she had befriended, and she and Grandville were happy and thriving. Drudging up their past would cause more harm than good at that point. Besides, she had already asked the Lord for forgiveness and prayed that it would be enough.

During their meeting with the psychiatric staff, Emily outlined the details of her post-discharge treatment plans. Juliette was put on a regimen of medications to help alleviate her PTSD symptoms. As a result, she had been sleeping peacefully at night and feeling much better. In addition, to regain her strength, she attended numerous group sessions with other psych ward patients. During that week, Juliette and Emily arrived at the conclusion that it was time for her to talk to Grandville about the issues surrounding her breakdown. Grandville had been coming to the hospital every day to see her. During their daily, hour-long visits, they'd focused their conversations primarily on their children.

"How are my babies?" Juliette would inquire.

"Missing their mom," Grandville would reply.

Grandville informed her that Jolene felt better and had been released after spending just one day in the hospital. During her hospitalization, she received a referral to see a hematologist. Juliette could tell Grandville was confused about Jolene's diagnosis and was trying to grasp what had been upsetting Juliette to the point that she needed to be hospitalized, but he was allowing her the space she needed to confront her demons.

When Grandville arrived for his daily visit, the team asked to meet with him regarding Juliette's discharge plan. When they sat down at the table in the small conference room, Emily took the lead.

"Mr. Stubbs, we asked to meet with you today to discuss Juliette's progress and her recommended course of treatment after her release," Emily said, garnishing a friendly smile. "During her stay, we've been able to help her pinpoint the source of her distress. Juliette has worked hard to find the strength, determination, and comfort level to share some things with you. She asks that you allow her the opportunity to tell you her situation in her own words and at her own pace. I'm going to allow you and Juliette some privacy but will return shortly with Juliette's treatment team." Emily made eye contact with them both before exiting, leaving Juliette and Grandville alone.

Juliette looked at her husband and saw the love and concern etched all over his face and felt her heart breaking. She hoped he still looked at her the same way once he learned the truth.

"Grandville, I want to start by thanking you for everything you do for me and our family," she began.

"Juliette, you don't have to thank me. I love you and our kids unconditionally, and I want you to know there's nothing you can do to make me stop loving and supporting you. This is what I *want* to do."

Grandville's words touched her to the point where tears suddenly poured down her face.

"Baby, tell me what's wrong," he pleaded. "Why are you crying? Talk to me and let me help you."

She took a deep breath and said, "Grandville, there's a lot that I need to tell you, and it's going to be difficult. But for now, I just need you to listen."

"Okay, I'm listening," he assured her.

"On the day we lost Jessica, I was beyond distraught. I'd lost both of you at the same time, and I had no idea what I was going to do. I was in a state of shock. One minute, we were riding high, and in a matter of moments, we were at the lowest point we'd ever been. The accident occurred on a Saturday afternoon, and your arraignment was the following Monday afternoon."

"Yes, I remember being stunned at how quickly everything happened after the accident," Grandville said. "I'd assumed Samantha pulled some strings."

"Samantha had nothing to do with it," Juliette replied. "She works in Cleveland County, and your case was in Lake County. I think they fast-tracked your case due to the court being smaller and out of fear of there being a media circus. Franklin took me to your arraignment while my mother stayed with the children at her house."

"Juliette, I was out of it. To be honest, the whole proceeding is a blur in my mind. I was also in shock, and I could barely comprehend what had happened. All I could remember was that the police took me from the hospital directly to the arraignment, and I pleaded not guilty."

"After Franklin dropped me off at home, I took an Uber to a bar downtown. I was a mess, crying and drinking when an attractive man sat down next to me. He was upset with his wife because he found out she had been cheating on him. We shared a few laughs, shed some tears, and enjoyed a few drinks before we eventually wound up in a hotel together." She paused and swallowed as the words seemed to lodge in her throat. She pulled in a deep breath, then continued, "I don't remember the sex, but I know that I woke up naked in the bed alone. My purse, keys, and clothes were on the chair, but the man—whose name I don't even remember—was gone."

She looked down at her hands, unable to bring her eyes up to meet his. Then she forced herself to continue. "I've been ashamed that I put myself in a position to have another man explore me emotionally and sexually. This is the main reason I didn't visit you at Oakhill. I hated myself, and I didn't think I could bring myself to look you in the eye. I promise, except for that night, I've never let anyone else touch me in an intimate or sexual way. All I can say is that I'm sorry for what I did, and I hope you can find it in your heart to forgive me." When she finally found the courage to look up at him, her tears blurred her vision.

Grandville just sat there staring blankly at her. He finally took in a deep breath and slid his hand down his face. His eyes dropped down to his lap as they began to fill with tears.

"Baby, please, say something," she pleaded. "Look at me."

Grandville kept his eyes down and shook his head. It was as if he had grown averse to the sight of her. She couldn't blame him, as there were days when she could hardly stand to look at herself in the mirror.

He shot up to his feet and walked over to the window. "We had just lost our daughter, and all you could think about was screwing some random dude?" He was seething as he kept his back to her.

"I'm so sorry," she said in a faltering voice. She got up and followed him to the window, keeping a safe distance in case he snapped. After giving him a moment to calm down, she allowed her quivering hand to gently fall on his shoulder, which he jerked away before chasing a tear from his face. "Please, don't hate me for this," she spoke barely above a whisper. "I never meant for this to happen. It happened during a moment of weakness. I'm not trying to make excuses. I'm just being honest. Finally."

Grandville released a deep breath before turning around to face her. "I know you didn't do this on purpose, and I'm sorry for judging you, especially after everything I've done," he said, finally drying his eyes. "I could never hate you after what I've done to Jessica and to this family. But that doesn't mean that this doesn't hurt because it does. It absolutely does."

"Please forgive me, Grandville," she pleaded as her eyes emptied down her cheeks to her quivering lips. Since his release from Oakhill, she hadn't seen him that upset. She didn't know if she should turn and run out of the room or try and comfort him. Before she could reach a decision, Grandville grabbed a tissue from the box in the middle of the table and wiped her tears.

"Sweetheart, please don't cry," he soothed through his own visible pain, which she greatly appreciated. "As hurt as I am to hear this, I feel responsible for putting you in a position to be drunk at a bar alone."

Of course, he would say that, she thought to herself as he dried her face. That's what she loved about him. He was so accountable and humble. Even though what he said was true about her not being in the position to be intimate with Franklin had he not killed Jessica, she couldn't let him take the blame for something she made a conscious decision to do.

"This is squarely on me, Grandville," she said. "I appreciate you trying to lessen my guilt. But you can't. I have to take full responsibility for this. All I ask of you is to try to put this behind us."

"Given how you've forgiven me for what happened with Jessica, how could I not return the favor?"

She nodded and smiled as the twinkle in his eyes returned. "Thank you, Grandville. I promise to make this up to you."

"I know you will. But I still have to wonder about one thing. Jessica's been dead for five years. What's making you reveal this to me now?"

His question caught her off guard, but she quickly recovered. "When we went to the opening of the clinic, everything fell apart, and I was forced to remember what I had done."

"Sweetheart, I'm sorry, but I don't understand. Apart from Jolene getting sick, we seemed to be having a great time."

"It started with Jolene's scream during the pool party," she recalled. "To me, it sounded so much like Jessica's screams on the day we lost her, and it didn't help that it was the anniversary of her death. The therapists and doctors believe the scream triggered some post-traumatic stress disorder symptoms. I have to agree because, up until that day, I was okay. Now, the slightest noise has me on edge."

"I agree that you've been jumpy since the evening of the opening. What else do you need to tell me?"

Juliette sighed and looked away to buy herself a few extra moments. She had to decide if she would go further and disclose the truth about Jolene's paternity. Given that Grandville was already in a forgiving mood, she figured she might as well tell him and get it over with. There would be no sense of having to hurt him all over again down the road.

"When I took Jolene to the ER, the pediatrician told me that he suspected sickle cell disease," she said, her gaze penetrating his soul through his comely hazel eyes. "He advised me to take her to a hematologist, and I was forced to face the fact that Jolene may not be your daughter."

Grandville lifted a brow and asked, "What do you mean?"

"I had both Jolene and Jenae tested by one of my friends, who is a hematologist. I learned Jolene has hemoglobin SC. I want you to understand that I was more than five months pregnant by the time I figured out I was expecting. I was hurt over Jessica's death, and when I learned I was going to have another baby, it was as though God was giving me another chance to be a mother. I prayed for a daughter, and when I learned that I was carrying twin girls, I was ecstatic. We made love the morning of the accident, so I assumed the babies were yours.

"When the babies were born, I took one look at Jenae, and I knew without a doubt that she was yours. Since Jolene looked more like me, I never doubted you were her father. When we decided to reconcile, I buried my infidelity, and I didn't think about it anymore. But when I learned of Jolene's diagnosis, I knew the likelihood that you were her father was low. You were tested when I was pregnant with Jessica and Jonah, and I know you're not a carrier of hemoglobin S, but I don't know if you are a carrier of hemoglobin C. So, there is a chance that you're not the twins' biological father. Ever since I found out this news, I've been barely holding on. Then I started having nightmares about Jessica and couldn't sleep."

Grandville lifted his head until his eyes scorched the ceiling. He pressed his palms against his eyes and held them there until he finally released a breath. When his eyes finally returned to hers, they were surprisingly full of understanding. However, there was a tinge of pain held within them—pain her actions caused.

"I'm so sorry, Grandville. Please, don't let this change the way you love the twins. This isn't their fault. It's mine."

Grandville reached across the table, grabbed Juliette's hand, and squeezed it as she sobbed quietly. "There's nothing that could ever change the way I feel about those girls or about you. Yes, this is going to take some time for me to work through, but I love you enough to do so, just like you've done for me. We'll get through this, one prayer at a time."

Smiling, Juliette reached and squeezed his hand. Her heart melted from the warmth of the smile on his handsome face.

"Juliette, I had no idea you were under such stress. You shouldn't have had to deal with this kind of stress alone."

She dropped her head in shame, only for Grandville to return her eyes to his when he lifted her chin with a curled finger.

"You made me promise not to keep secrets from you, but you've been keeping secrets from me for years."

"I know, and I feel like such a hypocrite. That's why I didn't want to be around my family or friends and was isolating myself. I've helped so many people in the course of my career, but I couldn't figure out a way to help myself. But I knew the only way I can begin to repair my life is to tell you the truth."

"I'm not going to lie; this is a shock to the system. But I love you, and as far as I'm concerned, both of the twins are my daughters."

"Don't you want a DNA test?"

"No, I don't need one. In my heart, those girls are mine in every way that counts."

"What are we going to tell people? The only way to have sickle cell disease is to have two parents who are carriers of the gene."

"I'm going to tell them that I'm a carrier."

"What about Greta? She'll know that isn't true."

"How? For all she knows, I got the gene from our father."

"I can't bear for anyone but you to know about what I did," Juliette cried.

"Listen, no one is going to know unless you tell them. Now, I know there's something else. Whatever it is, I can handle it. So please speak. I don't want any more secrets between us," Grandville said.

There was one last secret she felt the need to release from her conscience and it made no sense to withhold it anymore. "Sabrina asked me to find her son's biological parents," she admitted, which also allowed her to change the subject.

"Really? Were you successful?" he responded, seemingly just as happy to drop end the discussion of her infidelity as she was.

"Yes, I found them. But I haven't told Sabrina yet."

"Good. Sabrina is going to be ecstatic."

"We'll see. But I didn't want to share the news with her until I talked to you first."

"Why would you need to talk to me about finding George's biological parents?"

"Because George is your firstborn son. He's the one you had with Gina."

Chapter 34

I'm Yours

Grandville couldn't comprehend what he'd just heard. "What did you just say, Juliette?"

"George is your biological son, and he has no idea that Sabrina has been looking for his biological parents. She was able to get some of his DNA, and I forwarded it to an ancestry website. Your conviction gave them access to your DNA."

Grandville stared at her for a few moments, his broad shoulders squaring as he leaned back in his chair. "I-I...can't believe it. How long have you known about this?"

"A few weeks."

"A few weeks?" he asked incredulously as his voice raised a few octaves. "Why didn't you tell me as soon as you found out?"

"I was scared."

"Scared of what?"

"Your reaction, which is the same reason I was scared to tell you about the twins. You've been doing so well, and I didn't want to do or say anything that would cause you to have a mental or emotional setback. Ironically, the stress of learning this news and keeping it from you has caused me to have my own mental breakdown. I was just nervous and anxious about what you were going to do with this information."

"Well," Grandville exhaled loudly. "I'm going to make decisions with my lovely wife."

"If you tell George, he might have a negative reaction. Learning the circumstances of his birth could be traumatic. This could prove to be problematic for Franklin and Sabrina."

"I can see your points, Juliette, but if George really wants to find his biological parents, he'll just run his own DNA. Then he'll find out on his own that I'm his father. Look how easy it was for you to get the information. I think we should sit down with Sabrina and Franklin and tell them the truth. They can help us decide how we should handle this. Apart from you and Greta, Franklin is one of the only people who know what happened between me and Gina."

"Okay, I think that's a great plan."

"Juliette, do you see how easy that was? I want you to know that I'm not as fragile as you may think I am. You don't need to protect me. I deserved to know about Jolene's illness and George's paternity as soon as you learned about them. You've made yourself sick worrying when all you had to do was talk to me."

Juliette nodded and sighed. "You're absolutely right. And again, I'm truly sorry. However, what mostly contributed to my decline was knowing Jolene is dealing with a potentially fatal disease. As you know, my father passed away suddenly due to sickle cell anemia. I feel responsible for her pain and the possibility that it could shorten her life. I'm going to have to be a witness to her crises, and I don't know if I can do it. I'm terrified that she's going to die just like my dad and Jessica."

"Juliette, you're here because of your father. Sickle cell is a part of your heritage. I didn't know him, but I've heard enough about the type of man he was from you and your mother to know that he was strong. And despite his condition and the pain it caused him, he went to work every day to support his family. You and Jolene are products of that strength. We're going to teach Jolene how to persevere in the face of adversity. Also, we're all going to die, and we're not going to assume that Jolene's condition is a death sentence."

"I guess I've never thought it about it that way before," Juliette admitted. "I can honestly say I've been so consumed with guilt and shame that I haven't been thinking straight. You are right, we're going to tell her about my father and how strong he was, and I also think we should join a sickle cell support group to help us understand how to fully support her."

Grandville nodded. "I think that's a great idea. Research also shows many parallels to sickle cell disorders as well as mental health issues."

"I'm not seeing the parallels," Juliette commented.

"Both disorders are individual to the person and based on a number of factors. I suffer from bipolar disorder, but with the right support, I've been able to manage it. We're going to teach Jolene how to manage her sickle cell disease, and we're going to be there to help her find her strength."

"Indeed. Do you think you'll eventually tell Greta about George?"

Grandville paused thoughtfully before responding. "I don't know. I'm ashamed about having a child with a woman whom I now know was my sister. I don't know how I would face Greta's anger if she ever found out that I've known about this since my mother's passing and didn't tell her. Also, I'm worried about how George will receive the truth. It's one thing to fantasize that the people who put you up for adoption are off leading fabulous lives, but the reality is tragic. I just don't want to damage him. He's a victim of circumstance, and none of this is his fault."

"Grandville, I want to thank you for being so understanding and for forgiving me," Juliette said, giving her husband's hand a squeeze. "I've been so ashamed and afraid that you'd want a divorce once you learned the truth."

"Juliette, I love you, and I have no plans to divorce you. I want nothing more than to spend the rest of my days loving you. I just need you to promise that there'll be no more secrets between us."

"I promise," she replied.

After their private conversation, Emily and the rest of Juliette's treatment team filed back into the room and advised them that Juliette was being released.

"Juliette, you have worked really hard thus far. But, as you know, there is still more work to do," Emily remarked.

"Yes, I'm aware, and Grandville is too," Juliette said. "We've decided to no longer keep secrets from one another. We've vowed to deal with our problems together."

Emily smiled. "That's great."

"The kids and I really miss Juliette. Is she being released today?" Grandville asked.

"Yes. That's why we called you here today," Emily explained. "We have her discharge plan right here, and it consists of a combination of therapy and medication."

Grandville nodded. "Good, I think she'll do even better at home and surrounded by family and friends."

"We agree, and that's why the team has unilaterally concluded that Juliette is no longer a danger to herself," Dr. Menefee said. "Juliette, I have your signed release paperwork ready. Ms. McHall will continue your treatment on an outpatient basis. If you have any problems, please contact us right away."

"Thank you, Doctor, but I think that going home will greatly improve my mental health condition. I don't anticipate any further issues," Juliette said.

"Great. Take care of yourself." Dr. Menefee stood up and shook her hand.

"Juliette, we have a few papers for you to sign, and then the nurse will meet you in your room to get you discharged," Tasha said.

Later that evening, as he lay on his comfortable bed and watched his wife sleep, Grandville reflected on everything Juliette had told him that afternoon. He felt horrible that his wife had been dealing with so much pain and shame all on her own. He had been oblivious to it all. Additionally, he couldn't believe the day had finally come when the events of his past had collided with his future. The mystery of what had happened to the child that he and Greta had together had finally been answered. He was both excited and scared to learn how George would handle the news. From what he could tell, he appeared to be a smart, intelligent young man whom he wanted to get to know more intimately. But he knew in order to do everything the right way, he would need the approval of his best friend. Juliette woke suddenly and stirred slightly, catching him staring at her.

Worry etched her forehead as she asked, "Grandville, what is it? Are you okay?"

He smiled at her. "Yes, I'm good."

"What are you thinking about?"

"George. Now that I know he's my son, I want to get to know him better. But if he learns the truth about how he got here, it can cause irreparable damage. Then there are our other children. I don't want to have to explain the details to them of how George is my son," he explained.

"I think the plan we discussed earlier is the best course of action. You should talk to Franklin first."

"Okay, I'll do it first thing in the morning, when we're alone at the office."

The next morning, Grandville waited anxiously for Franklin to arrive. At about ten, he heard a key turn in the lock.

Grandville rose to his feet and called out, "Hey, you're awful late this morning. I've been waiting for you for quite some time. I need to holler at you about something."

"Great, I need to talk to you, too," Franklin said as he walked into Grandville's office with George following him.

Grandville swallowed as he laid eyes on his firstborn son.

"George is going to be working with us for a while. So, please come up with a list of tasks that you need for him to do, and I'll get him set up."

Chapter 35

Leave Out All the Rest

Melinia was caught off guard by Mimi's question and asked, "Mimi, you're my best friend and everything, but I need to know if I can trust you?"

"Are you for real, Melinia?" Mimi asked incredulously, raising an eyebrow. "After all we've been through together, you're actually questioning my loyalty?"

"Yes, because the last time I checked, your loyalty was exclusive to China white. As much as I love you, I can't trust that you won't sell me out for a hit."

"Of course, I won't sell you out. I give you my word on that."

"Your word means a lot to me, just like you do, Mimi. But you have to understand that this is my only chance to get out of here and make a life for me and my children. As much as I don't want to leave you behind, I have to think about them," she explained apologetically.

Mimi looked at her for a moment, then nodded. "I understand. I want you to know that I view you as much more than a friend. I see you as my sister, and I'll miss you."

"I feel the exact same way, and you know I don't want to leave you. But once that monkey gets on your back, we both know you'll do and say anything for a hit."

"You're right. That's why I don't want you to give me any details about your plan. Just promise me that you'll be careful and that you'll take good care of yourself and those kids."

"I promise. Now, I need you to make a promise to me," Melinia said with tears in her eyes.

"Okay, what is it?"

"I want you to promise that you will do everything in your power to kick this habit before you end up dead." Melinia took her friend's shoulders in her hands and shook her gently.

"Okay, I'll try," Mimi said, her eyes dazed and glassy.

"I'm going to miss you, and I'll be praying for your safe return one day, as well."

The two hugged and cried on each other's shoulder. When they pulled away from each other, they each dried the other's tears as they had done so many times.

Later that evening, Melinia helped Romanita pull together a dinner of beans and rice. Afterward, Roberto began patrolling the perimeter of the property with a plan for Julio to relieve him at midnight. There was no still no sign of Rique and the rest of the crew, and Melinia was fearful that they would arrive before she and Julio could make their escape.

At ten that evening, Melinia laid a sleeping Rafael beside her on the floor of the guest bedroom and promptly went to sleep. She had no idea what time it was when Julio gently shook her awake.

"Hey, Melinia, it's time for us to make our move," he whispered.

She slowly sat up and rubbed her eyes. "Okay."

She grabbed the small bag she had packed when no one was looking and scooped Rafael up before following Julio outside into the cool, pitch-black night.

"I know it's dark out here. Don't worry. I have a flashlight, but we can't turn it on until we get farther out," Julio whispered.

Cradling Rafael against her chest, she stepped carefully and asked, "How are we supposed to see where we're going without light?"

"Just follow me. I know the way."

After Melinia silently struggled to keep up with Julio for about ten minutes, she was completely winded. Due to her pregnancy, Rafael's dead weight seemed to grow heavier with each passing minute.

"Hey, Julio," she huffed. "Rafael is getting really heavy. I'm not sure how much longer I can go before I have to stop."

"I know, chica. Just hold on a little longer. We're almost there."

"Almost where?"

"Just be patient. You'll see soon."

Melinia decided to follow Julio's lead and hoped that he knew what he was doing. She was a bit apprehensive about having her son in the middle of nowhere with someone she had originally considered a friend but now realized she didn't know much about. All she knew about Julio was what he had told her. She had no idea where they were, and neither did anyone else. She concluded that she had no other choice but to go along and hope that her initial decision to leave with him had been the right one.

After walking for another fifteen minutes down a winding, sandy path lined with broken palm trees, Melinia thought her legs would give out. At that moment, they found themselves facing the back of a large resort. They approached a wooden shed that was partially shielded by palm trees and had a small searchlight on top. Julio opened the door, and they walked in.

Once inside, Melinia asked, "Julio, what is this place?"

"It's one of the gardener sheds where the resort groundskeepers store all of their gardening equipment."

"Yes, I can see that. But what are we doing here?"

"We're going to hide here until our cell service has returned. No one will be coming back here, and I plan to get into the resort and snag a uniform. That will make it easier for us to get to a phone inside so I can contact Polaris."

"Okay…and you couldn't think of a more comfortable place for us to hide?"

"Listen, Melinia, we need to plan two moves ahead, just like when we're playing chess. It'll be days before the resort can resume full operation, and that means very few people will be staying at this hotel. We can get food and clean water until we're rescued, and if the crew shows up and is looking for us, they won't be able to find us. No one knows we're here. Lastly, I guarantee you that the resorts will get their phone service restored before the rest of the island does," he reasoned.

"Okay, it seems like you've really thought this out. But how did you even know to come here?"

"Before I showed up at Romanita's, I stopped by this resort. I had to use public transportation to get to Romanita's house, and the bus stopped near here first. I got off the bus and walked into the lobby of the hotel and made believe that I was a rich American vacationing here," he confided.

"Not all Americans are rich. Many of us struggle, just like other people all over the world."

"I'm aware of this, but your idea of poverty would be considered as a luxury to myself and so many others," he argued.

Melinia raised an eyebrow. "I've been a sex slave for the past three years, so I think I know a little about poverty."

"I know for a fact that Rique never allowed you to see the kind of poverty that we were exposed to while living in the Dominican Republic."

"Whatever. Where should I lay Rafael?"

"Let's all lay down here," Julio said, pointing to space behind several leaf blowers.

Melinia passed Rafael to Julio and pulled out a small blanket from her bag to spread on the ground. She promptly sat down and took her sleeping son from Julio and laid him down next to her.

Melinia was peacefully sleeping when she felt Julio shaking her awake.

"Hey, sleepyhead," Julio said.

"Hey," Melinia replied groggily.

"I brought you both some food.

Melinia sat up and asked, "What time is it?

"Eight in the morning. I found my way into the hotel, and it's a ghost town in there. I was able to slip into the custodial closet, and I found this uniform."

Melinia looked at the skirt and matching blazer that Julio had in his hand and said, "But, it's for a woman."

"Yes, I know."

"What am I supposed to say if I get caught?"

"I don't know. Make something up. Now go behind that equipment and try it on."

Melinia stood and saw that her son was still asleep. She did as Julio said and was surprised that the uniform fit, and it was difficult to tell she was pregnant.

"See, you look adorable, and I know you can pull this off. I'll continue to try to slip into the hotel, but sooner or later, more people will return. So you'll have to go into the hotel when necessary." He gestured toward her chest. "There's something in the blazer pocket. What is it?"

Melinia reached in and pulled out a deck of cards. She opened the box and scanned the instructions. "I've never seen cards like this before. It says they're used to play a game called 'Naked Bootleg'."

"I don't get it. What is Naked Bootleg? Is it fútball? Does it have something to do with soccer?" he asked.

"Well, football in America is a completely different game than soccer. According to the instructions, I think this card game has something to do with American football. In American football, a naked bootleg is a trick play. But the instructions say anybody can play the game, even people who don't understand football. We can play it to pass some time during Rafael's nap this afternoon. I can also teach you about football, which you'll want to be familiar with as an aspiring American."

"I'm very serious about becoming an American and will do anything to get into your country," Julio affirmed eagerly.

"Your desperation to become an American is going to get you killed," she warned. "I don't know if you're aware of this, but your brother and his gang raped Romanita when she was pregnant with her first child. They killed her fiancé right in front of her. Because of that, she can never have kids. I believe Rique and the crew were going to exact their revenge on you."

Julio looked at her for a moment without responding. She could tell he was stunned by what she had just shared with him. But what she didn't expect was what he said next. "Chica, what you don't realize is I knew what my brother did. Like you, I willingly joined the crew, even though I knew the risks of doing so."

Melinia shook her head in disbelief. "But why? That doesn't make any sense."

"Because I wanted to protect my family. While I was away at school, I really had no idea that my only brother was a drug dealer. When I was forced to leave the university and returned home, I found out how he could afford to pay for my tuition and what he had done to Romanita. At that point, I decided to put myself in a position where I came to Rique instead of waiting for him to come to me."

"So, let me get this straight. You're saying you purposely placed yourself in Rique's possession?"

"Yes. I figured that was my best chance of getting into the United States was to use Rique and the crew to get me out of the DR. So, I focused on putting myself in the position I'm in now."

"To be shipwrecked on an island?" Melinia sarcastically replied.

"No, to be on the brink of putting myself in the same situation that you take for granted."

"I'm sorry, but I don't know what you mean. I'm not taking anything for granted."

"Chica, you're an American. You don't know how it feels to have to worry about being murdered at any moment and no one will do anything about it. In America, there's a justice system in place that will protect you."

Melinia laughed quietly. "Julio, you're so misguided on what life is really like in the United States that it's not even funny. Don't get me wrong; I love my country. But I've lived there, unlike you. I've seen all kinds of bad things happen in our precious land of milk and honey. People are senselessly murdered and raped daily, just like any other country in the world. Hell, we lead the entire world in the annual incidences of mass shootings. We have one of the highest crime rates of any industrialized country. African Americans are incarcerated at more than five times the rate of whites. You can move up if you work hard, but it costs more to be poor."

"I don't understand what that means."

"It means poor people in America have to spend more money to survive, including being forced into higher interest rate loans to purchase things like cars and houses. The problem is if you already don't have money, trying to make ends meet is even more difficult," she explained. "So, when you come to America, I hope you have a plan in mind to ensure you don't wind up reliant on the government to provide your needs."

Julio nodded while deep in thought.

Later, after Melinia had played with Rafael and put him down for a nap, she and Julio played the Naked Bootleg card game. While they played, she had a good time teaching him about football.

Afterward, Julio said, "It's time for you to put on the uniform and head over to the resort. You need to learn the layout and locate a phone, food, and water. Rafael is going to be waking up soon, and he's going to be hungry and thirsty."

Melinia headed out of the shed and followed the signs that led her to the entrance of the hotel. She wondered how she would react if she were to be stopped by someone who worked for the hotel. As she approached the front door, she hesitantly walked through it, entering a deserted lobby. Her breath caught when she saw a middle-aged white woman lounging on a couch. The woman stared at her as she walked toward what looked like a restaurant.

After peering inside of the closed restaurant's front window for a few moments, Melinia turned to walk away. She let out a yelp when she almost collided with the woman, who was now blocking her path.

"The restaurant is closed," she said firmly, her eyes studying her.

"Yes, I can see this. I was hoping it was open so I could eat before my shift began," Melinia lied.

The woman's brow lifted. "You're an American?"

"Yes."

The woman thought for a moment before saying, "You look familiar to me. Is your name Melinia?"

Melinia painfully swallowed past the growing lump in her throat, knowing that how she answered that woman's question would forever change her life.

Chapter 36

Can't Get Enough

Grandville was completely caught off guard. Now that he knew who George was, he couldn't stop staring at him.

"Hey, Grandville, are you okay?" Franklin asked, wearing a concerned expression.

"Yeah, frat, I'm cool," Grandville replied. "I was just caught off guard. Actually, I was just thinking how great it would be if we had an assistant to run errands for us like going over to Starbucks on ninth and picking up some coffee. Then you showed up with George. It's like you were reading my mind."

"You know what they say, great minds think alike," Franklin laughed before turning toward George. "Hey, can you get Grandville and me a couple of caramel lattes and get something for yourself?" Franklin handed George a twenty-dollar bill.

George nodded. "Of course. Do you guys need anything else while I'm out?"

"Come to think about it, we're having a morning meeting, so why don't you pick up some doughnuts, bagels, and fresh fruit at the market up the street," Franklin said, handing him another twenty.

"How many people are you expecting?"

"Only two."

"Okay. I'll be back in a few," George said as he headed out the door.

Franklin took one look at Grandville and asked, "Okay, what's up? You said you needed to holler at me about something?"

"Yeah, I wanted to talk to you about something super confidential, and I wanted to do it while we were alone," Grandville said.

"My bad," Franklin declared. "I should've given you a heads up that I was bringing George to work with me today. Sabrina's been bugging me about bonding with him. I'm really at a loss on how to make that happen with a grown-ass man. He was working on an accounting degree at Cleveland State University, but he took this semester off. Sabrina thought that coming to work with us could help motivate him to get back in school and finish. I promise I'll pay him for the work that he does out of my share of our profits."

"Frat, paying him is no problem. He'll be helping us both. He's actually who I wanted to speak to you about."

"Oh yeah?" Franklin asked, taking a seat in front of Grandville's desk.

"Yes. I'm not sure if you're aware, but Sabrina asked Juliette to help her find George's biological parents," Grandville said.

"No, I had no idea."

"Well, Juliette was able to locate them."

"That's fantastic, man. I can't wait to tell Sabrina."

Grandville leaned forward in his chair. "See, the thing is, I asked Juliette for the opportunity to talk to you about what she discovered before revealing the information to Sabrina."

"This news doesn't involve us. It's about Sabrina and George. So, why would you need to speak to me about it?"

"Franklin, do you remember when I discussed with you about what my mother told me on her deathbed?" Grandville asked.

"Yes, that your cousin, Gina, who had been sexually abusing you, was actually your sister," Franklin said.

"Yes, and I also shared that Gina and I had a son that I never knew about until right before my mother died. She and my mother put him up for adoption without my knowledge.

"After my mother told me about my son, she passed away, and I drove myself mad with worry, wondering if my child was deformed or unstable due to his parents' genes being too similar." Grandville shook his head. "Well, it turns out that George is my biological son. The only person who knows the complete truth, other than you, is Juliette. But I didn't tell her until she visited me at Oakhill."

"I can't believe this. It's almost too much," Franklin said, shaking his head.

"Who are you telling, frat? I'm overwhelmed, too, but I'm glad to finally know my son is doing okay. I want to get to know him but not to the detriment of him and the rest of my kids. Withholding this information from me was what partially contributed to Juliette's breakdown. She was hesitant to tell me because she was afraid of my reaction and that the news would trigger me to experience symptoms related to my bipolar disorder. I'm more concerned about this news causing George mental and emotional issues."

"Damn, frat. This is a lot to lay on me this early in the morning. Let's grab lunch after our meeting and discuss how we're going to handle this since we need to finalize our proposal for this potential client," Franklin advised.

"Who are these people again?"

"They're from a small business that manufactures plastic screws," Franklin explained. "We're looking at representing them and receiving a monthly retainer that would include representation during their new contract negotiations. In addition, we would process their employees' personal taxes as a perk. There's only ten of them in total."

"Nice. We can teach George how to do simple taxes and pay him to assist us," Grandville suggested.

"Great idea."

After their morning meeting concluded, they sent George to get Franklin's car washed and detailed while they had a working lunch.

"Those ideas you pitched to the U-Screw company were excellent," Grandville complimented his partner as he bit into his sub sandwich. "You saw how quickly they signed on the dotted line for our services."

"Thanks, Grandville. Honestly, all I could think about throughout the whole presentation was George and how we should handle this situation. George is adopted, so I guess I should have guessed he was your son as soon as I saw him. He looks just like you."

"I admit, he does. But, for whatever reason, I never fathomed that he and I were connected. I'm not sure I'm ready to explain to everyone how George is my son. I don't want to lie, but I'm not ready to face George or Greta just yet. Greta doesn't even know Gina and I have a child. I also don't want you to start your marriage off with dishonesty."

"How's Juliette dealing with this news?"

"She's better. She was under a lot of stress trying to carry this secret and worrying about Jolene and her sickle cell diagnosis. But telling me about my relation to George has lifted a huge weight off her. She's a woman of her word, and she hated not telling Sabrina what she learned as soon as she found out. But she felt like she owed it to me to see what I wanted to do beforehand."

Franklin nodded. "I agree with Juliette's decision. This whole situation is about you, so I don't think we should tell Sabrina or George until you're ready."

"Are you sure? Because I don't want to be the cause of you keeping secrets in your relationship," Grandville said.

"Honestly, Grandville, it's your news to tell. You should do it whenever you're ready."

"Thanks, Franklin. I plan to tell George and Sabrina everything in the future, but I want to get past Greta's wedding in order to avoid the craziness. It's in two weeks, and I'll be walking her down the aisle and giving her away. Afterward, I'll work on finding the strength to tell both George and my sister the truth."

"Take as much time as you need,"

That evening, Grandville shared the details of his conversation with Franklin with his beloved.

"I knew Franklin would agree with me," Juliette said. "I think you should start working with a counselor to help you explain to George, Greta, and our children the truth about what happened to you," she said with concern in her eyes.

"I agree, babe. I'll start looking for one tomorrow."

"I'm so glad we're on the same page."

"Me too," he returned with a smile.

"Also, I don't know if I told you, but on Friday, Greta wants me to go on a girls' trip with her, Sabrina, Samantha, and Maria. We're going to fly to New York and spend the weekend shopping and relaxing. She booked us all an appointment at an exclusive wellness spa. Do you think you'll be okay taking care of the children for the weekend?"

"Of course, I will! That sounds like exactly what you need, babe. I know you're a little nervous about leaving, but I encourage you to do so. Spend some time with your friends, and don't worry about anything back here while you're gone."

"You're right. I am a little nervous. This is going to be the first time I'll see any of my girls since I was discharged. To be honest, I'm a little embarrassed about everything that's happened. And then there's the fact that I wouldn't know what to tell Sabrina if she asks about the status of finding George's biological parents."

"First of all, Juliette, you don't have anything to be embarrassed about. There are a lot of people who would fall apart if they had to deal with a third of what you've been dealing with. Your friends love you and want to be there for you. So, let them. Second, tell Sabrina you're still working on it and leave it at that. Everything is going to be okay."

Juliette, who seemed comforted by his words, rested her head on his chest. As they snuggled together, he hoped and prayed that his words would prove to be true.

Chapter 37

Despacito

Melinia was completely caught off guard by the unknown woman's question but did not let her unease show on her face. "I'm not Melinia, but I may know where you can find her. Who are you, and why are you looking for her?"

"My name is Helen, and the business that I have with Melinia is private. I'm staying here at the hotel in room two-fifteen. If you see Melinia, will you let her know I'm looking for her?"

"I doubt I'll be able to convince her to come here if she doesn't know who's looking for her and why."

"Listen. Please let Melinia know that if she comes and meets with me, she will be pleasantly surprised because I have something that I think she wants," Helen said.

"Okay. When I see her, I'll let her know. I have to see if it's time to start my shift. See you later."

As she rushed away, she racked her brain to figure out who Helen was and what she wanted with her. She wondered if Helen worked for Rique and was suddenly afraid because it would mean that Rique knew where she was hiding. She still had to find food and water for herself, Julio, and Rafael. She also wanted to get back to the shed in case Rique and the crew came to the hotel looking for them.

In her haste, she accidentally ran right into a tall, dark man wearing a hotel uniform when she turned a corner. He stopped dead in his tracks and with a heavy Bahamian accent, said, "I'm glad you were able to get here..." He strained to read the name tag on her lapel. "...Angelique. Go to the back kitchen and deliver a tray to room five-twelve. They've been waiting on their room service for at least a half an hour. Hurry before the food gets cold."

Without a word, Melinia hurried toward where she thought the back kitchen might be. After ten minutes of wandering around the hotel, she finally stumbled onto it. She timidly nudged the swinging double doors open and peeked inside the large, industrial kitchen. There was a tall, round man stirring a large stew pot. He stopped and looked up at her once she stepped all the way inside.

"Hello, I was told to take a tray to room five-twelve," Melinia said timidly.

"Yes, please hurry. I'm the only one here, so please get back here as soon as you deliver the food because I've received other orders. Because of the hurricane, we don't have any staff and couldn't open the restaurant. But we still have guests who couldn't get off the island. Hopefully, you'll make some great tips." He wiped his hands on his apron and handed her a tray with what looked like vegetable stew, a side salad, and oyster crackers.

Melinia nodded as he said, "There's the cart. To the right is the service elevator. It's running on the generator."

She put the tray down on the cart and rolled it out of the kitchen. It didn't take her long to find the service elevator, and before she knew it, she had delivered eight trays and made fifty dollars in tips.

When she came to pick up the last delivery, the cook said, "This is the last delivery for the lunch rush. We can't keep the room service open all day because we have a limited menu. We'll reopen at five this afternoon. I made you some lunch. It's in the brown bag on the back counter. After you deliver this tray, you can leave, but come back here at five for the dinner rush."

Melinia thanked him quickly, and after delivering the last tray, she took the bag and hurried out of the hotel. She found the employee break room and grabbed a few water bottles and found a small bag of cookies in someone's lunch in the refrigerator. Then, she headed toward the street before doubling to the back of the hotel to the hideaway shed to make sure no one saw her. When she walked in, she spotted Julio and Rafael playing with his matchbox cars.

As soon as Julio saw her, he said, "Chica, what in the world took you so long to get back? I was worried to death. I didn't know if I should take Rafael and come into the hotel to look for you or not. If you hadn't returned in the next hour, that's exactly what I was going to do."

"I'm sorry," she breathed. "I think the other hotel staff really thought I was an employee. Or maybe not and they were just desperate. There were still guests there, so I delivered food to some of the rooms and made fifty dollars in tips. The cook packed lunch for me, and I was able to swipe a few other items. Let's see what we've got."

The large bag had enough food to feed the three of them. There were rice and beans and conch fritters, which were island staples. While they ate, Melinia filled Julio in on her encounter with the unknown woman.

"Do you know if she's staying in the hotel?"

"She said she was staying in room two-fifteen."

"Well, we're going to her room."

"I don't know if that's a good idea, Julio," she warned. "She might be working for Rique and the crew."

"Yes, she could be, but the odds of that are very low."

"Why do you think so?" Melinia asked, opening the package of cookies for Rafael.

"It's highly unlikely that a white American would consent to come to a place experiencing a hurricane just to find you," Julio argued. "Chica, the longer I live, the more I realize that life is a whole lot like a good game of chess. Sometimes the best defense is an aggressive offense."

Melinia let his words set in for a moment before responding. "Okay. I saw the layout of the rooms while I was delivering the food. Room two-fifteen is at the corner. When we show up there, you and Rafael will hide at the end of the hallway, so when she looks through the peephole, she'll only see me standing there. When she opens the door, you'll help me storm into her room. Once we're all inside, we'll force her to sit down and tell us exactly what she wants from me."

"Excellent plan, chica," Julio said. "We won't be violent, and hopefully neither will she, especially with Rafael being with us. The goal is to talk to her peacefully to get to the bottom of her motive for wanting to see you. Maybe you should sit down and rest. At four, we'll go back to the hotel."

Melinia took Julio's advice and took a power nap. At exactly four, the three of them slipped back into the hotel. Julio quickly changed in the break room before they took the back staircase up to the second floor. As Melinia had said, the stairwell was close to room two-fifteen. Julio cracked the door open so he could see her from where he and Rafael hid in the stairway. Melinia took a deep breath and knocked on the door. It only took a few moments before she heard the lock turn.

"Melinia, I'm so glad that you're here. Please come in," Helen said in an inviting voice.

As Melinia appeared to hesitantly enter Helen's room, Julio, who was carrying Rafael, quickly ran in behind her before Helen could close the door.

Before she could cry out, he clamped a hand over the woman's mouth.

"Listen, Helen. This is my friend, Julio, and my son, Rafael. If you promise not to scream, he'll let you go. We don't want any problems."

Helen nodded, and Melinia looked at Julio for a beat. Julio dropped his hand from her mouth. Helen quickly wiped her face and silently glared at Julio.

Melinia stepped closer to Helen. "I just want to know why you're looking for me and who sent you. Please start by answering what you have for me that you said I would want."

"Melinia, I'm from the Human Trafficking Task Force," Helen said. "I believe you want your freedom, and I am here to give it to you."

Chapter 38

Coming Home

Juliette looked in the mirror and admired how she looked in her new off-white pantsuit. She looked great, but, unfortunately, wasn't feeling as good as she looked. She was actually a nervous wreck. This was the first time that she would be hanging out with her girls since being hospitalized. Greta had gone all out and arranged for a limo to pick them up from their homes and take them to Burke Lakefront Airport. Then, she'd chartered a private plane to take them to New York. The flight was approximately forty-five minutes long, and they would be staying at the Ritz Carlton. Although Juliette was excited about the five-star experience that lay ahead of them, she was nervous about leaving Jolene as well as being around her friends.

Grandville came into the bedroom and hugged her from behind. "You look great," he purred, sniffing her neck. "Is this a new outfit?"

"Yes, it is. Thanks for noticing," Juliette said, smiling back at his reflection.

"I notice everything about you, including the fact that you're stressed out right now. You don't need to focus on anything except relaxing and having fun with your girls. Please stop overthinking. And when you get back from your trip, you and I are going to have our own little private party," he murmured in her ear.

"Now *that's* something I can't wait for," Juliette said and turned around to kiss her man on the lips. "The limo will be here in a few minutes, so let me say my goodbyes to the children. Grandville, please make sure Jolene takes her vitamins every day. I also left the number for the sickle cell clinic on the refrigerator, just in case she has a crisis."

"Hey, I said not to worry. I got this, babe."

"Thanks, Grandville. Of course, you do." Juliette smiled at her man before walking into the family room where the kids were watching television.

"Hey guys, I want you to be good for your father. I'll be back home in a couple of days."

"Are you going to bring us something back from your trip?" Jabari asked.

"It depends on if you guys behave. I don't want to hear that you all acted up while I was away. And Jabari, I expect you to be your dad's right-hand man," Juliette said.

"No problem, Mom," Jabari said. "Dad and I already had a long talk about that. We're good."

"Great! Now, come over here and give your mother a hug," Juliette said to her kids. She gave each one a hug and a kiss right as the doorbell rang.

"Hey, babe, your ride is here," Grandville announced. "Let me help you with your coat. Now be sure to call me when you touch down," he said as he kissed her on the lips. He then passed her an overnight bag and gently pushed her out the door.

As Juliette walked toward the limo, her friends let down the windows and stuck out their heads.

The sunroof opened, and Greta popped her head out and yelled, "Girl, let's get this party started right! Juliette, get your beautiful self into this limo because it's time for a girls' trip!"

The limo driver stepped out and took her bag before opening the rear door for her. Once she stepped inside the vehicle, her friends jumped up to hug her.

"Hey, girl! We're so happy to see you," Greta said. "Get ready to turn up because this weekend, we're celebrating my birthday and my bachelorette party at the same time."

She uncorked a large bottle of champagne and poured it into four flutes. Maria's was the fifth flute to be filled, but with chilled sparkling grape juice instead of champagne. "Let's have a toast to friendship and fun!" Greta declared.

The ladies all clinked their glasses together, and the driver turned on '90s R&B. The ladies had a great time laughing and catching up. Before they knew it, they were pulling up at the airport.

"Hey, Maria, are you sure you're okay to fly? That baby must really be growing. You're all belly," Samantha teased.

"I'm seven months along, but my doctor gave me permission to fly," Maria replied. "Besides, it's a pretty short flight."

"Good, because I'm not trying to have Sabrina deliver the baby on the plane," Samantha joked.

"Girl, don't be putting out those vibes," Greta playfully warned. "We're going to have a great time that doesn't include Maria giving birth. I paid for pre-check for all of us, so getting in and out of the airport should be a breeze."

"I'm officially on vacation, so all I want to do is have fun and get ideas for the wedding," Sabrina said as they stepped out of the limo.

"Do you have a particular theme or style for the wedding yet?" Juliette asked.

"No, not yet. But we were thinking of a late fall wedding. I love the fall season, especially that time of year when the leaves all change colors," Sabrina said.

Inside the airport, they quickly passed through a private security screening before boarding a small plane. It was beautifully decorated with lush, soft oversize leather reclining seats. The stewardess came out to greet them and take their drink orders. Just before the plane was due to take off, the pilot came out and greeted the ladies.

"It'll only take us about forty-five minutes to arrive at New York City. So you ladies can sit back and enjoy the quick flight," she said.

"Thank you," Juliette said while winking at the ladies. "Looks like we have an all-female cast, ladies!"

Maria winked back and shimmied her shoulders. "Yes! That's a great sign!"

"Come on, ladies, gather around before we take off for a selfie," Samantha said excitedly, pulling out her phone.

After they posed for a few pictures, Juliette buckled herself in and prepared for takeoff. Once the plane smoothly took off, the ladies began chatting like schoolgirls.

"Juliette, I'm so glad you were able to come with us," Greta cheered. "I know you've been feeling under the weather, and I'm grateful that you're doing better. You know we wouldn't have gone without you."

Juliette smiled at her sister-in-law. "Yeah, I'm doing better now. And I just want to let you know that Grandville and I appreciate you giving us space as we dealt with multiple issues. As you all may know, I was hospitalized for psychological issues."

"Juliette, you are one of the most stable people I know. I just don't understand what could have happened to make the doctor refuse to let you leave," Samantha said.

"Honestly, I was in a bad way. Jolene has been diagnosed with sickle cell disease, and I was afraid she would die like Jessica did."

"But why would you think that? There are thousands of people with sickle cell disease who lead full, productive lives," Sabrina said.

"Yes, that's true. But I guess since my father passed away from complications of sickle cell disease, it greatly impacted how I felt."

"I was shocked when Grandville told me about Jolene's condition," Greta shared. "I had no idea that sickle cell was even in our gene pool. I guess that's why it's so important to know your genetic background. Grandville and I didn't know our father, so we had no idea what kind of issues we'd inherited from him. This helps to underscore the fact that I need to get genetic testing because Derek and I want to start a family, and I want to be aware of any potential problems."

"That's a great idea. Franklin and I just had it done, and we learned that Franklin is also a sickle cell carrier. I was tested, and I don't carry the gene, but is always a good idea to be informed before starting a family," Sabrina said.

The mentioning of Franklin's genetic profile sent a chill down Juliette's spine as it further confirmed what she had already accepted in her heart: that Franklin was Jolene's father.

"Luckily, this won't be an issue for me because I'm never having kids," Samantha announced while all the ladies laughed. They were all clear on Samantha's stance on parenthood.

The women continued their playful banter for the entire short flight. Before they knew it, they exited the plane and were whisked away to the Ritz Carlton via limo.

On the ride to the hotel, Greta made an announcement, "I'm so glad that my sister-girl circle consists of you beautiful, talented women. I want to thank each and every one of you for accompanying me on this trip. To further show my love and gratitude, I've secured us front row tickets to see *The Color Purple* on Broadway."

The women all cheered and clapped, hugging Greta, and each other. After the ladies quieted down, Greta continued, "The show is at seven-thirty. Let's meet in the lobby at the bar to have a drink at a quarter 'til six so we can ensure that we'll have plenty of time to get to the show. This is Manhattan and the traffic in this town is outrageous, so I want to get an early start."

Once in her room, Juliette reflected on the conversation with her friends, and it gave her an idea. So many people had little awareness of their genetic predispositions. She was deep in thought about how she could raise awareness of sickle cell disease while using the concepts that her friends discussed. Suddenly, a knock sounded at the door. She looked through the peephole and spied Sabrina, who looked stunning in a royal blue dress. She took a deep breath and let her in.

"Hey, Sabrina, come on in. I'm just putting the finishing touches on my makeup," Juliette said as she stepped aside to allow Sabrina into her suite.

"Hey, lady. I was hoping to catch you alone before the group linked up downstairs. I love your dress, girl. You're looking fierce in that magenta," Sabrina complimented.

"Thanks. And you're looking like royalty in your blue," Juliette said.

"So Juliette, I hope you haven't put a lot of work into looking for George's biological parents because I've decided that now is not the right time to pursue it," Sabrina said, taking a seat on the edge of the bed.

"Actually, I didn't get the opportunity to do much investigating, given everything that I've been dealing with lately. But why have you changed your mind all of a sudden?" she asked.

"I just need to focus on planning my wedding. I'm afraid that if I learn who George's biological parents are, I'll get caught up with helping him deal with everything. I don't mean to sound selfish, but my wedding should be about me and Franklin," Sabrina said. "I've spent half of my life making sure that my mother and George's needs were met while neglecting my own. For the next year, I'm going to enjoy planning the wedding and all that comes with it. And I'm not saying that I won't want to pursue the search in the future, but just not right now."

"I totally understand," Juliette said with an inward sigh of relief. "And that's not selfish. It's called self-care. And you deserve it, my friend."

Downstairs, the ladies had a great time drinking and laughing at the bar. Samantha pulled out a Bride-to-Be sash and put it on Greta. "You're wearing this the whole trip because this is one big bachelorette party," she said while the ladies clinked their glasses together and cheered.

After an hour of bumper-to-bumper traffic, the ladies arrived at the theater. The play was wonderful, and their center front row seats blew their minds. As directed, they had turned their phones off during the show, but once they emerged from the theater, they turned them back on.

"Hey guys, I've got a voicemail from my assistant. She knows I'm here and rarely calls on the weekend, so it must be important," Samantha announced as she stepped aside to listen to the message.

The ladies were laughing and discussing the show when Samantha returned, looking like she'd seen a ghost. They could instantly tell that the message had been dead serious.

"Oh my God, Juliette! You are not going to believe this," Samantha said. Her face changed, suddenly shining with excitement.

"What? Did your office finally hit the Mega Millions? You all have been paying into that pool for years," Juliette joked.

"No, even better," Samantha said.

"What could be better than winning millions?" Juliette asked.

"Juliette, the Human Trafficking Task Force found Melinia in the Bahamas. She's been examined and will be flown into Cleveland on Wednesday with her son and unborn child," Samantha announced.

The women stood in stunned silence for a moment, still attempting to process the full meaning behind the news. Then they each turned to hug Juliette while she released tears of joy in the middle of Broadway. She was overcome with immense gratefulness, knowing that God had finally granted her favor by answering her unending prayers.

Chapter 39

Everybody Business

Melinia felt grateful and blessed to arrive safely back home in Cleveland. There had been many changes during the three years she had been away, and most of them had occurred within herself. She was a different person, as evident by the scars her heart bore from the wreckage of her past. She was resigned to the fact that it would take some time for her to get reacquainted with most of the people who were eager to welcome her home. Hopefully, she would have all the time she needed to heal, and the party that Juliette and her family were having for her would assist her with rediscovering what being loved and feeling welcomed was like. As she looked at the faces of those who had gathered in her honor to celebrate her rescue, she couldn't help but feel an overwhelming sense of appreciation.

During the three weeks since her rescue, she'd had to get used to resting in a soft bed and the absence of a swaying boat rocking her to sleep. Her nose had to readjust to the smog of the city and her ears to the noise and commotion that came along with urban living. She was enjoying all the home-cooked meals, and the quick ten pounds she'd put on since being back home was evidence of that. But the most difficult and fulfilling adjustment she had to make was being a full-time mother.

While the melodic tune of smooth jazz filled the air of Juliette and Grandville's expansive finished basement, Melinia smiled as Rafael climbed down from her lap and made his way toward Juliette.

As Rafael drew closer to Juliette, she knelt and opened her arms, which she used to engulf him into a huge bear hug. He giggled as she kissed him and hoisted him up into her arms, grunting playfully at how big and heavy he was for a three-year-old. A fit of anxiety washed over Melinia as she watched her cousin carry him away where she could no longer see him. She began rubbing her hands up and down her thighs while rocking in her chair, trying to resist the urge to chase after Juliette.

"Are you all right?" asked Mabel, Melinia's mother. "You look troubled all of a sudden."

"I'm fine, Mom. Thanks."

Mabel raised her chin but kept her large owl-like eyes locked onto her, which was usually a sign that the sixty-four-year-old elementary school secretary wasn't buying her story. "Melinia, I know when there's something wrong with my child. You don't have to tell me what's wrong, but don't tell me that nothing is wrong when there clearly is."

"It's not important, Mom."

Mabel gave her a side-eye. "It's important to me, Melinia."

Melinia blew out a deep breath. "We'll talk once we get back home. I don't want to get into this right now. The last thing I want to do is ruin my own party."

Mabel nodded her acceptance of her daughter's compromise and squeezed her hand gently. The subtle gesture put Melinia at ease as the last thing she wanted was to upset her mother, whom she had missed dearly while in captivity.

After chatting with one of her distant cousins for a few minutes, Melinia excused herself to go empty her bladder. The few moments alone in the bathroom allowed her the opportunity to purge her mind of the dark thoughts that were plaguing her. But no matter how much she tried not to think about Rique or Lovelle showing up to hurt her, she just couldn't put it out of her mind. She hardly slept from waking every half hour to make sure that Rafael was safe. Although she appreciated every aspect of her freedom, she struggled with how to exist in her hometown when she knew that Lovelle may still have a hit out on her. When she was on the boat with Rique, she enjoyed guaranteed protection she didn't have in Cleveland.

As she exited the restroom, she looked around before feeling secure enough to proceed back to the carpeted section of the basement where her family and close friends continued partying. She jumped and shot her hands to her mouth when Greta nearly bumped into her.

"Oh. Sorry," Greta said, laughing. "I didn't mean to startle you. Guess I shouldn't text and walk at the same time."

"You're good," Melinia breathed, clutching the fabric of her pearl-white cowl-neck sweater dress. "I was off in another world myself."

Greta's hazel eyes bored into her as if she were scanning the depths of her soul. "Your son is so freakin' cute and adorable, Melinia."

"Thank you, Greta. I'm so happy to have him back."

"I want you to know that if you and Rafael ever need anything, you can always call on me and Derek. Rafael is just the most handsome little man, and he reminds me of someone, but I can't put my finger on who," Greta laughingly said.

"Thank you, Greta," Melinia returned in a faltering voice as tears welled in her eyes. "I appreciate that."

Greta placed a hand on her arm and smiled, just as a giggling Rafael came racing around the corner with Juliette in hot pursuit. Rafael jumped up into his mother's arms moments before Juliette tickled his stomach, which made him squeal out louder in laughter. When Juliette ran off, Rafael jumped back down and chased after her,

Greta threw her arms around her shoulders and pecked her on the cheek. "Welcome home, Melinia. It's good to have you back."

Greta marched away as if she were on a mission, only to stop abruptly and spin around on her stiletto heels. Melinia narrowed her eyes as Greta slowly approached her.

"How old is your son again if I may ask?"

"Almost three."

"Hmmm." Greta nodded and turned to walk away, leaving Melinia to ponder how long it would be before Greta and the rest of her family and friends would start to have suspicions regarding Rafael's paternity.

When she returned to her seat, her mother was embroiled in a juicy conversation with Juliette's mother, Nadine. "Ah, you finally made it back," her mother said. "I was just about to send Grandville to check on you."

"I'm fine. I just ran into Greta on the way back."

"Say no more," Mabel said. "We all know how Greta likes to talk."

"Mabel," Nadine scolded playfully. "Behave and be nice. That's your niece's sister-in-law."

"I ain't studdin' her. She thinks she's better than everybody because she got a few coins in her purse. If it weren't for Rayshawn, she wouldn't even have that."

Nadine rolled her eyes and returned her attention back to Melinia, who couldn't help but nod in agreement with her mother. "Are you hungry yet, Melinia?"

"And you better not say no," Mabel said, rubbing Melinia's belly. "You're eating for two, so you gotta be hungry."

"Sure," Melinia returned with a smile. "I am kinda hungry."

Juliette, Samantha, Sabrina, Greta, and Maria set the food out on the covered pool table along with dishes and silverware. After Grandville made the announcement that the buffet line was now open, Mabel escorted Melinia and Rafael to the end of the long banquet table near the center of the room to be seated. Juliette brought Melinia a plate of tempura butterfly shrimp, her favorite dish, along with coconut and curry basmati rice. She finished her plate before everyone moved through the line and was on her second serving by the time everyone was seated.

"I guess you really were hungry," Mabel teased as she sat with Rafael astride her lap, watching him pick over his food.

Melinia laughed and turned her attention to her phone as a WhatsApp message popped up.

Julio: Hey. How's the party? How are you and Rafael doing?

Melinia: The party is nice. It's good to see everyone again. Rafael and I are doing fine. Can't wait until you can join us once your citizenship paperwork is complete. Have you heard anything about Rique and his crew?

Julio: That's great. I'm looking forward to it as well! No, I haven't, thank goodness. Have you heard from Mimi?

Melinia: No, I haven't had any contact with her. She might have gone back home to Detroit.

The thought also crossed her mind that maybe Rique and his boys had found her or vice versa, but she didn't want to speak that into existence. The mention of Mimi's name filled her with guilt about not doing more to help her best friend. She still hadn't forgiven herself for not allowing her to come with her and Julio to the hotel. Although she felt she was being responsible by looking out for the safety and well-being of herself and Rafael, she still felt bad for leaving Mimi behind. If she didn't understand how it felt to be a slave to the China white, she might have been more accepting of Mimi's presence and brought her along. But it was too late now. She could only hope that Mimi had made it off the island and found her way back to the United States. She knew Mimi would be on her own for the rest of the way. And for that matter, so was Melinia.

"Who are you texting that's got you grinning and blushing over there?" Mabel said loudly, drawing everyone's attention to her. "Is that the new baby's father?"

Melinia rolled her eyes and smiled but gave no answer.

"Is that the Dominican guy we're sponsoring?" Grandville asked after taking a sip of his non-alcoholic beer.

"Can I have just a teeny bit of privacy, please everyone?" Melinia said with a smile that was in contrast with the slowly boiling anger within her. "If and when I'm ready to disclose any of personal business, I'll do so at the time of my choosing."

The table got quiet as people exchanged uncomfortable glances with each other.

"I apologize for being intrusive," Grandville said. "I didn't mean to poke and prod in your personal affairs."

"I apologize as well," said Aunt Mabel as she raised her hand in the air. "We don't mean any harm, baby. I guess we're all just a little overprotective and excited to have you back."

Melinia nodded, wiped her mouth with her cloth napkin, then quickly excused herself from the table. She climbed the steps and made her way out onto the sun porch. She didn't care about the freezing temperature or the fact that she could see the steam from her breath.

All that mattered was that she was alone with her thoughts and away from her prodding family and friends. She knew they all meant well, but they were annoying, nonetheless.

She sat in one of the chairs on the sun porch and gazed up at the early February moon that illuminated the quiet Saturday night sky. As she stared at it, she wondered where Mimi was and tried to block out visions of her being back on the boat, performing sex acts for a hit of China white. Her mind ventured off to thoughts of both Rique and Lovelle coming for her and her children or perhaps her mother and other family members. She wondered if coming home was a good idea, as she worried about putting those she loved and who'd never stopped looking for her in danger.

Maybe I'll leave and settle down in another city with Julio, she thought. *I'll go someplace safe where no one will even bother to look for us. This time, I'll keep in close contact with my family. I won't put them through the pain of worrying about my whereabouts and safety again.*

"Hey, cuzzo," Juliette said after pulling the door open and stepping out onto the porch to join her. Rubbing her arms for warmth, she approached slowly and sat down next to her. "What are you doing out here in the cold all by yourself?"Melinia shrugged and sighed. "I just felt the need to have a quiet moment alone. I'll be back down soon. I hope people don't think I'm being rude and ungrateful because I'm not. It's just that—"

"I get it, Mel," Juliette cut in. "We were all being a little overbearing. It's just that everyone is so worried about you. We want to make sure you're good."

"I know."

Melinia reached over and hugged her favorite cousin, trying her best not to dampen her blouse with her tears. After a few minutes of quiet contemplation, Juliette stood and offered her a smile. "Well, I'll leave you to your thoughts. Just make sure you don't stay out here too long. We don't want you dying of frostbite before we can enjoy you being home," she joked.

"Jules wait," Melinia called out just as she pushed the door back open to re-enter the house.

Juliette turned around and made her way back toward her. Melinia stood and met her halfway. "I need you to talk to Grandville for me."

"Okay. About what?"

"I'm worried about Lovelle, Rayshawn's cousin coming after me now that I'm back home. I still owe him a lot of money, plus I did something really foul to him."

"Okay. I'll talk to him. But what exactly should I say?"

"I need him to talk to Rayshawn about telling his cousin to leave us alone and that I'll repay him as soon as I find a job."

When Juliette asked how much she owed him, Melinia couldn't provide an answer, as she honestly couldn't remember. "I'll have Grandville find out what your debt is, and we'll settle it for you."

"Jules, I can't ask you and Grandville to do that. This is something I did that I have to fix."

Juliette placed a hand on her shoulder and smiled as she peered into her eyes. "Listen, Mel. If keeping you safe means having to cough up some money, then that's what we're going to do. We can use the reward money we raised for your return to help pay off your debt. If you're serious about fixing this, then you can pay *us* back when you get back on your feet."

"You'd really do that for me, Jules?"

"Absolutely. We're family, and you're my favorite cousin."

The two embraced, and Melinia did exactly what she said she wasn't going to do, she deposited tears on her all over her cousin's blouse.

"Come on, cuzzo," Juliette said. "I'm freezing, and we have a cake to cut in your honor."

"Thanks, Jules. It's great to be home."

"It's great having you back, Mel. You were sorely missed."

Epilogue

Grandville stood in the foyer of the church and watched the processional that signaled the commencement of Greta's wedding. The historic Catholic church, housed in wall-length stained glass windows, high ceilings, and marble floors, was the perfect place for his twin and her fiancé, Derek, to begin the rest of their lives together. The church was filled to capacity and music from a large, majestic organ filled the air.

Juliette, Greta's maid of honor, looked breathtaking in her emerald gown. She confidently strolled toward the front of the church, grasping the arm of one of Derek's groomsmen. As Grandville gazed upon her beauty, he thought about all they had endured since Jessica's name was commemorated with the opening of the clinic at Oakhill. As he watched his beloved wife, his heart rate rapidly increased, and he remembered to take deep breaths. His anxiety slowly dissipated and the love he felt for her calmly filled his spirit. He silently wished it was him standing at the front of the church, waiting to marry her all over again.

The passing of their oldest daughter had caused his wife to lose some of her sanity. This realization somehow brought them closer together. Juliette knew how it felt to mentally snap under the weight of worry and anxiety borne out of the fear of hurting him. That alone had brought their kindred spirits closer together. He had put her through a lot in his attempt to protect her from his past, but he now realized that Juliette had done the very same thing to him during their Oakhill visit. She'd been protecting him when she hadn't told him there was a possibility that he may not be the twins' biological father or about her one-night stand. He'd hated the thought of someone else intimately touching what, according to God's law, was exclusively his. But, in some ways, he felt somehow responsible for her infidelity.

Juliette wasn't a loose woman and she wasn't a big drinker, so he knew in his heart that her transgression was not intentional. He knew she wouldn't have been at a bar alone, drunk, and talking to a stranger had he not accidentally killed Jessica and unwittingly set off a chain of events that still impacted him and his family. His drinking and failure to deal openly with his past abuse at the hands of his deceased cousin and sister, Gina, and the news that a child was born out of their illicit copulation had been the catalysts that had sent him over the edge.

He didn't begrudge Juliette for anything that had happened. He admired her strength, knowing that the secrets she harbored in her heart, along with the news of Grandville's son, had refined her into the strong woman she had become.

His attention was captured by the laughter of the wedding attendees as they watched his beautiful twin daughters skip down the aisle. His heart swelled with love as he watched them in their identical replicas of Juliette's dress. He looked on as they threw rose petals onto the floor in unison and couldn't help but feel blessed. After all that had occurred, God still saw fit to bless him with two more beautiful daughters. For him, the circumstance behind their conception didn't matter.

Since Jolene's hematologist had confirmed that he was a hemoglobin-C carrier, he had little doubt that Jolene was his biological daughter. Only one out of forty people are carriers of the genetic disorder. However, there was still a possibility that the man that Juliette had a one-night stand with was also a hemoglobin-C carrier and was one or both the twins' biological father. It was something that he would never ever know for certain. Regardless of the twin's paternity, in his eyes, they would always be his daughters. A DNA test wouldn't change how he felt in his heart, so he decided that, no matter what, he would never have a test done.

As he watched his daughters prance toward the front of the church, he vowed to always love, protect, and provide for them. He thanked God every day for allowing him the opportunity to watch them grow and to be a part of their lives.

As Granville's eyes scanned the church, he spotted George sitting with Franklin and Sabrina. He marveled at how much George's physical appearance mirrored his own. As he watched him from afar, he wondered how George would react when he eventually learned that he was his biological father. He was sure George would want to know details about his biological mother and why he had been placed for adoption. He dreaded the day he would have the conversation, but was glad that Franklin would be there to help him when the time came. He and Franklin had made the decision not to tell Sabrina and George about the details, but they'd decided to revisit the subject in the near future.

Grandville had always felt close to Franklin, but he felt even closer once he learned that he was also a hemoglobin-C carrier. Franklin had shared that because Sabrina was not a carrier, which meant that there was no chance that any children they produced would have sickle cell disease. Franklin had also been supportive and understanding that Grandville had not told Greta the truth about impregnating Gina. He didn't want the stress of disclosing it at this time to negatively impact Greta's wedding day, so they decided to break the news to her after her honeymoon.

His smile broadened when he spied Melinia sitting between her mother and his mother-in-law. Melinia looked happy as she held her son on her lap and looked around the church with wonder. Juliette and her family were shocked that Melinia had a child while in bondage and that she was carrying a second one.

Juliette had recently shared that Melinia regretted her decision to voluntarily place herself into bondage to evade a local drug dealer. Grandville was well aware of the sex tape Melinia made with Lovelle and Rayshawn and her attempt to blackmail Lovelle with it. Consequently, her plans backfired, thus resulting in Lovelle ordering a hit on her.

Grandville, to his dismay, broke the code he'd made with Juliette by electing not to disclose the hit on her with Juliette or her family. Melina had sworn she was off the drugs for good and all she wanted was to be a good mother for her children. Grandville could only hope that Lovelle would leave the situation alone and wouldn't attempt to harm Melinia or her children. He made a mental note to ask Rayshawn about attempting to convince Lovelle to call off the hit, per Juliette's request.

Grandville scanned the church once more and spotted Montell, Monty, and a very pregnant Maria sitting in the back pew. Montell and his family were very excited to learn that their new addition was a girl and she would be making her way into the world in the next few weeks. According to Montell, Monty was super excited to become a big brother and the family had planned for both Montell and Monty to help deliver the baby.

Samantha and Jared were sitting in the middle of the church and Grandville watched with amusement as they held hands. According to Juliette, he'd asked Samantha to move in with him and she was seriously considering his offer.

Juliette knew that as time passed Jolene's need for blood and other treatments would increase. In response, Juliette had come up with a sickle cell campaign called "Know Your Sails" which was aimed at raising awareness about sickle cell disease. Due to her father's unfortunate passing, Juliette was very aware of sickle cell anemia, but it wasn't until Jolene's diagnosis that she became aware of the various forms of the disease. She decided to use her experience to help her community by teaching people about the importance of knowing if they are sickle cell carriers.

As the wedding march began to play, Greta appeared next to Grandville looking beautiful in her off-white Vera Wang gown. Grandville took her arm and the two began their stroll down the freshly rolled white carpet toward the front of the church. They both gazed out at the sea of their close family and friends watching them in awe. When they stood before Derek, who was patiently waiting, Grandville beamed at his future brother-in-law. He placed Greta's hand into Derek's, and after announcing he was the one to give Greta away, stepped back so that the service could begin.

With tears of pride and joy brimming in his smiling eyes, Grandville found his seat next to Juliette's mother and clutched her hand. Seeing the elation in Greta's hazel eyes reminded him of the way Juliette once looked at him. He longed for the days when that sparkle would return to his beloved wife's eyes.

Suddenly, he felt Jessica's warming undeniable presence. As he continued to gaze at his wife, he gasped in response to the sparkle that shone in her eyes as she returned his gaze. She was back, and he had God and Jessica to thank for that. It was then that he knew in his heart that the future would have its challenges, but with the help of his family, friends, and God, he would be just fine.

Grandville was so caught up in the beautiful moment that he had missed the minister asking if there was anyone who felt the need to protest Greta and Derek's union.

"I protest," a loud, familiar voice rang out from the back of the church. Grandville, along with every pair of eyes in the church, turned and shot their gazes back toward the sound.

As he took in the identity of the speaker, Grandville couldn't believe his eyes or his ears. He turned around to look back at the couple. Judging from their slack-jawed expressions, neither could they.

Author's Note

During tumultuous times, we often find ourselves under spiritual attack, similar to many of the scenarios portrayed in this novel. Melinia, Grandville, and Juliette all leaned on a favorite scripture of reference for overcoming the spiritual attacks presented in this story. I would like to share this scripture with you, in hopes that it is applicable and relevant to helping you overcome the many life struggles to come.

Be blessed and thank you for reading this heartfelt story.

The Whole Armor of God
Ephesians 6:10-20 (NIV)

10 Finally, be strong in the Lord and in his mighty power. 11 Put on the full armor of God, so that you can take your stand against the devil's schemes. 12 For our struggle is not against flesh and blood, but against the rulers, against the authorities, against the powers of this dark world and against the spiritual forces of evil in the heavenly realms. 13 Therefore put on the full armor of God, so that when the day of evil comes, you may be able to stand your ground, and after you have done everything, to stand. 14 Stand firm then, with the belt of truth buckled around your waist, with the breastplate of righteousness in place, 15 and with your feet fitted with the readiness that comes from the gospel of peace. 16 In addition to all this, take up the shield of faith, with which you can extinguish all the flaming arrows of the evil one. 17 Take the helmet of salvation and the sword of the Spirit,

which is the word of God. 18 And pray in the Spirit on all occasions with all kinds of prayers and requests. With this in mind, be alert and always keep on praying for all the Lord's people. 19 Pray also for me, that whenever I speak, words may be given me so that I will fearlessly make known the mystery of the gospel, 20 for which I am an ambassador in chains. Pray that I may declare it fearlessly, as I should.

If you enjoyed this novel, please share it others and let me know by leaving a review on Amazon and Goodreads.

Fondly,

JJ Winston

Melinia's Playlist
While in Captivity

1. "Collide" Tiana Major9 and EARTHGANG

2. "She" Stokley

3. "Something About Us" Daft Punk

4. "Beyond" Leon Bridges

5. "Grown Folks" The Bar-Kays and The Unknowns

6. "Let It Ride" Robert Glasper Experiment and Norah Jones

7. "You Know I'm No Good" Amy Winehouse

8. "Where Are We Now" David Bowie

9. "No Halo" BROCKHAMPTON

10. "Moral of The Story" Ashe

11. "Bad Guy" Billie Eilish

12. "Lose Yourself To Dance" Daft Punk and Pharrell

13. "What I've Done" Linkin Park

14. "Add to Me" Ledisi

15. "Bobby James" N.E.R.D.

16. "The Other Side" SZA and Justin Timberlake

17. "High Right Now" Tyla Yaweh and Wiz Khalifa

18. "All Your Friends" Coldplay

19. "1000 X's and O's" Prince

20. "Something Keeps Calling" Raphael Saadiq and Rob Bacon
21. "Believe in Us" Mint Condition
22. "My Life" Mary J. Blige
23. "Dazed and Confused" Teddy Byers
24. "The Journey Home" Tim Matson
25. "Senorita" Shawn Mendes and Camille Cabello
26. "Secrets" The Weeknd
27. "When I Was Your Man" Bruno Mars
28. "Slow Down" Skip Marley and H.E.R.
29. "Pity Party" Melanie Martinez
30. "Know Your Worth" Khalid and Disclosure
31. "Anyone" Demi Moore
32. "Tomorrow" The Roots f. Raheem DeVaughn
33. "Come to The Light" Jill Scott
34. "I'm Yours" Antoine Dunn
35. "Leave Out All the Rest" Linkin Park
36. "Can't Get Enough" Tamia
37. "Despacito" Luis Fonsi featuring Daddy Yankee
38. "Coming Home" Anthony Hamilton
39. "Everybody Business" Kehlani

Acknowledgments

It is my belief that we all have been put on this planet to fulfill a purpose. For me, my purpose is to use my education and knowledge from my over twenty-five-year behavioral health and legal experiences to write fiction that is true to life. My goal is to help my readers remember that we are all a curious blend of good and bad. Though we are imperfect, every one of us has a talent or a gift bestowed upon us from the Lord above. I want to thank God for blessing me with the gift of imagination and the vision, which has allowed me to continue Grandville and Juliette's fictional story in *The Commemoration*. I explored the real-life subjects of mental health, substance abuse disorder, human trafficking, and sickle cell disease.

I would like to thank my editing and proofreading team. A sincere thank you to my editor and writing coach, Eryka Parker of Lyrical Innovations, LLC, for her dedication, persistence, love, and support in ensuring that this novel represented my very best work. The many hours that she spent on my manuscript is a testament to her work ethic and is much appreciated. Special thanks to Ann Weatherhead for blessing me with her editing skills and for her encouragement and support. Sincerest thanks to Michael Payne for the time he spent reading, proofing, and aiding me with the editing process and for his excellent suggestions. Heartfelt thanks to Stephie Walls of Wallflower Edits for proofing this project and Tayvon Jackson of Jackson Publishing for laying out my novel and setting up the Kindle version of this novel.

We are all only as good as our team, and I have been blessed with many friends, colleagues, and loved ones who have gone above and beyond to ensure that my dream of being a writer was fulfilled. Some of these individuals include my significant other—Douglas Winston, who is the love of my life, my mother, my children, my siblings, my sorority sisters, co-workers, and friends. Much gratitude to my personal cheering squad, which includes Tonya Bennett, Beverly Byers, Pinkey Carr, Jeanetta Johnson, Tonya Jones, Sunia Marsh, Melissa Stallings, Camille Warner, and Terry Winston, for their love and encouragement. Sincerest appreciation to Dave Van Horn of the Cleveland Writers Group for the numerous hours spent mentoring me on the art of marketing. I would like to extend a most special thank you to Leonard "LC" Collins for the original drawing that is my book cover and for his friendship.

About the Author

JJ Winston has worked in Behavioral Health for over twenty years and now serves as a Family Court Magistrate Judge in Cleveland, Ohio. JJ Winston is a licensed Independent Social Worker and Attorney in the state of Ohio. She is an avid reader whose hobbies include fishing, watching movies, writing fiction stories touching on social issues, and spending time with family and friends.

JJ Winston is the author of *The Anniversary* and *The Anniversary: Guide to Behavioral Health Workbook*. *The Commemoration* is the sequel to *The Anniversary* and her second fiction novel. For updates on upcoming projects, please follow JJ Winston on Facebook or Instagram at Novelist JJ Winston.

www.ingramcontent.com/pod-product-compliance
Lightning Source LLC
Chambersburg PA
CBHW050510270326
41927CB00009B/1982